The Communist Manifesto
by Karl Marx and Frederick Engels

WITH RELATED DOCUMENTS

SECOND EDITION

Edited with an Introduction by

John E. Toews
University of Washington

bedford/st.martin's
Macmillan Learning
Boston | New York

For Bedford/St. Martin's

Vice President, Editorial, Macmillan Learning Humanities: Edwin Hill
Program Director for History: Michael Rosenberg
Senior Program Manager for History: Laura Arcari
History Marketing Manager: Melissa Rodriguez
Director of Content Development: Jane Knetzger
Assistant Editor: Melanie McFadyen
Associate Editor: Mary Posman Starowicz
Content Project Manager: Lidia MacDonald-Carr
Senior Workflow Project Supervisor: Joe Ford
Production Supervisor: Robin Besofsky
Media Project Manager: Michelle Camisa
Manager of Publishing Services: Andrea Cava
Project Management: Lumina Datamatics, Inc.
Composition: Lumina Datamatics, Inc.
Director of Rights and Permissions: Hilary Newman
Permissions Manager: Kalina Ingham
Senior Art Director: Anna Palchik
Cover Design: William Boardman
Cover Art: Strike (oil on canvas)/Kustodiev, Boris Mihajlovic
   (1878–1927)/State Russian Museum, St. Petersburg, Russia/Bridgeman Images
Printing and Binding: LSC Communications

Manufactured in the United States of America.

2   1   0   9   8
f   e   d   c

For information, write: Bedford/St. Martin's, 75 Arlington Street, Boston, MA 02116

ISBN 978-1-319-09483-6

Acknowledgments
*Text acknowledgments and copyrights appear at the back of the book on page 183,
which constitutes an extension of the copyright page. Art acknowledgments and copyrights
appear on the same page as the art selections they cover.*

   At the time of publication all Internet URLs published in this text were found to
accurately link to their intended website. If you do find a broken link, please forward the
information to history@macmillan.com so that it can be corrected for the next printing.

Foreword

The Bedford Series in History and Culture is designed so that readers can study the past as historians do.

The historian's first task is finding the evidence. Documents, letters, memoirs, interviews, pictures, movies, novels, or poems can provide facts and clues. Then the historian questions and compares the sources. There is more to do than in a courtroom, for hearsay evidence is welcome, and the historian is usually looking for answers beyond act and motive. Different views of an event may be as important as a single verdict. How a story is told may yield as much information as what it says.

Along the way the historian seeks help from other historians and perhaps from specialists in other disciplines. Finally, it is time to write, to decide on an interpretation and how to arrange the evidence for readers.

Each book in this series contains an important historical document or group of documents, each document a witness from the past and open to interpretation in different ways. The documents are combined with some element of historical narrative—an introduction or a biographical essay, for example—that provides students with an analysis of the primary source material and important background information about the world in which it was produced.

Each book in the series focuses on a specific topic within a specific historical period. Each provides a basis for lively thought and discussion about several aspects of the topic and the historian's role. Each is short enough (and inexpensive enough) to be a reasonable one-week assignment in a college course. Whether as classroom or personal reading, each book in the series provides firsthand experience of the challenge—and fun—of discovering, recreating, and interpreting the past.

Lynn Hunt
David W. Blight
Bonnie G. Smith

Preface

The passing of the Cold War era and the explosive, conflict-ridden, global expansion of finance capitalism in the twenty-first century has opened up the possibility of reading the *Communist Manifesto* in new ways. This familiar, "classical" text could be, and has been, relegated to the status of an object of "merely historical" antiquarian curiosity and appropriated as an object of nostalgia or radical-chic conspicuous consumption. But the historical uncoupling of the *Manifesto* from the world in which it could inspire fear and fanatical commitment need not end in irrelevance and trivialization. The text still has the power to speak against its transformation into a commodity marketed to grace the coffee tables of the wealthy and the privileged, and to open up an intellectual space in which the world of financial markets and commodified forms of life is placed in critical perspective. And it sustains such power precisely as a historical text. This second edition is intended to engage students and teachers in the imaginative task of reconstructing the historical meaning of the *Communist Manifesto* as a communication from the past that can stimulate historical reflection and critical self-understanding in the present.

In the preface to the 1872 German edition of the *Manifesto,* Karl Marx and Frederick Engels claimed that the passing of a quarter-century since its first publication had turned the *Manifesto* into a "historical document," which, even as the original authors, they "had no longer any right to alter." Sweeping changes in European and global politics and the "gigantic" development of the system of modern industrial capitalism had made the specific historical references of the text irrelevant and left its political program "antiquated." What remained, untouched by the passage of time, was a statement of the principles informing the communist movement. Aside from a few brief weeks during the revolutionary turmoil of 1848, the *Communist Manifesto* has exerted its historical presence not as a political program but as pedagogical instrument, as a condensed, eloquent account of the theoretical and historical foundations of Marxism. Although this edition of the *Manifesto* in the Bedford Series in History and Culture does not ignore the immediate historical contexts of the writing and publication of the *Manifesto* as a political act in 1848, it is organized around the question of the historical character of the principles informing the *Manifesto*'s specific interpretations and programmatic recommendations. The selected documents and the introduction suggest guidelines for reading the "principles" embodied in the *Manifesto*—assumptions about liberty, community, productive labor, and history—as themselves historical.

The revised Introduction in Part One continues to provide context on the political, social, and intellectual background of the Manifesto, with new emphasis on the trajectory of Marx's thought from the 1830s onward. The main document in Part Two, the Manifesto, is accompanied by the related documents in Part Three, which now include documents by Hess and Tocqueville. These additional documents illuminate the contexts and interactions that influenced the original formation of the Manifesto. Together, the introduction and related documents focus primarily on the historical formation of the theoretical premises informing the arguments, metaphors, narrative accounts, and description of the Manifesto. The last section of the introduction and a number of documents from the period after 1848 (Documents 20–25) also allow for an examination of the place of the Manifesto in the historical development of Marx's thought. A Chronology, new Questions for Consideration, and an updated Selected Bibliography provide further pedagogical aids for student comprehension of the content and context of the main document. This edition can be used by students and instructors as a historical introduction both to a specific text and more generally to the intellectual career of its primary author. The purpose of placing the text in its various personal and cultural contexts, however, is not only to illuminate its status as a document that can tell us something about the past and about its author, to help conjure up the world of the dead, but to clarify its message as an act of communication to the living and for the present.

A NOTE ON THE TEXT

The text follows the English translation by Samuel Moore of 1888, which was edited, annotated, and authorized by Engels and has over the past century taken on the status of a standard edition. Engels's own annotations from the 1888 edition are included with the text. These are marked with asterisks or other ornaments. Also included are annotations by the editor, which are numbered. The text contains many, mostly

minor, modifications of the original German version. The Moore translation has been compared in detail to the German version published in
February 1848, but only those changes judged by the editor to have a
potentially significant influence in construing the meaning of the text
have been noted.

ACKNOWLEDGMENTS

I would like to thank Natalie Davis for suggesting the idea for the first
edition of this book and Katherine Kurzman of Bedford/St. Martin's
for encouraging me to pursue it. The readers assigned to review the
manuscript provided invaluable criticism and suggestions. I am especially grateful to Jonathan Sperber for an incredibly detailed and very
critical reading, which helped me to define my own positions, and to
David Luft, Paul Breines, Kevin Repp, John McCole, Eric Weitz, and
Helmut Smith for pushing me to formulate those positions more
clearly for an undergraduate audience. The manuscript would never
have reached completion without the following people from Bedford/
St. Martin's: Program Director for History Michael Rosenberg; Senior
Program Manager Laura Arcari; History Marketing Manager Melissa
Rodriguez; Assistant Editor Melanie McFadyen; Associate Editor Mary
Posman Starowicz; Content Project Manager Lidia MacDonald-Carr;
and Cover Designer William Boardman. I also owe a great deal to the
students in my undergraduate and graduate classes over the past twenty
years who have helped me formulate the perspectives on history and
on Marx that inform this volume. Finally, I must thank Eleanor Toews
for knowing me well enough to insist that I finish this little book before
submerging myself once again in the big one.

John E. Toews

Contents

Foreword   iii

Preface   v

ILLUSTRATIONS   xi

PART ONE

Introduction: Historical Contexts of the
Communist Manifesto   **1**

Immediate Historical Contexts of the *Manifesto*   6

Historical Premises of the *Manifesto*   21

Specters of Politics and Ideology   48

From the *Manifesto* to *Capital:* The Lessons of History
and the Laws of History   52

PART TWO

Manifesto of the Communist Party   **61**

I. Bourgeois and Proletarians   64

II. Proletarians and Communists   76

III. Socialist and Communist Literature   84

IV. Position of the Communists in Relation to
    the Various Existing Opposition Parties   94

PART THREE
Related Documents 97

1. Alexis de Tocqueville, From *Recollections: The French Revolution of 1848*, 1847–1848 98

2. Frederick Engels, *Draft of a Communist Confession of Faith*, June 9, 1847 100

3. Frederick Engels, From *A Letter to Karl Marx*, November 23/24, 1847 105

4. Frederick Engels, From *The Condition of the Working Class in England*, 1845 106

5. Robert Owen, From *Report to the County of Lanark*, 1820 111

6. Charles Fourier, From *The Theory of the Four Movements and of the General Destinies*, 1808 114

7. Charles Fourier, From *The Theory of Universal Unity*, 1841–1843 116

8. Robert Owen, From *Report to the County of Lanark*, 1820 118

9. *The Six Points of the People's Charter*, 1838 120

10. James Bronterre O'Brien, *Private Property*, 1841 122

11. G. W. F. Hegel, From *Reason in History: A General Introduction to the Philosophy of History*, 1837 124

12. Ludwig Feuerbach, From *The Essence of Christianity*, 1841 126

13. Karl Marx, From *Contribution to the Critique of Hegel's Philosophy of Law*, 1844 127

14. Karl Marx, From *On the Jewish Question*, 1843 129

15. Ludwig Feuerbach, From *Principles of the Philosophy of the Future*, 1843 131

16. Moses Hess, From *A Communist Credo: Questions and Answers*, 1844–1846 133

17. Karl Marx, From *The Economic and Philosophic Manuscripts of 1844*, 1844 136

18. Karl Marx, *Theses on Feuerbach*, 1845 141

19. Karl Marx and Frederick Engels, From
    The German Ideology, 1845–1846   144

20. Karl Marx, From *The Class Struggles in France,
    1848–1850*, 1850   148

21. Karl Marx, From *The Eighteenth Brumaire of Louis
    Bonaparte*, 1852   151

22. Karl Marx, From *Inaugural Address of the Working
    Men's International Association*, October 1864   155

23. Karl Marx, *Afterword to the Second German
    Edition of* Capital, 1873   156

24. Karl Marx, *The Fetishism of Commodities and
    the Secret Thereof*, 1867   158

25. Frederick Engels, *Speech at Karl Marx's Funeral*,
    March 1883   169

APPENDIXES

Chronology for the Historical Contexts of the
Manifesto (1765–1895)   171

Questions for Consideration   177

Selected Bibliography   179

Index   **185**

Illustrations

1. Frederick Engels in the mid-1840s   14

2. Cartoon by Frederick Engels of the Prussian King Frederick William IV   20

3. Portrait of Marx as a university student, 1835–1836   25

4. Prometheus Bound: Allegory on the prohibition of the *Rheinische Zeitung*   27

5. Karl Marx in London in 1861, during the time he was working on *Capital*   56

6. Title page of the first German edition of the *Manifesto of the Communist Party*, February 1848   62

7. A page of the original draft of the *Communist Manifesto*   63

8. A page of the manuscript of *The German Ideology*   146

Introduction: Historical Contexts of the *Communist Manifesto*

The *Manifesto of the Communist Party*,[1] commonly known as the *Communist Manifesto*, is both a historical product and a historical action. As a historical product, it not only gave specific shape to the personal intentions of its authors, but it also embodied in its descriptions, metaphors, and arguments the more broadly shared perspectives and values of its time and culture. As a message that was meant to connect its authors to an audience of readers, the *Manifesto* gathered much of its original meaning from the historical contexts in which it was written and in which it was intended to be read. However, the *Communist Manifesto* was more than a product of specific historical circumstances, more than a mere mirror of the world from which it arose. As a creative action, it refashioned its historical conditions into a historical event that marked the entry of something new into the world. As a critical reinterpretation of established cultural meanings for the historical tendencies transforming nineteenth-century Europe, it opened up new possibilities for making sense of those tendencies. The *Communist Manifesto* was meant not to confirm but to transform the way in which its readers understood their experience and convince them to change their present conditions and join in the revolutionary creation of a new world. Since its original publication in February 1848, the power and influence of the *Communist Manifesto* has been in its ability to awaken such critical self-recognition and guide such action.

In the wake of the end of the Cold War and the collapse of the communist regimes in the Soviet Union and Eastern Europe, the *Manifesto*'s ability to provide meaning for the experience of large groups of people and to effectively guide collective action has come into question in a much more radical and universal way than ever before. The globalization and structural transformations of capitalist modes of production and control have increased the sense that the *Manifesto* has become a purely historical document. In many ways it has been reduced to a message from a rapidly receding, increasingly opaque past, which can be understood only through a reconstruction of the historical contexts in which its meanings seemed obvious, whether as an inspiring or a threatening document.

In 1872, less than twenty-five years after its publication, its authors, Karl Marx and Frederick Engels, suggested that the *Manifesto* had already become a historical document. They explained that parts of it would need to be revised to fit the changing historical circumstances produced by the continuing evolution of industrial capitalism, the expansion of political and trade organizations among working people (parliamentary parties and labor unions), and the accumulated experience of political events such as the European revolutions of 1848–1849 and the Paris Commune of 1871.[2]

This type of self-consciousness concerning the *Manifesto*'s historical limitations continued among Marxists into the twentieth century. The *Manifesto*'s analysis of existing historical conditions and its political proposals and strategic advice required constant reconsideration and revision in the light of new developments. The adaptability of the message of the *Manifesto* was considered to be a sign of its continued vitality as a map of the world and a guide for conduct. In 1919, the Hungarian Marxist philosopher Georg Lukács claimed that Marxism would still be "true" even if every one of its specific historical claims turned out to be empirically false.[3] The basis for this manner of evaluating the *Manifesto* as a historical document had been defined by Marx and Engels in 1872 in terms of a distinction between general organizing principles and specific, historically bound details. "However much the state of things may have altered during the last twenty-five years," they wrote, "the general principles laid down in the *Manifesto* are, on the whole, as correct today as ever."[4]

More than a century later, in the 1970s and 1980s, the *Manifesto*'s vision of capitalism's collapse and the triumph of communist world revolution could still be conjured up on both sides of the Cold War as the description of a reality that either promised or threatened the achievement of human freedom, social order, and world peace. Editors of English editions of the *Manifesto* in the early 1970s repeated Marx and Engels's

1872 claim that the principles of the text retained their validity in spite of changing historical contexts.[5] In the 1980s, President Ronald Reagan still found it politically advantageous to raise the specter of world communist revolution to rally support for his foreign policy in Central America and his domestic tax policy.

One might say that historical events of the late 1980s and early 1990s emancipated the *Communist Manifesto* from the historical burdens created by its status as a foundational text for twentieth-century communist movements and regimes. Having lost its ability to justify the authority of existing political power structures, inspire devotion to revolutionary change, or arouse fear of an insidious external threat to the conditions of one's own existence, the *Manifesto* could be viewed as also having lost its relevance and interest. Neither the desire for social salvation nor the need to muster a defense against threats to individual liberty and happiness are likely to drive a citizen of the contemporary Western world to study this text. The contemporary issue in interpreting the *Manifesto* historically is no longer simply one of examining the empirical validity of its historical descriptions in detail or testing the adaptability of its principles to new historical circumstances. Instead, it is important to look at the historical nature of the principles themselves.

Pursuing the notorious, familiar metaphor with which Marx began (and concluded) the *Manifesto,* one could say that it no longer arouses the "specter" of a communist revolution that would define the world in a qualitatively different way. That specter has apparently been exorcised and laid to rest. As the specter has dissipated, however, it may have become easier to examine the motives that produced it in the first place. There may never be a better time to confront the *words* of the *Manifesto*, rather than the specters that hope and fear have created from it, and to let the words speak for themselves, unencumbered by the dogmatic commitments and political loyalties that have accumulated around them.

Read as a message from the past, the *Manifesto* reveals the distinctive historical particularity of its construction. Rather than self-affirmation or fear, historical wonder is the appropriate response to a communication from a past that has become strange and different. In what kind of a world was it possible to construct history and society in this fashion? From what premises could this constructed world be imagined as a true description of the real world? As the *Manifesto* becomes increasingly historical, its value is tied more closely to the production of our distinctive historical self-consciousness in the present, to a recognition of both the differences between the present and the past and the continued power of the past in the present. It is this very relationship of distance that makes possible a critical perspective on our own historical assumptions, that brings into focus the boundaries of our own historical world. Instead of being read within the context of a dramatic confrontation between "us" and "them," perhaps the *Manifesto* can be read within the internal drama of the tension between "then" and "now."

The specter of communist revolution conjured up by the *Manifesto* is increasingly a ghost of the past. But ghosts from the past can also haunt the present, and it would be foolish to exaggerate the historical distance that separates us from the worlds assumed by and imagined in the *Manifesto*. The world in which Karl Marx wrote in 1848 has not completely disappeared during the past 170 years. The historical world, or aggregate of social, political, and cultural contexts he inhabited, is not totally incommensurable with the world we inhabit today. And the map his images and arguments construct from his place and moment in history has not completely lost its interpretive power. The passages in the *Manifesto* that describe the revolutionary global effects of industrial capitalism and market relations can still be read for their prophetic insights into a future (now our present) in which all fixed social and political relations dissolve under the relentless pressure of changes in systems of production and all human relations tend to be defined as relations among commercially exchanged products or commodities. Even the emergence of a new global incarnation of Marx's revolutionary proletariat with the potential to create a post-capitalist egalitarian and democratic commonwealth has established a presence in some spheres of the current historical imagination, and produced new forms of calls to action that echo some of the rhetoric of Marx's and Engels's original *Manifesto*.[6]

A complex combination of obvious difference and lingering identity defines our relation to this historical text. As we read Marx's text as an action in a foreign world, we may come to understand our reading of it in this fashion as itself a motivated action in our own world, as an attempt to make the *Manifesto*'s words bend to our own desires in the present. Consigning the *Manifesto* to a historical scrap heap of antiquated curiosities may just be another way of avoiding listening to those messages that resonate disquietingly among the unquestioned assumptions of the present, of obscuring or breaking a mirror that retains the power to induce disconcerting moments of self-recognition.

In the opening paragraphs of the *Manifesto,* Marx's use of the term *Gespenst* (meaning "specter" or "ghost") indicates some of the complexities of the historical relationship between imaginary fictions that obscure reality and mental models that can function as viable maps of real worlds. The specter of communism that is haunting Europe, Marx suggests initially, is not a representation of a known reality but of an imaginary entity. It is a "nursery tale"[7] created out of both fear of internal weakness and the desire to inspire fear in others. It has been conjured up for the specific purpose of dismissing and controlling opposition to established political and cultural powers. But Marx goes on to say that this fiction, this fairy tale, does in fact refer to a historical actuality. The specter haunting old Europe is a specter of its future, and this specter does have a reference point in present reality. Hiding behind the specter of communism is an actual communist movement, which possesses the power to assert its own reality. The imaginary stories circulating in the minds of the ruling powers hide a historical reality that the publication of the *Manifesto of the Communist Party* will finally bring to light.

This previously hidden historical reality, however, retains some of the characteristics of the imagined specter. Real historical communism, like the imaginary subject of the fairy tale, is also a product of the powers that rule Europe—a product not of their imagination, but of their very concrete, earthly social practices. The existing social order, as Marx contends later in the text, produces the conditions of its own destruction. It creates its own "grave diggers." Like a sorcerer who has lost control of the specters he has conjured up, old Europe has conjured up a reality that it can no longer control and that marks its own demise. The threat is real and should cause the "ruling classes" to "tremble." The aim of the *Manifesto* is not simply to dissipate or exorcise the specter but also to unveil the reality it hides. Similarly, the *Manifesto* seeks to liberate the oppressed from the illusions of their own fairy tales of a utopian liberation from oppression and to unveil the actual historical forces that will transform the hopes embodied in the specters into a historical reality.

Pushing this line of analysis one step further, one could say that the events of the late twentieth century are the final act in a long historical process in which the power of events and the emergence of powerful alternative maps and stories (maps of religious and cultural division, stories of national self-determination and identity, for example) have unveiled Marx's own realities as historical fictions. But is our own construction of the meaning of the *Manifesto* and its vision also not subject to such unveiling? What "truths" about "reality" undergird the confidence of our current exercises in historical exorcism? Could present self-confidence in relegating the views of the *Manifesto* to the status of myth not be based on historical assumptions that later generations may also unveil as mythical? Does the unveiling of the historical conditions motivating the fairy tales of the *Communist Manifesto* also involve seduction by a particular cultural construction of history, a fairy tale of our own? By becoming itself a part of our history, the *Manifesto* places one of its central contentions in our own court: The meaning of the past is a product of the present. What does the story we tell about the *Manifesto* tell us about ourselves?

The collapse of the ideological and political scaffolding that defined the cultural meaning of the *Manifesto* for a century has made it possible to encounter the Marx behind Marxism, to uncouple the texts of Marx from the historical reality of communist movements and communist regimes. By breaking this connection, the *Manifesto* more obviously becomes a part of our own past, conjuring up specters from within that can no longer be easily reduced to images of an external power. Reading the *Manifesto* today may turn us back on ourselves to question the historical conditions and motives that have suddenly made it seem so convincingly real, obvious, and natural to construe the *Manifesto* as mere fiction. Rereading the *Manifesto* as a "mere" historical construction should bring us back to a recognition of our existence as "merely" historical beings limited by our own fairy tales about the world. Perhaps the words with which Marx prefaced his masterwork *Capital* still hold true: *de te fabula narratur*—"this story is about you."[8] At least it is a question worth examining.

To come to a reasoned judgment of the extent to which the *Manifesto* can still speak to us, it is important to frame its message within the historical contexts in which it was written, to reconstruct the principles and meaning of the "story" that confronts us in the text. That is the purpose of this introduction.

IMMEDIATE HISTORICAL CONTEXTS OF THE *MANIFESTO*

The *Communist Manifesto* was composed by Karl Marx between late December 1847 and early February 1848. It was written during a period of intense expectation of imminent revolution in Western and Central Europe and was printed in London at the moment when events in Paris marked the fulfillment of such expectations and inaugurated a new season of revolutionary turmoil in France, the German Confederation, and the Austrian Empire. The *Manifesto* was not an extended historical investigation or a systematic theoretical treatise, but a compressed historical and theoretical summary for rapid popular consumption and immediate tactical guidance. Although Marx wrote the *Manifesto* at his temporary home in a suburb of Brussels, it was published as the collective expression of a political organization called the Communist League, which was headquartered in London and had commissioned Marx to compose the work. When the personal authorship of the *Manifesto* was publicly disclosed a few years later, it was presented as a collaborative work of Marx and his close associate Frederick Engels. The most immediate context of the *Manifesto* consisted of the alliance between Marxian theory and the Communist League; the intimate collaboration of Marx and Engels, which helped to negotiate this alliance; and the atmosphere of revolutionary expectancy leading up to the events of 1848, which provided much of the historical pressure and motivation for bringing the negotiations to a successful conclusion.

The Alliance between Marxian Theory and the Communist League

In the *Manifesto,* the Communist League was rechristened the Communist party and portrayed as the political arm of the European proletariat—the international wage-earning working class of a modern capitalist, industrial economy. This self-representation of communism in early 1848 was a claim on future reality, a historical construction rather than a description of an existing state of affairs. Even the name did not stick. The Communist League continued to exist under its original name until its dissolution in the early 1850s. Engels admitted, in an 1890 preface to a new German edition, that the *Manifesto* originally resonated only among "a not very numerous vanguard of scientific Socialism."[9]

The historical roots of the Communist League were not in the factories of the emergent industrial economy, but in expatriate communities of German intellectuals and handicraft workers. The former group was composed of two groups: (1) journalists and writers attempting to escape German censorship laws and (2) political radicals threatened by more direct political persecution. The latter group also consisted of two parts: (1) traditional communities of traveling journeymen, primarily craftsmen such as tailors, cabinetmakers, watchmakers, and printers, whose livelihoods were threatened by industrial organization, technology, and free-market relations; and (2) artisans who had become refugees from political persecution because of their participation in populist movements of political opposition to the conservative, authoritarian regimes in central Europe. In organizational terms, the Communist League was a descendant of the *Bund der Geaechteten* (League of Outlaws), a society of exiled radicals formed in Paris in 1834, and its successor the *Bund der Gerechten* (League of the Just). The League of the Just split off from its parent society in 1836 when many of the original members, supported by a growing number of refugee artisans, turned away from the political goal of creating a democratic republic through political agitation and toward the social goal of creating an egalitarian society organized around the principle of communal property ownership.

The League of the Just was a secret society that allied itself with analogous French groups in planning for a violent overthrow of the existing order, but it also maintained ties to the broader, public societies of handicraft workers whose activities were centered on mutual aid and self-education. In 1838, the League found a charismatic spokesperson in the exiled artisan philosopher Wilhelm Weitling, whose programmatic pamphlet, *Mankind as It Is and as It Should Be,* projected a future society in which the religiously grounded ethical principle "all men are brothers" would attain historical reality through communal ownership of property. Weitling's amalgam of communist theory and a religious vision of the imminent establishment of a "new Jerusalem" maintained a powerful hold on the leaders of the League into the mid-1840s.

Participation in an abortive uprising in Paris in 1839 forced many of the leaders of the League to flee to London. The London branch of the League of the Just soon developed the two-dimensional organization that was to become characteristic of communist organizations. The League itself was organized as a secret, hierarchically structured political society built on local cells of five to ten individuals, circles composed of delegates from these cells, and a Central Committee elected from the circles. At the same time, the League joined or established Worker's Educational Societies, where recreational and social activities aimed at forging working-class solidarity and a common cultural identity were combined with popular political education and the teaching of various theories of social change and historical transformation. The Educational Societies constituted the popular working-class base for the smaller circle of political activists and theorists within the various committees of the secret society. Unlike many other movements for radical social transformation in the 1830s and 1840s, the League of the Just had organizational ties to a social group outside the tiny circles of conspiratorial revolutionaries and social theorists. This popular base was small, but it provided a link between disaffected middle-class intellectuals and working people outside the dominant social and political elites. But this popular constituency was not at any time during the 1840s composed of wage earners within the new industrial enterprises. Its members were workers whose traditional forms of production and exchange were being undermined by industrial capitalism. They were more external victims than internal products of the new system of production.

The London branch soon assumed a leadership role in the League of the Just. Connections were forged with non-German radical groups, with circles of exiles from other countries (such as France, Italy, and Poland), and with local English organizations. The legally protected freedoms of speech and association enjoyed in England allowed for more open relationships among political organization, ideological education and propaganda, and the everyday concerns of a working-class constituency.

Although Marx and Engels had frequent contact with leaders of the League in both Paris and London from the time of their own exile from Germany after 1842–1843, they did not at first join its ranks. Working on the formation, clarification, and defense of their own theoretical positions, they created their own organization, dominated by refugee intellectuals, called the Communist Committees of Correspondence in 1846. As they searched for the appropriate agents to put their theories into social and political practice, they focused on the League of the Just. It was a working-class organization committed to the general principles of communist revolution and with at least the beginnings of an international constituency extending beyond the narrow circles of German intellectuals in exile. At the same time, the London leadership of the League initiated attempts to create a more practical and unified program for its organization. The moral pronouncements and messianic prophecies of Weitling had lost much of their attraction by 1846. In addition, the French branch of the League seemed to be floundering in its eclectic mixture of theories derived from utopian traditions calling for social revolution based on a transformation of moral or religious consciousness. In 1846, Marx's invitations to the Paris and London branches of the League to join his Communist Correspondence Committees were reciprocated, with the League asking Marx and Engels to join in its process of program formation and political reorganization. The Brussels Committee of Correspondence, led by Marx, joined the League in early 1847, becoming one of its circles and forming a local Worker's Educational Society on the League model.

The alliance between the two groups, combining the theory of Marx and the social and political activity of the League, took the new name *Bund der Kommunisten* (Communist League) at two major congresses held on June 2–9 and November 29–December 8, 1847. During these conferences and the debates among members of the individual societies that took place during the months between them, Marx and his associates were able to convince the leaders of the League to accept the fundamental theoretical tenets of his position. By the fall of 1847, the motto of the League of the Just—"All Men Are Brothers"—had been changed to "Proletarians of All Countries, Unite!" and the universalistic utopian principle of community of property had been reformulated in the specific historical terms of an abolition of bourgeois, capitalist, "private" property. This process of accommodation was difficult and gradual, as documents outlining the statutes and programmatic drafts from the two congresses reveal.

At the first congress, the draft statutes began with this principle: "The League's aim is the emancipation of mankind from slavery through the dissemination of the theory of the community of goods and its most rapid possible practical realization." After the second congress, this principle had been changed to: "The purpose of the League is the overthrow of the bourgeoisie, the rulership of the proletariat, the abolition of the existing society which rests on the foundation of class opposition and the founding of a new society without classes and without private property." The shift was drastic: from a vision of communism as a moral principle based on the nature of man to a class-based program in which communism embodied the historical viewpoint of a specific group within society whose victory over its oppressors would produce a new classless society governed by the communal ownership of property and the collective control of the processes of production and exchange.[10]

The translation of Marxian theory into the political program of a working-class movement is most evident in the various drafts of a communist "confession of faith" or "catechism," which preceded the commissioning and publication of Marx's *Manifesto* in early 1848. At the June 1847 congress, the *Draft of a Communist Confession of Faith* (see Document 2) presented for discussion in the local circles was still marked by an awkward combination of different perspectives. Drafted by Engels in the catechism format of question and answer, the June confession began with the claim that the aim of the communists was to organize society according to the principle of community of property so that individual freedom would be compatible with social harmony and the welfare of all. Two justifications for the abolition of private property were presented. The first was the Marxian historical claim that the development of an industrial, capitalist economy had produced the necessary material conditions for communal ownership of property. The second returned to the "irrefutable" basis of universal human principles, such as "the happiness of the individual is inseparable from the happiness of all." Engels himself was clearly dissatisfied with this compromise, and in his discussion with the Paris chapter of the League during the fall, he revised the Confession to conform more consistently with the Marxian position that communism was "the doctrine of the conditions for the emancipation of the proletariat." This proposition defined communism as an understanding of history emerging from the experience and consciousness of a particular social class, and its effective presentation demanded a historical narrative of the development of the conditions of emancipation. It was not comfortably squeezed into the question-and-answer format of a catechism or confession of faith. In late November, just before the second League congress, Engels wrote to Marx that he should use the programmatic materials from the League's discussions to write not a catechism or confession of faith, but a "manifesto" that presented the historical viewpoint they had developed over the past five years (see Document 3).[11]

The *Communist Manifesto,* as composed by Marx and accepted by the Communist League as its collective program in February 1848, was therefore the product of a series of negotiations that connected Marx's theory of society and history to the practical agency of a political movement with a working-class constituency.

The Collaboration of Marx and Engels

In the complex negotiations and discussions that culminated in the commissioning and publication of the *Manifesto,* Frederick Engels played a critically important role. At the congress of June 2–9, 1847, which Marx did not attend, Engels represented Marx's position to the League delegates. He drafted two important preliminary versions of the *Manifesto* in June and November 1847, which Marx used among other materials in composing the published version. In the preface to the English translation of the *Manifesto* by Samuel Moore in 1888, Engels acknowledged that the text was a "joint production," yet he insisted that "the fundamental proposition, which forms its nucleus, belongs to Marx."[12] This nuclear proposition, which Engels compared in its importance to Darwin's theory of evolution, was actually an interlocking set of propositions: (1) a theory of society, politics, and culture as effects of specific historical modes of economic production and exchange; (2) a conception of class antagonism as the motor of historical development; and (3) a view of human emancipation as the historically conditioned emancipation of the proletariat from the capitalist system of production and the politically enforced class domination of the bourgeoisie. According to Engels, Marx had already worked out this theory when they began their period of intensive collaboration in the winter of 1844–1845. What Engels brought to the relationship and to the theory was not just an affirmation of the Marxian "truth" but also the ability to make the theory accessible to a broader audience than exiled German philosophers and cultural critics, to apply it to the empirical reality of the historical transformation of material conditions and social life by the forces of industrial capitalism, and to grasp its practical implications for the working-class politics that had begun to emerge in Western Europe, especially in England and France, during the 1830s and 1840s.

During the 1960s and 1970s, an influential component of Western European and American scholarship interpreted the relationship between Marx and Engels in dichotomous terms: as an uneasy alliance between thinkers with theoretical and historical perspectives opposed in decisive ways. This interpretation became the basis for blaming Engels for the later fateful directions of Marxism toward authoritarian politics and a closed and dogmatic "scientistic" worldview governed by assumptions that merged knowledge of relations in the world of natural objects with an understanding of relations among human beings as active historical agents or "subjects." This interpretation served the purpose of salvaging a "humanist" Marx from the appropriation of Marxism by Soviet-style communism, but it also distorted the relationship between the two close friends and lifelong collaborators and confused transformations within Marxism after 1848 with differences in the personal perspectives of the two men. Engels was certainly not Marx's clone, but there is no convincing evidence that disproves Engels's claim that he and Marx were in essential agreement, especially during their close collaboration between 1845 and 1848, and that this agreement was achieved through Engels's subordination of his own research and argument to the framework provided by Marxian theory as it had evolved up to 1845.

Karl Marx and Frederick Engels were both natives of Prussia's westernmost province, the Rhineland, an area of Germany that had been under French rule during the Napoleonic period and had been incorporated into the Prussian state by the Congress of Vienna in 1815. The Rhineland was the Prussian province most transformed by the legal and political changes represented by the French Revolution. It was also the province most affected in its social development by the consequences of commercial market relations and industrial production, both through competition with English products and through the beginnings of a transformation of the systems of economic exchange and production within its own borders.

Marx (born in 1818) and Engels (born in 1820) were also members of the same historical generation, having passed their childhoods in the period of conservative restoration between 1815 and 1830 and become adults during a time in which the restoration began to unravel due to socioeconomic and political change during the 1830s and early 1840s. The cultural perspectives or intellectual maps that were available to them as they tried to make sense of a world involved in rapid, confusing change overlapped to a very large degree. Both first tried to express their experiences in literature. During the late 1830s and early 1840s, however, both turned to the philosophical tradition of the German Hegelian school to gain a conceptual mastery of their historical environment and a critical view of current conflicts and future possibilities.

As in any productive collaboration, that between Marx and Engels involved not only mutually recognized agreements but also complementary differences. Engels was the eldest son of a prosperous Protestant mill-owning family in the Wuppertal, a region of textile manufacturing that was undergoing the first stages of industrialization. His formal education was cut short at the age of seventeen so that he could pursue a practical education in the family business—first in the local factory, then in an export office in the port city of Bremen, and finally as an accountant in the English branch of the firm of Ermen and Engels at the center of the British Industrial Revolution in Manchester. Engels was a voracious reader and a precocious journalist who participated actively in contemporary literary and philosophical debates, but his education was clearly marked by his intimate experience of religion and politics as effects of changes in the processes of economic production and exchange. From the time of his youth, he was acutely aware of the changes in the physical and social environment produced by the new technologies and methods of production in the textile industry, as well as by the expansion of the commercial networks in which commodities were exchanged. His first significant publication was an extended essay on both the destructive effects of industrialization in his home region and the ideological uses of religion to divert attention from, and provide moral justification for, these effects.

When Engels decided to collaborate with Marx in 1845, he had just finished a large-scale study, *The Condition of the Working Class in England* (1845), which critically described the social and political consequences of the Industrial Revolution at its global epicenter (see Document 4). Having spent two years (1842–1844) observing factory production, class polarization, and labor unrest in Manchester, Engels brought personal observation and experience to bear on the processes that Marx had previously known only theoretically, or from the

Figure 1. Frederick Engels at the time of his first collaboration with Karl Marx in the mid-1840s.
Hulton Deutsch/Getty Images

perspective of a radical intellectual theorist. Moreover, Engels played a significant role in directing Marx's attention to the theoretical conceptualization of the production, accumulation, and distribution of wealth within a free-market system as it had been developed in the British tradition of "political economy." In his "Outlines of a Critique of Political Economy," published in 1844, Engels critically described the evolution of economic theory from Adam Smith's *Wealth of Nations* (1776) to the early-nineteenth-century works of Thomas Malthus, David Ricardo, and James Mill. He judged this body of theory as a pseudoscientific justification of the practices of greed and exploitation that characterized economic relations in a system based on the private ownership of property and free competition among property owners.[13]

Marx carefully studied and excerpted Engels's works. Both Engels's critique of the premises of the science of modern free-market economics and his descriptions of the actual living conditions of the new industrial working class were decisive influences in guiding Marx to consider relations within the system of production as the primary site where the drama of human suffering and human emancipation was being played out.

After 1845, Engels threw himself with self-abnegating enthusiasm into the task of clarifying and defending Marx's views against all alternative positions. Soon he developed exceptional skill in employing Marxian principles in the detailed analysis and interpretation of contemporary history. However, his work on Manchester, as well as his formulations of a Marxian version of the communist credo in the summer and fall of 1847, reveal his tendency to read historical processes as technologically determined and to see the process of liberation in terms of a quantitative expansion of the possibilities of industrial production. In Engels's words, the communist revolution sometimes appeared like a managerial solution to the inhibitions on industrial growth created by the capitalist system. Marx's prose was usually murkier and more convoluted but strongly resonant with both connections and contradictions that Engels barely noticed.

The predominating influences in Marx's early development came less from the consequences of the new modes of industrial production than from the legal and political changes inspired by the French Revolution. Benefiting from French rule on the left bank of the Rhine from 1792 to 1814, Marx's father was among the first generation of German Jews to enjoy equal status under the law with his fellow German subjects and to experience personal freedom in the choice of residence, occupation, and professional education. The young Marx

experienced both the exhilaration and anxiety created by this emancipation. In an early high school essay, he seems almost overwhelmed
by the burdens of assuming personal responsibility for his "vocation"
in society.[14] Moreover, the experience of his father, who had used the
new freedoms to forge a professional identity as a respected lawyer, as
well as the advice of other childhood mentors and teachers, strongly
suggested to Marx that enjoyment of the new freedoms was connected
to assimilation to the cultural values and ethical rules of the larger
non-Jewish world into which he had been granted entry. In fact, Marx's
whole family "converted" to Protestant Christianity to ease this process of assimilation.

Intense reflection on the conditions of personal freedom and community membership pervaded Marx's educational development. Much
more than in Engels's writing, Marx's discussions of liberation and community resonated with an acute self-consciousness concerning the labor
of self-making and the tensions of achieving full participation and recognition in the political and cultural community. At the time (during the
early 1840s) when Engels devoted himself to an examination of both the
theory and the practice of the Industrial Revolution (in England), Marx
threw himself into an examination of the theory and practice of the political revolution (especially in France). Both focused on the fate of their
homeland from the perspective of exile, but Marx saw that homeland
from Paris rather than Manchester.

The publication of the *Communist Manifesto* was a culminating
moment in the intellectual marriage between Marx and Engels, but
even this moment of close cooperation and apparent total agreement
revealed signs of implicit tensions in the differences in content and style
between Engels's drafts and Marx's final version of the text.

The years between 1845 and 1848 were not years of intellectual creativity or theoretical innovation for either Marx or Engels. Instead,
during this period, the two men clarified and explicated their positions
in relation to theoretical competitors and in the search for an audience
of historical agents that would demonstrate the validity of their theoretical commitments in historical practice. In relation to their theoretical
competition, Marx and Engels were intent on displaying the superior-
ity of their own "historical" conception of communism to any position
based on subjectively held moral or religious principles. Their first
collaborations in 1845 involved a critical accounting with the German
philosophical radicalism they had left behind. Their old Hegelian commitments were now unveiled as illusions that hid the real conditions of
historical existence. In the years immediately preceding the writing of

the *Manifesto,* both Marx and Engels were especially concerned about differentiating their positions from other forms of socialism that shared their belief that private property (or at least certain forms of it) must give way to communal ownership and market competition to cooperative management, but did not share their view that the class conflict emerging from the inner contradictions of capitalist production was the necessary historical condition of a socialist or communist revolution.

The last section of the *Manifesto* summarizes the results of this history of self-differentiation and criticism. Marx and Engels were convinced that any attempts to ground the transition to a communist society on a return to the past or on the alleged universal power of love, reason, justice, or faith would collapse before the irresistible power of the historical evolution of structures of economic production and exchange. Any theory that could not explain and thus master this historical process would be quickly revealed as the nostalgia or defensive reaction of a social group whose time had passed, or as an isolated, personal vision without the historical power to provide the working masses with a mirror of their own situation and a guide to their historical future. Although they appreciated the incisive criticism of free-market economics and bourgeois society in utopian works such as those by Robert Owen and Charles Fourier (see Documents 5 and 6), they were contemptuous of attempts to create model communities on the basis of a new "science" of society. Like Fourier, Owen, and other utopian socialists, Marx and Engels believed that the task of constructing a viable, harmonious community demanded a transformation of social relations and especially a reorganization of the conditions of human labor. Both the high evaluation of labor as an essential human activity and the belief that labor had somehow been corrupted or perverted under the rule of the free market were broadly shared among socialist thinkers such as Fourier and Owen (see Documents 7 and 8). The Marxian theory was distinguished by its claim that it embodied the historical perspective of the social class that contained the future in its current productive practice, that it was not a mere theory about the world, but a self-understanding of the real everyday practices of the actors who were transforming the world.

Marxian theory thus claimed an inner bond with a powerful collective historical agent. In fact, it claimed to be the voice of historical judgment itself. Its theoretical criticism of the existing order was empowered by the practical criticism of that order in the experience of an oppressed class destined eventually to encompass the majority of humankind. The goal was to appropriate the term *communism* for the Marxian position and to present communism as the legitimate self-understanding of the global experience of the historically progressive working class. In pursuing this goal, Marx and Engels needed to establish their position in the context of the radical political movements that had mobilized workingclass discontents during the late 1830s and early 1840s and had begun to regain some of their vigor during the period of devastating famine, poverty, and unemployment in 1846–1847. The Chartist movement in England and the "red" republican or social democratic movement led by Alexandre Ledru-Rollin (1807–1874) and Louis Blanc (1811–1882) in France combined a democratic critique of existing constitutional arrangements with promises of social and economic reform for the benefit of the working classes (see Documents 9 and 10). The term *socialism* had emerged in public discourse in the 1830s to designate a conception of social reform that opposed the principle of competitive individualism on the basis of the principle of association or cooperation. The term *communism* had emerged in the 1840s to designate the insurrectionary activism of a working-class politics seeking some form of public control of the world of economic production and exchange. Marx and Engels aimed to appropriate the latter term for their own position. In polemical terms, this was the assertion of the *Manifesto:* Marxian historical theory is communism, and communism articulates the revolutionary consciousness of the social class that essentially defines the productive process in capitalist society—the wage-earning industrial workers, or proletariat.

The polemical battles for the right to speak for the historical agent of emancipation in the 1840s took place in an atmosphere heavy with the expectancy that a period of revolutionary turmoil and transformation was imminent. It was this historical expectancy that fueled the furious journalistic skirmishes Marx and Engels fought with proponents of alternative forms of socialism, as well as their critical dismissal of all attempts to restrict the historical realization of the ideals of freedom and community to the political sphere.

Revolutionary Expectancy

The signs of approaching crisis in European politics and society that marked the years between 1845 and 1848 were certainly not easy for contemporaries to read as items in a single story or dimensions of a unified historical process. Events such as the calling of the first United Diet in Prussia, the organization of political resistance to the French monarchy (in the form of raucous reform "banquets," or demonstrations), the extraparliamentary agitation by British liberals to repeal the tariffs on imported grain, and the successful revolt of the liberal cantons within the Swiss Confederation in 1847 suggested the emergence of a new surge in the ongoing battle to create, reform, or solidify the political and legal institutions of middle-class liberalism. Political agitation by more inclusive, populist movements, such as the British Chartists or French and German democratic radicals, who represented constituencies outside the privileged circle of established constitutional politics, pointed toward a process of democratization that would undermine the privileges of wealth and education through broader definitions of citizenship and use the powers of the state to mitigate the social effects of free-market economics and industrial production. Political turmoil fueled by nationalist sentiments in Austria's Polish and Italian provinces, as well as national gatherings of German leaders of the liberal and radical opposition movements, raised the specter of cultural nationalism as an organizing principle of popular mobilization and political community. At the same time, the vast migration (and thus sudden visibility) of destitute populations into the cities or overseas, because of devastating food shortages and the collapse of traditional artisan production and cottage industries under the pressures of free trade, indicated the existence of economic and social problems that could no longer be resolved within the political frameworks of the existing regimes.

Did the disparate and scattered signs of immiseration, the bouts of unemployment and waves of migration among the lower classes, and the periodic crises of overproduction in the system of exchange indicate a general economic crisis? Were these birth pangs of the new industrial capitalism as it struggled for dominance with older systems of production, or early death throes of the new system, revealing its inner contradictions? Did the political turmoil and agitations in various places throughout Europe portend a major shift in the general political landscape? Marx and Engels were certainly not the only writers and social observers who felt that European society was on the verge of revolution in late 1847 and early 1848. In fact, the widespread fear of revolution inspired their own hopes. During the weeks in which the *Manifesto* was being conceived and produced, the French liberal social theorist Alexis de Tocqueville warned his fellow members in the French Chamber of Deputies against falling asleep "over an active volcano." Hoping to arouse his colleagues to a spirited defense of property rights and individual liberties against the threats of communist revolution, Tocqueville noted that the ground was "trembling" once again in Europe and a "revolutionary wind" was in the air. "There is a tempest on the horizon, and it is moving towards you. Will you let it take you by surprise?"[15] (see Document 1)

Ich und Mein Haus, Wir wollen dem HERRN dienen.

Figure 2. Cartoon by Frederick Engels of the Prussian King Frederick William IV, surrounded by his aristocratic entourage, addressing the opening session of the United Diet in Berlin, April 1847. The phrase from the King's speech cited under the cartoon represents the alliance of throne and altar on the political Right: "I and my House, we will serve the LORD."

Marx and Engels were convinced that their theory provided a guide for reading all these signs of the times as part of one story, decoding all the clues as indicators of a general European and even global crisis. In politics, the long process of legal and political emancipation inaugurated by the French Revolution was relentlessly breaking down the order of legal privilege and exclusive definitions of citizenship. This process also was creating political communities defined by equality under the law and inclusive rights of participation in the making of law. Every assertion of a claim to extend voting rights, to reform legislative bodies so as to broaden the class of political participants or ensure the responsibility of governments to peoples, or to extend the rule of general laws over the last bastions of privilege and customary rights seemed a part of this single story of what we might call the "long"

French Revolution. At the same time, displacement, unemployment, and poverty among the working classes in both urban and rural areas, as well as the volatility of the market regulation of production and consumption both within and between countries (expressed in periodic recessions or commercial "crises"), pointed toward a general crisis in the system of industrial capitalism as it spread from Great Britain to the European continent. Turmoil was produced both by the impact of the new system of production on traditional patterns of work and exchange, and on conflicts and contradictions within the new system itself.

During the late 1840s, due to the impact of the political French Revolution and the British Industrial Revolution, European social relations appeared to be entering a new era of uncertainty, change, and danger. Marx and Engels possessed a highly developed critical theory of what was historically problematic in bourgeois society and in the processes of political liberation and economic production that constituted that society's foundations. At the same time, however, their critique was organized around certain assumptions about liberty and community, about work and social relations, which they shared with many of their nonsocialist and noncommunist contemporaries. Although the *Communist Manifesto* claimed to speak for a class that had no stake in the existing order, that had nothing to lose but everything to gain through a total transformation of its social world, it was in fact deeply committed to bringing the fundamental principles informing that world to full fruition. The *Manifesto* was, in many ways, not only a critique of the foundations of bourgeois society and culture but also a profoundly "bourgeois" work. The political and economic revolutions that had created the society that Marx and Engels rejected, because it was opposed to the full realization of freedom and community, also informed the fundamental values of the world that they envisioned as its successor.

HISTORICAL PREMISES OF THE *MANIFESTO*

The map of the world constructed in the *Communist Manifesto* was shaped by a number of fundamental assumptions or unquestioned premises. These assumptions or premises were also derived from the cultural context in which the *Manifesto* was written, even if less obviously than its immediate political intentions, personal motivations, or specific historical references. Construing the meaning of the *Manifesto* one and a half centuries after its creation requires some understanding of the assumptions about freedom, labor, community, and history that operated at an unself-conscious, subterranean level in shaping its descriptions, metaphors, and arguments.

The Principle of Emancipation:
The Theory and Practice of Freedom

In the *Communist Manifesto,* the coming communist revolution is presented as the historical culmination of the process of human emancipation, as the liberation of the creative powers of humankind from the "fetters" of historical oppression and servitude. Communist revolution would break the chains that had held humanity in a state of dependence and had prevented the full development of its potential powers of creativity and self-government. The *Manifesto* is a manifesto of liberation, an heir and successor of previous movements of emancipation, from the Protestant revolt against the medieval Catholic Church in the sixteenth century to the political revolts (in England, America, and France) against arbitrary royal power and encrusted social privilege beginning in the seventeenth century and culminating in the French Revolution at the end of the eighteenth century. At the same time, however, the *Manifesto* presented its intentions in terms of a critique of all previous emancipations. It unveiled the historical process of emancipation as one in which repeated claims of a general liberation emerged as illusions hiding new forms of enslavement. The future communist revolution was pitted against a regime that itself articulated freedom as its highest value.

The *Manifesto* thus constructed itself around a paradox of liberation. It described a historical process culminating in a society that defined freedom as free trade, or the free competition of commodity exchange in the global marketplace. The unleashing of individual self-interest in a market society liberated the individual from all previous forms of dependence—from servitude to the gods, customary privilege, and personal authority; from the ties of kinship; from the duties of social or professional calling; from the given "natural" identities imposed by sex, age, and ethnicity or race; from subservience to the powers of nature outside of man. Individuals were left free to define their own value through the unrestricted pursuit of personal interest, through the free and rational "egoistic" exploitation of their own natural energies and accumulated property. Participation in this process of liberation, however, entailed the reduction of the individual human agent to a commodity in market exchange and defined freedom as the freedom of a mere object, whose value was determined by impersonal, raw, "callous cash payment."

Bourgeois freedom was thus reduced to servitude to the impersonal flow of capital, to dependence on market forces outside the individual's control. What appeared to be individual freedom to seek recognition on the basis of achieved merit within a system of fair competition was in fact submission to the mechanism of the market and the rules of capital accumulation that determined which acts of individuals would be recognized as valid or meaningful.

At the same time, Marx insisted that the liberation achieved in bourgeois society had established, or was in the process of establishing, the necessary conditions for the emergence of an authentic self-determination, a true emancipation of humankind from the chains of natural and cultural determination. Bourgeois emancipation was both the negation of true freedom and its historical condition. Informing this opposition was a particular conception of liberation as self-determination and self-sufficiency that Marx had absorbed from his own historical experience and that he had examined and critically developed within the terms of the German intellectual heritage he had assimilated between 1835 and 1845.

During his university years in the late 1830s, Marx discovered a powerful conceptual framework for articulating his experience of individual emancipation and communal participation in the political and cultural philosophy of Georg Wilhelm Friedrich Hegel (1770–1831) (see Document 11). Marx's initial public commitment to the ongoing process of human emancipation occurred as an intense engagement in the liberation of secular human self-consciousness from the chains of religious faith, particularly Christianity. His own choice to pursue a career in philosophy was a choice, as he proclaimed in the preface to his doctoral dissertation in 1841, for the cultural party that fought under the banner of Prometheus, the Greek hero who defied the gods, stole their heavenly fire, and brought it to earth to construct a self-sufficient human realm. Prometheus was the "most eminent Saint and Martyr on the Philosophical Calendar" because he belligerently rejected humanity's dependence on any knowledge or power outside itself and actively worked to create a world on the basis of this defiance.[16] Philosophy in its Hegelian form was for Marx a defiant claim that human self-consciousness was grounded within itself and could determine the principles of its own creative activity.

Once human thinking had freed itself from the seduction of faith in heavenly powers, Marx claimed, it was the task of philosophy to build a human world according to its own principles, to work toward the creation of the human community not as an association dependent on an authority outside itself but as a free association of moral beings, who affirmed their own independence as they joined together to create a world according to the immanent, purely human criteria of rational thought. Having clarified and grasped the principles of its own activity, human consciousness turned its attention to the world to remake that world to conform to its own principles. Once the philosopher had grasped the basis of his philosophical activity, he became an activist, a critic of the world, a reformer of the world. For the young Marx, philosophy as a career ceased to be an academic discipline concerned only with itself and became public critique and popular education, a form of theoretical practice.

As a young philosopher, Marx assigned himself the task of making philosophy real by creating a world defined by self-determination rather than relations of dependence, by working toward the creation of a secular, "free" democratic state. Freedom was here defined as self-sufficiency and self-determination, as the creation of the rules of one's own activity. But such freedom was within and of a community, a freedom realized in "the free association of moral beings."[17] In acts of freedom, human beings discovered their true essence, attained self-realization, and integrated their actions with their nature. Authentically liberated human beings were free to express their own inner beings as self-legislating persons. Their task was not just to throw off the chains of dependence on any and all forms of external authority but also to discipline the merely self-interested freedom of the calculating individual ego and subject its actions to the self-imposed laws defined by the collective, public ego, the general human reason of the state. True freedom was expressed in those acts of public self-determination that created a human world in defiance of the gods.

In the early 1840s, Marx gave two distinct meanings to the emancipation process to which he had committed his talent and energy. First, emancipation involved human liberation from the self-imposed enslavement of religious faith. It was a heaven-storming activity insisting that human salvation — full self-realization — must be built within the earthly human realm as a self-creation. In an introduction to a critique of his Hegelian heritage written in 1843 and published in exile in 1844, Marx provided a condensed and polemically forceful statement of this humanistic concept of liberation (see Document 13).

Second, emancipation from religious dependence produced a commitment to democratic politics, to the formation of a state in which the progress toward secular self-determination found its natural fulfillment in a moral association of free beings who recognized their freedom as

Figure 3. Portrait of Marx as a university student, 1835–1836.
PAGES Francois/Getty Images

self-legislating subjects. Freedom in community took precedence over the purely self-interested freedom of the particular ego. The moral freedom of the citizen as a member of a political association that made and administered the laws of its own members was a higher form of freedom than the freedom of the individual to move unhindered by others in the selfish pursuit of personal merit in the economic and social marketplace. Achieved freedom for Marx was thus, from the beginning of his career, tied to the achievement of a public consensus based on the common human essence of liberated individuals. Making freedom real involved an inner transformation of the individual into a moral and rational being obedient to the rules that followed from the essential nature the individual shared with other human beings.

As Marx turned away from academic philosophy and to the practical tasks of educating his fellow Germans to recognize their duties as autonomous moral beings and to create a secular, democratic state, he soon developed a more critical perspective on the claims of political emancipation. The revolutionary and reformist movements of the previous generation had, in his view, created a divided world in which the competitive egoism of civil society regulated by market relations was opposed to the rational and moral community of the state, in which human beings employed their reason to forge common rules for their activity and to motivate obedience to those rules. In historical practice, however, the individual "selfish" freedoms of civil society overrode the moral autonomy and rational consensus of the political sphere: the "bourgeois" trumped the "citizen."

In an 1843 analysis of the classic texts of liberal democratic politics and the eighteenth-century revolutionary tradition included in a review of the particular issue of Jewish emancipation (see Document 14), Marx presented a principled critique of political emancipation. The civil emancipation of the individual as guaranteed in the human rights proclaimed by various American and French constitutions, he noted, marked the emancipation of the self-interested, isolated ego from all social bonds. Individual liberty in the liberal democratic canon was simply the liberty of man "regarded as an isolated monad, withdrawn into himself." Legal rights marked the boundaries preventing such monads from harming each other in their self-interested pursuits. Citizenship rights—the rights of participation in the association of free beings creating the laws governing their own activity—were reduced to the limited purpose of guaranteeing and protecting individual rights. The collective or communal self-represented by the state served and protected the interests of the isolated ego.

The claim that the secular democratic state was a moral community in which individuals elevated themselves to their higher public selves as autonomous, self-legislating agents was, therefore, an illusion. In fact, Marx noted, inequalities of power and wealth, which allowed some groups to dominate others, were not abolished by the new constitutional rights but guaranteed and promoted by those rights. Religious freedom under constitutional liberalism was not freedom from

Figure 4. Prometheus Bound: Allegory on the prohibition of the *Rheinische Zeitung*. As the editor of this liberal newspaper, which was forced by Prussian authorities to cease publication on March 31, 1843, Marx identified himself with the mythic Greek hero Prometheus, here depicted as chained to a printing press and attacked by the royal Prussian eagle.

the chains of religious belief but the freedom of every individual to enslave himself or herself to religious illusions without outside interference. The association of individuals in the public identity of the state was merely a formal artifice that served the preservation of the selfish ego's free movement according to the rules of market exchange. In their everyday activities as sensuous, interested, producing, desiring beings, human individuals found that the real content of their lives was determined by the unequal productive and exchange relations of civil society. The citizen was a formal abstraction, and the self-interested, egoistic "natural man" of civil society was the real human individual, despite an ideology that portrayed the citizen or communal being as the real, or essential, human individual. In civil society, human beings were enchained, not self-determining or self-sufficient, but subjected to rules of production and exchange over which they had no apparent individual or collective control. These rules thus appeared to them as "natural" or "divine" laws, as rules imposed on them from outside the processes of their self-determination.

In this programmatic statement, Marx defined his generation's distinctive path in the modern tradition of human emancipation. His chosen vocation was to unveil the illusions of political emancipation and inspire commitment to a process of liberation that would make the principle of self-determination a reality in the actual existence of individuals in their activities as producing, exchanging, sensuous beings: "Only when the real, individual man re-absorbs in himself the abstract citizen. . .will human emancipation have been accomplished."

Marx thus affirmed that the principle articulated in the concept of political emancipation — that human beings attained self-determination as members of a community of self-legislators (that is, through an identification process that formed their individual egoistic wills into the consensual collective will of a moral association) — was correct. The problem was that this principle could not be made into an experienced reality within the realm of legal and political relations. The ideology of political emancipation was illusory not because its view of emancipation was wrong, but because it expected this emancipation from politics. As Marx looked to human relations within civil society as the site where the edifice of mutual identification (community) and self-determination (freedom) would have to be built, he thus continued to affirm his inherited notions of liberty. The emancipation that communism was imagined to produce would retain the claim that self-determination became real only on the basis of association or identification. Marx never wavered from this commitment to the belief that emancipation was an elevation into a state of self-recognition in which individual freedom was merged into an identification with the "associated individuals" (to use the terms of the *Manifesto*) who formed the human community.

Marx's rejection of political emancipation as inadequate to the inherent human drive for freedom as self-determination produced a view of the political sphere that remained a permanent part of his theory and is present throughout the *Manifesto*. Politics is defined as a realm of illusions in the sense that the promises of universal equality, freedom, and community cannot be fulfilled there. The political community is not the place where these goals can be achieved. There is no inherent human value in equality under the law or in democratic political institutions. Rather, politics is reduced to a means of achieving the French Revolution's ideals of liberty, equality, and fraternity in the area where they must be established to become a daily lived reality—the realm of social and economic relations in civil society.

This cynical, disillusioned conception of politics as a means to other ends was applied critically to the analysis of the past and the present. The liberal democratic state, even in its most advanced contemporary forms, could be nothing more than an instrument for furthering the interests of the dominant groups in civil society, a means for class domination. It was also applied to the strategies for the ongoing process of human liberation. Political strategy was a sphere in which manipulation, compromise, and deception could justifiably operate in service to a higher goal. Working-class parties could ally themselves with their political opponents to create a situation in which they might triumph over these opponents.

Politics was, of course, terribly important in organizing and achieving revolution, as an instrument for destroying the old society and opening a space for the conditions of the new order to develop. But in a society of free beings, politics itself disappeared. Human association found its essential place in social life, and "government" became a mere management of technical processes, not an association of citizens making their own laws.

In the wake of his disillusionment with political emancipation as human emancipation in 1842–1843, Marx made a decisive choice for the direction of his theory. By reducing political and legal phenomena to secondary expressions of relations and conflicts rooted elsewhere, he opened himself to a sentimental misreading of power and politics as a realm of specters that would dissolve once the reality behind them was transformed. At the same time, he encouraged a cynical view of politics as a means toward higher ends. The upshot was that Marxism had little to say about law and politics per se, and it provided little room for the creation of a world in which differences might be regulated rather than integrated, in which conflict might be subjected to rules rather than dissolved in total consensus or covered up by assertions of unity. The rejection of politics as a site for community was ultimately and implicitly the rejection of a vision of a society of differences, of multiple social and cultural identifications whose relation to each other could only be negotiated in a more formalized public sphere encompassing them all.

As Marx made the transition from politics to society as the primary site of the achievement of human emancipation, he engaged in a difficult creative process of translating and revising two major assumptions of his intellectual inheritance. The description of human essence as self-determination, creativity, and self-creation was translated into the economic terms of production, or labor, and the idea of community as a consensus among self-determining agents in making the rules for their own activity was reconceptualized as the mutual identification of producers in the social associations of class. Labor, not power, defined that core human agency whose emancipation would be synonymous with human emancipation. "Class," not the "people" or the "public," represented the collective historical embodiment of human agency. "Proletarians of All Countries, Unite!" not "All Men Are Brothers" was the battle cry of emancipation.

Productive Labor as the Organizing Center of Human Existence

Marx's relocation of the primary site of the historical struggle for human emancipation from politics and law to the economic and social relations of civil society was first clearly enunciated in an unfinished, untitled collection of writings that, since their publication in 1932, have been known as *The Economic and Philosophic Manuscripts of 1844* (see Document 17).

Written in Paris in the spring and summer of 1844, this dense and roughly drafted series of analyses and commentaries display Marx reconceptualizing his project from two perspectives. In 1842–1843, Marx had used the classic texts of the formation of the modern state and of the liberal democratic movements of the eighteenth century to frame his critique of contemporary history. The constitutions produced by the American and French Revolutions, and the political and ethical writings of the theorists of liberal politics, such as Rousseau, Kant, and Hegel, guided his perceptions of what was central to the realization of freedom and the construction of community in his own time. The manuscripts of 1844 show Marx looking elsewhere for his descriptions of contemporary human reality—to the political economists who described the workings of market relations and industrial modes of production, and to the socialist critics of contemporary society who focused on property relations and the processes of human labor as the core determinants in human history. Marx's starting point, his "premises" in these manuscripts, was, he claimed, simply taken from the texts of the political economists. He accepted their "language" and their "laws," simply assuming that their descriptions of private property, the separation of wages and profit as forms of property under capitalism, and the process of market exchange that produced increasing class division and increasing poverty and degradation among wage earners were valid. His task was not to give a new empirical description of the workings of the market and the impact of the Industrial Revolution, but to unveil the inner meaning of the descriptions at hand—to show the inner logic that tied the various elements together in a dynamic fashion and thus pointed the way to an "internal" historical critique of the system as a whole. What the political economists presented as a world of hard facts produced by the universal human motives of greed and competitive war among the greedy was to be unveiled and explained as a "historical form," as a stage in the development of human self-determination and social identity.

The conceptual framework for this unveiling of political economy's secret meaning was derived from German philosophy, particularly from the most recent phases in the critical development of the Hegelian tradition by the philosopher Ludwig Feuerbach (1804–1872). Through his transformative translation of the Hegelian metaphysical account of the self-determination of "spirit" into the everyday terms of a "positive, humanistic, and naturalistic" theory, Marx contended, Feuerbach had provided the basis for a revolutionary understanding of contemporary historical reality (see Document 15).

At the center of Marx's revisionist interpretation of his Hegelian inheritance was the definition or discovery of the real meaning of human subjective agency in the work process. The human essence, that which defined human beings as a distinctive species within the natural world, was the transformation of inherent creative power into products, the constant realization of inner subjective agency or energy in the making of external objects, the recognition by the self of its own nature in its products, and the constant appropriation of the world outside the self as material for self-expression. In acts of labor, human beings "objectified" themselves in the world. As productive, laboring beings, they developed and thus revealed the inherent possibilities of their universal identity as members of the human race, of their "species-nature," and of their essence as "species-beings," and thus they created themselves not only as individuals but also as exemplars and members of the community of humanity.

At the same time, acts of labor transformed the objects of the world external to human beings into human products. Labor thus humanized the world, making it familiar and turning it into a human "home," as it progressively came to mirror the expressive potentialities of its makers. The human was made into a world of things, and the order of natural things was "humanized."

Labor was the activity that defined "real" life—concrete, sensuous existence in civil society—in contrast to the purely abstract formal life of the citizen in the sphere of law and political institutions. This identification of human species-being with labor marked the conclusion of a rather lengthy process of reductive interpretation and "translation" of Hegelian concepts in which Marx had participated since about 1840. Hegel had defined the distinctiveness of human beings as participation in the universal activity of thought, an activity that he identified with divine "absolute" reality (see Document 11). In the first phase of Marx's Hegelian discipleship, he had joined in the demystifying, secular critique of Hegel's more radical students, which had stripped the Hegelian notion of "spirit" of its theological and metaphysical center and recreated it in purely humanistic terms. Man as creative, self-conscious spirit was primarily imagined as a producer of himself in the symbolic meanings of the cultural world. In the creation of myth, religion, art, science, ethical and philosophical systems, and so on, the human species made its inner potential into something external and "objective" and came to understand what was implicit in its own freedom (see Document 12). It made present in the world of cultural meanings the potentiality of its own creativity, then recognized this world as a self-expression, as its own creation, by coming to grasp or know it. The goal of the historical process from this perspective was the freedom of self-recognition that emerged when the world of cultural objects was recognized as a self-created world, a home that did not restrict one's freedom but instead gave shape to it.

In Feuerbach's work, this humanist critique was driven a step further in the sense that human agency was defined in terms of the active and passive elements of human sensuous existence—as processes of passive experience and active passion, involving all of the physical senses. The defining element in human nature for Feuerbach was the sensual act of love in relation to another human being, the experience of oneself as an object under the desire of the other, and the experience of oneself as subjective agent in the passionate desire to possess the other. For Feuerbach, this reciprocity of passive and active relations in sensual desire most clearly exemplified the subjective and the objective, and also the individual and the social, nature of the human species (see Document 15).

Marx enthusiastically took up the Feuerbachian focus on concrete ("positive") and sensuous existence in dynamic interaction with others as defining human essence. However, in the light of his own studies of political economy and his growing recognition that the world in which real human beings lived was being transformed by the processes of industrial production, Marx chose labor rather than love, work rather than sex, as the defining center of sensuous existence (see Document 16). The archetypal human being, the authentic representation of what it meant to be human, was not the desiring and feeling lover but the productive worker. Civil society was not fundamentally defined by the war between the sexes or the dialectic of sensual desire, but by the war between economic "classes" and the inner contradictions of the work process. In the making of products, human beings gave expression to their potential powers and came to an awareness, a self-consciousness, of their own creativity and freedom as producers. Man, Marx claimed, did not work merely to sustain his physical being but also to make his own nature real in the world, to affirm his creative powers as a producer.

Moreover, in the work process, human beings bridged the gap between themselves and the world of nature—in two senses. First, their own physical bodies became artistic instruments affirming the productive powers of the species. Second, human beings possessed the world outside the human realm and remade it into "human artifacts," and thus into a world of "art." The body became an agent of creativity rather than a burdensome thing, and the world became a self-affirming mirror of human powers. In a sense, Marx suggested, Hegel had already grasped the meaning of labor and had expressed the viewpoint of modern political economy. But he had defined labor as mental labor, as the work of thought attempting to articulate its inner principle and possess the object outside itself. Thus, he had not grasped the path to the achievement of the goals of self-determination and social identity through a transformation not of thinking, but of the labor process within the real, sensuous, practical relations of civil society.

The texts of political economy, however, described a world in which this process of human self-creation and affirmation had gone awry. Labor under capitalism was, as Marx wrote, "estranged" or "alienated" from itself, as well as from the world it had produced. The freedom and mutual recognition that were the implicit aims of all production were transposed onto the products themselves, leaving the producer fragmented and determined, isolated, impotent, and opaque to his or her own nature. Under the conditions of the capitalist economy, laborers confronted the products of their labor as independent powers that did not affirm the creativity of the laborers or create a humanized world in which they could feel at home. As components of the accumulated capital owned by the employer of labor, labor's products confronted the laborer as alien objects, as oppressive powers controlling a world in which the laborer was reduced to a dependent physical object in a hostile environment. While the laborer's products entered into a variety of relations of exchange with the products of other laborers, the laborer himself or herself remained isolated. Instead of affirming his self-determination in the making of himself, the worker found himself in servitude to the external forces of the market and to the power of capital possessed as private property by the class of employers.

Under the conditions of capitalism, the creative powers of labor were strangely perverted. Instead of humanizing the world by shaping it into a world of human production, labor found itself alienated from and dependent on the world of nature. In this relationship, human labor itself became a mere physical object, an industrial "hand" forced to expend its energies in monotonous, degrading work to sustain its merely "animal" existence. For individual human laborers, their essential creativity became a burdensome object that they had to peddle competitively in the employment market. Social relations were not marked by the mutual self-recognition of creative productivity and the collective wonder of transforming external nature into a human environment, but instead wracked by competitive hostilities in the quest for physical survival. In the books of the political economists, the Promethean creative essence of man had been transformed into an impersonal production machine, crushing human self-determination and abolishing mutual identification and recognition.

The central social institution enforcing this perversion of human selfcreation was private property. Abolish private property, and the human laborer would be able to recognize the natural world as material for creative humanization, the other laborer as a common creator of a human world, and the world of objects as the self-affirming expression of individual and common labor power. If laborers would not have to sell their laboring capacity—their human essence—as objects to others, they would in a sense recover ownership of themselves and the essential humanity they shared. If the products of their own labor were not taken from them as the property of others and added to the capital that controlled the employment of their labor, they would recognize themselves in the world of products.

In 1844, this repossession of labor's activity and its products—humankind's "return" to itself in an act of self-recognition and affirmation of its freedom as the creator of self and world—was described by Marx as the "positive transcendence of private property or human self-estrangement" in a communist revolution. Such a revolution would qualitatively change the nature of human experience in the world. It would thus constitute the "real *appropriation* of the *human* essence by and for man," the "*genuine* resolution of the conflict between man and nature and between man and man." The reality of human emancipation defined as both self-determination and reconciliation with the natural and social worlds would finally be accomplished, and the "riddle of history" would be solved.[18]

The utopian quality of Marx's projected hopes was grounded in a set of philosophical beliefs. In his texts, human essence or species-being as laboring activity was present as a real collective being, as a kind of "universal" or "absolute" self whose scope was universal in terms of both cultural space and historical time and that developed according to an inner logic of self-realization. Marx admitted at one point that he was reading the facts of human industry as an "esoteric psychology"[19]—that is, he was interpreting the history of production as the external representation of the subjective process of self-realization. Specific acts of production in specific times and places were seen as embodiments of a single process of human labor proceeding through the necessary stages required to achieve the goal of self-determination.

Within a few months, Marx would have second thoughts about the residues of metaphysical faith still so evident in these manuscripts and contemptuously reject all talk of human essence and the personification of conceptual abstractions as if they were real historical subjects acting in historical time and space. But despite this self-criticism, the primacy of productive labor remained central to Marx's conceptions. It marked the site in civil society where transformation would have to occur for self-determination and community to be accomplished. The revolutionary task was not to liberate the individual from oppressive governments, but to emancipate labor from its chains. The activity of labor as both self-production and the production of a world that mirrored the creative powers of its producer, the belief that human emancipation was synonymous with the emancipation of the laboring process, and the conviction that production was the motor of all historical development continued to dominate Marx's writings until his death in 1883.

What did this theoretical and personal choice entail? For Marx, it meant first of all that he was able to construct a series of hierarchical distinctions in the analysis of human experience. The core reality of human existence was the sensuous, bodily practice of appropriating the natural world and realizing potential, "subjective" powers in the production of objects. Labor as objectification and appropriation was the reality behind the deceptive veil of the phenomena presented to us in experience. All other dimensions of human culture, all other forms of human life were secondary derivatives of this primary activity and could be fully grasped only in relation to it. Labor was the palpable reality beneath the deceptive illusions of religion, politics, and the myriad forms of cultural and ethical meaning. To believe in the separate, substantial reality of these human creations was to believe in ghosts, to bow before specters. The goals of freedom and fraternity, of self-determination and community, were achievable in reality only through the transformation of the laboring process by overcoming the estrangement of the laborer from himself or herself and the alienation of the product from the producer. It was thus only in the transformative fulfillment of human laboring activity that genuine liberation, and a genuine reconciliation with nature and between human beings, could be achieved. The only authentic revolution, the only revolution that addressed the question of human emancipation at its core, was a revolution of the system of production.

The exemplary human being was like the proverbial artist who finds fulfillment only in his work, achieves happiness only in a world that mirrors his own creativity, and is driven to subordinate every other dimension of human life to the central task of aesthetic production. However, the distinction expressed in Marx's theory of labor was not just between the "real"—defined as sensual, concrete, embodied, or practical—and the illusory or spectral, but also between different dimensions of sensual, embodied existence. Marx's rejection of Feuerbach was a rejection of both sexual desire ("love") and passive reception or consumption as defining activities of humans as members of the species. Satisfaction in love emerged from the qualitative transformation of the mode of production. Experiencing the world as a home rather than a prison, or consuming it as a "human" world and not greedily as a world of objects, was a consequence of the transformation of the production process. The relations between men and women, brothers and sisters, parents and children were determined by forms of work and by the social relations constructed within the productive process.

Similarly, Marx integrated the will-to-power—the drive toward self-assertion, control over oneself, and domination of the other (whether nature or other humans); and the drive toward mutual recognition or identification with others—into the more fundamental creative activity of production. In the process of production, human beings created themselves as real, "objective" beings in the world and transformed the world outside them into an expression of their freedom. Once self-determination in production, mutual identification in society, and the humanization of external nature had been achieved, no reasons or motivations remained for exerting power over others.

Thus, Marx single-mindedly pursued a construction of reality modeled on the principles of productive labor. At the organizing core of the *Communist Manifesto* is a choice to subordinate all human activity to the activity of productive labor and to write a story of humankind's development that relentlessly pursues the logic of this choice. Sex, power, race, and ethnicity are not issues that can be easily integrated into the Marxian theory (unless they are perceived as subordinate, derivative issues) without dissolving this core. Many of the exclusions that this construction entails would come back to haunt Marxism and fuel both internal and external criticism throughout its history. In the late nineteenth century, social democratic Marxists in Germany, England, and Austria attempted to insert the autonomy of political identification and ethical commitment into Marxist ideology, but they inevitably found themselves at odds with the core of the Marxist vision of labor and production. Feminist, Freudian, and existentialist versions of Marxism in the twentieth century came to a similar impasse. Once power, sex, gender, ethnicity, and nationality were allowed to assert their autonomy within Marxist movements, the disintegration of Marx's original vision was well under way.

Class and Community, or Why "Working Men Have No Country"

The theory of class formation and class conflict that informs the analysis of bourgeois society and the narrative of historical development in the *Communist Manifesto* emerged from a process of conceptual development that can be traced back to Marx's years as a philosophical radical and political democrat in the early 1840s. In 1841–1842, during the period in which he was convinced that political emancipation was the primary historical path toward human emancipation, Marx tended to interpret the conflict moving the historical process forward as a conflict between rulers and ruled, governors and governed, the "state" and the "people." He criticized Hegel's political theory for identifying the state as the source of emancipation and community, and the groups that embodied the state—the class of civil servants—as the universal class whose activity carried the ideas of freedom and community into the historical arena. Marx insisted that it was not the state or state class but the people, the subjects administered by the state, who were the historical agents of human emancipation. "Democracy starts from man and makes the state objectified man," he wrote in a typical passage identifying the people as the representation of the species.[20] The struggle to include all human beings as active citizens in the making of their own laws was directed toward the creation of a community in which the general will would not be imposed by one group on another but would emerge as the self-determination of the associated citizens.

In the wake of his disillusionment with politics as the site of emancipation in 1842, Marx focused on defining those critical groups within civil society that determined the process of human emancipation as experienced and pursued by individuals in the concrete, sensuous individuality of their daily social existence.

In his initial attempts to define the revolutionary class in civil society, Marx was above all interested in finding a class whose interests were synonymous with a general emancipation and whose triumph would accomplish a final and total human emancipation. In past revolutions, Marx noted with special reference to the French Revolution, specific classes (the bourgeoisie in this case) had instigated revolutionary processes in the pursuit of their particular interests and goals. To accomplish the overthrow of their class enemies, they had appealed to the population at large and defined their own class interest as a universal interest and that of their enemies as a particular, and thus a one-sided, antisocial, and oppressive, interest. His task in the present was to define that group within civil society whose interest was in fact universal, whose class enemies were in fact the oppressors of human emancipation per se, and whose liberation as a class would be synonymous with human liberation. Such a class, he claimed, was at least embryonically present in the "proletariat."

In the first formulation of this position, Marx's rhetoric indicated that this class was still more of a historical construct than an identifiable reality:

> A class must be formed which has *radical chains,* a class in civil society which is not a class of civil society, a class which is the dissolution of all classes, a sphere of society which has a universal character because its sufferings are universal, and which does not claim a *particular redress,* because the wrong which is done to it is not a *particular wrong,* but wrong in general.

As a class that was totally dispossessed, whose impoverishment was not "natural" but historically or "artificially produced," the proletariat represented a "total loss" of humanity and could achieve emancipation for itself only by a "total redemption of humanity." The proletariat thus emerged for Marx as the agent of a total, human revolution, as the practical negation or dissolution of existing society, before he had actually examined in any detail the actual relations of production under modern capitalism. The proletariat was the "material weapon" of the philosophical ideal of human emancipation: *"Philosophy* is the *head* of this emancipation and the *proletariat* is its *heart."*[21]

One of the indications that Marx's identification of the proletariat as the representative and agent of universal emancipation occurred as a theoretical assertion, before much empirical study of actual productive relations, was his claim that the total, human revolution would occur in Germany. There the most advanced forms of theoretical self-consciousness (in Hegelian philosophy and its various humanist translations) could combine with a social group that had no stake in the existing order, that had "nothing to lose." The proletariat in Germany was not an industrial wage-earning class, but simply the class of the displaced and homeless whose traditional forms of life and work had been undermined by population growth and international market forces. What defined the proletariat, in this first definition, was not its role in industrial production but its absolute "suffering" as a group that had been banished from the circle of human association.

As Marx worked his way into the writings of political economists such as Adam Smith, David Ricardo, and James Mill in 1844, he fleshed out his theory of class conflict in terms of his conceptions of the selfestrangement of labor within the capitalist economy and bourgeois society. The proletariat now gained positive significance as the class of productive labor. It embodied or represented the universal interests of humanity not only because of its immiseration and exclusion from the material, social, and spiritual content of a full human existence, but also because it was the incarnation of the human essence as laboring activity. "The emancipation of the workers," he wrote, "contains universal human emancipation—and it contains this, because the whole of human servitude is involved in the relation of the worker to production, and all relations of servitude are but modifications and consequences of this relation."[22]

In the manuscripts of 1844, Marx conceived the class conflict between the proletariat and the bourgeoisie as a social and historical expression of the internal dynamics and contradictions of the laboring process, as the objectified reality of "estranged" or "alienated" labor. The wage-earning working class under capitalism represented the essential human powers of production dispossessed of the product in which it manifested these powers. By contrast, the owners of private property, who appropriated the products of labor and controlled the laboring process, represented the alienated product in its separation from the producer. Classes appeared as the external representation of an internal contradiction in the dynamic process of the development of human essence in history. In 1845, he wrote, "The propertied class and the class of the proletariat represent the same human self-estrangement."[23] The conflict between classes was grounded in the internal contradictions of the act of labor. The internal dynamics of the self-realization of "man" or the human essence as productive activity was made "manifest" in the conflict between the class of wage earners and the class of the owners of capital. The historical agent pushing class conflict to its extreme form and preparing the condition for a general human emancipation or "redemption" was, in Marx's 1844 terminology, "man" as a "species-being." The forces driving the historical process emerged from an internal necessity that drove this essence to become real in the world, to attain its full self-affirmation in the creation of a world that reflected its inherent nature.

By the time of the *Communist Manifesto,* Marx had dropped the conceptual structure and rhetoric of human essence, or human species-being, from his analysis and dismissed it contemptuously as the metaphysical residue of a theological tradition from which German philosophical radicals were unable to free themselves. He rejected it as unnecessary baggage from the "old world" of his philosophical heritage. Marx's theory of class, however, maintained the idea of human community as a process of subjective identification that he had brought with him from his philosophical education. The goal of human history was the creation of a universal human community, a single world in which every individual would feel completely at home and recognize himself or herself in the acts and products of every other individual. Marx tended to ignore the importance of national and ethnic processes of identification because he was so firmly convinced that the need articulated in those identifications, the need to experience oneself as a participant member of a subjective community, was already fully satisfied in the self-conscious association of producers. The community of class grounded in the productive process was more universal than not only the family, kinship group, or tribe but also all groupings based on language, ethnicity, religion, or politics.

Politics and theoretical education brought the implicit identification of individuals within social productive practice into visibility and self-conscious awareness. With its political triumph over the bourgeoisie, the proletariat would constitute itself as the nation. But community was already implicit in the everyday material activity of producers. In laboring activity, individuals carried their "community" within themselves, always present, as the very center of their lives. "The individual *is the social being,*" Marx insisted in 1844. Even if the individual's life activities were not directly and visibly social—that is, "carried out in associations with others"—they expressed and confirmed the individual as inherently, essentially social.[24]

In the *Manifesto,* there is evidence of the difficulty Marx experienced in adapting his theoretical identification of the proletariat as the agent of universal human revolution to the empirical evidence he possessed about the actual wage-earning classes in the new industrial enterprises. In the *Manifesto,* Marx admits that industrial capitalism has produced a wage-earning class composed in its majority of women and children. Yet the proletariat he envisioned as emerging from the factories to take up the revolutionary battle was modeled on the male artisan culture that the new system of production was displacing. He also asserts that capitalism has both produced "the men" who would turn its weapons against the bourgeoisie and displaced male labor with "that of women."

Just as Marx could not fully shake off a vision of working-class politics formed by the patriarchal artisan culture of a preindustrial period, so his general analysis of capitalism and of the progress of world history continued to operate within the distinctions of, and according to, the goals he had first formulated during his philosophical apprenticeship. The past was more difficult to abandon than Marx first imagined.

History as the Reality of Human Existence

The historical narrative that informs the first section of the *Communist Manifesto* summarizes descriptions and assessments that Marx, with Engels's collaboration, worked out in 1845, first in a series of aphorisms criticizing Feuerbach's ahistorical form of materialism (see Document 18) and then in a massive manuscript known as *The German Ideology* (see Document 19). These manuscripts were not published during Marx's and Engels's lifetimes. *The German Ideology* had been voluntarily abandoned to the "gnawing criticism of mice," Marx later recalled, because it had already served its main purpose of "self-clarification" through a "settling of accounts with our erstwhile philosophical conscience."[25] The reflective "self-clarification" of *The German Ideology* involved a systematic analysis of the premises of a theory of history that would not depend on metaphysical notions such as "spirit" or "human essence." This analysis of assumptions or premises, however, was not included in the text of the *Manifesto,* which displays only the results of Marx's rethinking of historical development, not the theoretical commitments that undergirded those results.

In *The German Ideology*, Marx claimed that the premises on which he based his conception of historical development were "not arbitrary ones, not dogmas, but real premises from which abstraction can only be made in the imagination." These premises were "the real individuals, their activity and the material conditions of their life, both those which they find already existing and those produced by their activity." Historical understanding had to begin with the physical reality of existing human individuals as parts of nature and the acts of production and reproduction through which these individuals differentiated themselves from other parts of nature and generated their own self-identity.

According to Marx, human beings did not possess a universal essence that sought concrete realization in the particular circumstances of time and place, but instead were finite beings whose activity in the world created the characteristics of a shared humanity. A common humanity was a *result,* rather than the cause or inherent goal, of their activity. By producing their means of subsistence, human beings shaped themselves into a "definite form of expressing their life." In setting their physical energies and skills in motion in the world to produce food, clothing, and shelter, human beings constantly changed both their own beings (their "inner" natures), the world around them ("external" nature), and the relations between these two dimensions of existence. Each generation creatively worked over their heritage of skills and products and left it as a historically defined reality for the next generation. Every generation inherited its "humanity" as a historical legacy from its ancestors. At the same time, the productive relationship between individual human beings and the natural world constantly created new forms of interaction (social intercourse) and new forms of communication and self-understanding. Every generation thus created a new historical "humanity" to pass on to the next generation. The defining character of human beings, their "nature," was always changing, inherently historical.

In 1845, Marx could no longer accept any explanation of this historical process that attributed its shape and direction to an inner logic of self-determination, self-estrangement, and self-restoration. There was no collective being called "man" that could function as the agent of the historical process. The historical narrative could not simply be read or reconstructed as the story of a singular humankind passing through various stages of development, but it would have to be constructed on the foundations of the separate acts of human individuals as they came into relation to the natural world and to each other. The individuals did not express a universal meaning within which their actions were determined. Instead, their actions created connections and relations that eventually produced a common history. The apparent necessity of historical development that transformed individuals into mere carriers of collective forces emerged as a consequence of the contingent acts of the individuals themselves.

The organizing conception of this historical narrative was not self-estrangement or self-alienation of the human essence as laboring productivity, but the division of labor that occurred as human beings pursued the task of fulfilling and redefining their needs in the process of social production. Division of labor emerged within nature from the differences created by the material conditions of human reproduction and the concomitant relations between fathers, mothers, and children grounded in physical difference, age, and role in sexual reproduction. Fathers controlled the means of production, subordinated women and children to their rule, and presented themselves as representatives of the family unit and of the community that encompassed the different roles and reciprocal relations of family members. In complicated ways, fueled by specific events, this pattern continued, but in a less natural and more "artificial" or cultural form, in the historical evolution from tribal communities, through ancient city-states and feudal aristocratic kingdoms, to modern national states.

"Alienation" found its empirical reality in the gap between the individual's experience as an isolated and dependent member of a system of social relations, emerging from the natural and material conditions of production at any given time, and the common or "general" interests embodied in the system as a whole. The real content of human community at any historical moment was present in the totality of productive forces (techniques of production and material resources) and social relations or "forms of intercourse." "The sum of productive forces, capital funds, and social forms of intercourse which every individual and generation finds in existence as something given," Marx argued in *The German Ideology,* "is the real basis of what philosophers have conceived as the 'substance' and 'essence of man.'"[26] The process of historical development was "nothing but the succession of the separate generations, each of which exploits the materials, the capital funds and productive forces handed down to it by all preceding generations."[27] The world individuals confronted in their struggle to develop their own powers was a human world, a world created by the productive social practices of human individuals up to that moment.

Because of the division of labor, however, every individual experienced this human "community," the inherited social substance of their existence, as dependence on a system of relationships outside their control. The mutual interdependence of human beings appeared to them individually as something alien to their self-determination. The totality appeared only in an illusory form, as the claim by the dominant class or classes in the system of production to represent the whole and as the oppressive weight of enforced unity for the subordinate classes. Myths, religions, and systems of ideas claimed universality from the perspective of specific ruling classes that controlled the techniques and resources of the creation and communication of ideas. Political communities or states represented "humanity" as the instruments of social classes that manipulated the means of social control and physical coercion.

In *The German Ideology,* as in the *Communist Manifesto,* Marx's description of the early stages of human history was rather sketchy. His main interest was the historical emergence of an industrial, capitalist economy and the social and political rule of the bourgeoisie, the class that possessed the techniques and resources of production in this economy. The bourgeois revolution in both texts was presented as the historical development that brought the quantitative patterns of previous developments to their ultimate conclusion, preparing the way for an apocalyptic, transformative, qualitative change in the nature of human existence.

Through the extension of capitalist market relations to global dimensions and the penetration of those relations to every sphere of human experience, the bourgeois era had transformed the process of the division of labor. Any residues of a natural determination of different roles in the system of production had been dissolved. The determination of role in the system of production was completely artificial, totally market driven. For example, women became the majority among the hired "hands" in textile mills not because they were somehow naturally suited for the assigned tasks, but because their labor was a cheaper commodity than adult male labor. The result was a global system in which, beneath the appearance of separate functions, there emerged the reality that all these functions were historically determined and temporary.

In the global market, choice of profession—the determination of who one was by the specific tasks one was forced to do to produce the means of subsistence—was arbitrary. Every individual confronted the possibility of moving from task to task, of experiencing the particular one-sidedness of the division of labor as a given fate determined by the competitive forces of the world market. Thus, the potential for the "all-round" individual could not be realized or made actual. It existed as a kind of empty possibility. The freedom to experiment with all shapes of life and work, and thus fully to express the possibilities inherent in human existence as productive labor, was denied to the individual producer. The freedom from determination by a specific social role was experienced as the necessity to take any job that the market offered.

Bourgeois society reduced the universal laboring capacity of human beings to the one role of wage labor. The full dimension of possible self-realization was reduced to a class uniformity determined by "callous cash payment." As wage earners, the proletariat experienced the universalization of their productive capacities and the transformation of their labor into a pure productivity that could be applied to any task as an oppressive necessity controlled by the world market.

At the same time, the expansion of industrial capitalism to all corners of the globe, and its unstoppable erosion and dissolution of all other productive and social relations, finally did create a common humanity. The many isolated, fragmented histories of the past became a single history, not as the expression of one human essence but as the result of human productive activities. Under world capitalism, the individual faced the system that controlled his or her fate—the universal that opposed his or her singularity—as a truly global system of relations, as the totality of human productive and social relations. "The transformation of history into world history is not indeed a mere abstract act on the part of 'self-consciousness,' the world spirit, or any other metaphysical spectre," Marx concluded, "but a quite material, empirically verifiable act, an act the proof of which every individual furnishes as he comes and goes, eats and drinks, and clothes himself."[28] But the individuals in bourgeois society faced this reality as the world market—as an opaque, apparently "natural" system that was alien to them, controlling their choices rather than opening up their possibilities. Overcoming estrangement and restoring the full content of the historically created human world to the enjoyment of the individual producer thus involved the act of taking control of this system of productive relations: "All-round dependence, the natural form of world-historical cooperation of individuals, will be transformed by the communist revolution into the control and conscious mastery of these powers, which, born of the action of men on one another, have until now overawed and governed men as powers completely alien to them."[29]

Marx envisioned the progress toward the creation of one "human" history and the production of individual lives as shaped by all-around dependence on the powers they had produced as an empirically verifiable, factual development. Similarly, he portrayed as an empirically verifiable process the creation of the agency that would restore the alienated world to the individual, fill his or her life with the richness of the human production of previous generations, and transform all-around dependence into all-around independence and self-determination.

The competitive forces of the world market increasingly simplified group alignment in the world into two classes—those who owned the means of production and those who had only their own labor to sell in the marketplace. The creation of a world proletariat composed of the vast majority of human individuals at the same time imbued those individuals with the characteristics that would qualify them collectively as the agency of the individual's fulfillment as a self-determining being. The process of production would be controlled by the associated individuals whose historical experience had already transformed them into "free" or "pure" labor. The struggle to survive within the pressures of a global market would lead to increasing confrontation between wage labor and capital, increasing exploitation and impoverishment of the wage-earning classes, a growing consciousness of identity of interests among these classes, and their formation as a single global proletariat. The increasing severity of crises of overproduction would provide the opportunities for the revolutionary act. The internal logic of the contradictory forces within the capitalist system of production would bring about the conditions for a qualitative transformation of the human condition.

The developmental pattern in historical events was available not only to those with esoteric knowledge but also to any unprejudiced observer. Once the distorting class lenses of bourgeois ideology had been thrown away, the reality behind the specter showed itself. The meaning of history did not need to be "constructed" by the historian, but could be discovered by anyone with an interest in seeing clearly.

In one sense, Marx did imagine his historical account of the production of human powers and their restoration to the producers as a subjective "construction." The trajectory of history was not a predetermined consequence of human nature or the necessary actualization of the human essence, but the cumulative creation of specific productive social practices. Human beings created their essence as they reproduced themselves, as they created the means for their subsistence and struggled to objectify their creative energies in the world of created things. Knowledge of human history was thus a conscious recognition by laboring human beings of the products of their own labor, a form of self-understanding of the actual history they had constructed in their social practices. In historical knowledge, human beings came to grasp who they were and to recognize their own identity because history itself consisted of the series of actions in which human beings made themselves and created their own shared humanity.

For the proletariat, the class of human labor and thus the embodiment of human existence as productive creativity, the Marxian theory of history would or should appear as a self-recognition of the meaning of their own collective practice. Yet Marx insisted that this "practical" construction of a single human history and of the appropriation of external nature as a human product—the creation of a world that human beings could enjoy as their collective home—was empirically observable in a scientific sense. The Marxian theory of history was presented as an objective truth that overrode the empirical resistance of individuals who refused to recognize themselves in its story. For the individual worker, this story of the estrangement of individuals from the freedom and community inherent in their laboring activity, and of the ultimate return of the substantial content of their humanity in the associated self-conscious management of the collective process of production, might very well be experienced as an "alien" story imposed on him or her by Marxist intellectuals and Communist party leaders. Yet Marx's notoriously acerbic satire and critical acumen were not applied to his own creation, or at least not self-consciously. As we have seen, Marx did criticize his own former positions, but always in the guise of attacking others who had shared those positions with him. In 1845, Marx had tried to clarify the general principles that grounded his dismissal of all religious and idealistic philosophies of histories. By leaving this self-clarification to be criticized only by mice, Marx opened himself to an uncritical belief in the objective validity of his own, however brilliant and provocative, construction of the past, present, and future.

Between 1845 and 1848, however, Marx was primarily interested in making history rather than writing it. Despite its reductive theory of politics, the *Manifesto* is a political work. In its pages, the political organization of the present plays a dominant role in order to control the immediate future. And it is this dimension that has made the *Manifesto* so problematic. As a guide to action, the *Manifesto* transformed its interpretation of the world of the past into the reality on which one must stand in order to risk oneself in action today and tomorrow.

From this perspective, perhaps it does not matter a great deal whether or not Marx saw the historical conceptualizations of the *Manifesto* as an objective science of historical reality, starkly contrasted to the utopian dreams of his rivals, or as a collective construction of the universal class of human labor, whose own "construction" of the world would, by definition, become the way the world actually was. In both cases, whether Marx spoke as an impartial observer of objective historical processes or as the spokesperson for a historical collective agent, he ignored the historical particularity of his own finite and limited perspectives. The story told in the *Communist Manifesto* is not presented as "just" a story, as an experiment in making sense of some important dimensions of experience, but as the story, a metastory or framing story that contains the real truth of all other stories, that encompasses them within itself and provides them with the appropriate categories for their correct interpretation.

SPECTERS OF POLITICS AND IDEOLOGY

The second section of the *Communist Manifesto* opens with a series of sweeping, almost breathtaking claims about the relationship between the Communist party and the global wage-earning working classes, or proletariat. According to these claims, communism represents a completely novel form of political organization and ideological expression.

In Marx's critical analysis of bourgeois society and all previous historical social and cultural forms, politics and ideology are presented as illusory forms of community and cultural meaning. In all previous history, political organization represented itself as embodying the unified identity of the community, in contrast to the actual fragmentation of individuals living in their sensuous reality within the relations of production and social exchange. These false representations emerged from and were imposed by specific class domination. The perspective of a particular group was imposed on all individuals as the perspective of the community as a whole.

In the *Manifesto,* Marx insists that the Communist party represented the common interests of the proletariat as a whole, that the political claim of a unified community expressed the real experience of the global proletariat. The difference between the ideological claims of the Communist party leaders and the actual experiences of individual proletarians in the present was a difference not between illusion and reality but between the inevitable future (already implicit in the present) and the empirical present.

At the same time, Marx is forced to admit that this claim does not conform to what appeared to be the case in the world, where different political organizations and an array of socialist ideologies competed for the loyalty of various working-class constituencies. By devoting the last third of the *Manifesto* to a historical critique of these competitors for working-class loyalty, Marx indirectly reveals the gap between Communist party hopes and historical realities. The claim that the Communists spoke for the proletariat per se and simply enunciated the proletariat's own perspective was a historical project, a possibility that must be made actual in the world. Regardless of what individual workers might think or imagine, according to Marx the reality of their existence could find its only appropriate organizational form through membership in the communist movement.

This claim that the Communist party was the only authentic political representative of the proletariat was tied to the ideological claim that the theory produced by party intellectuals constituted the true meaning of the proletariat's experience. Members of the party leadership had the "advantage" over the mass of actual laborers of "clearly understanding the line of march, the conditions and the ultimate general results of the proletarian movement." According to Marx, the theory of the Communist party was no ordinary theory. It was not a particular interpretation of the world, but a true reflection of the historical process of social production. Marx disavows individual responsibility for his historical claims, saying that they were not invented out of thin air or forced onto empirical reality but simply expressed in general conceptual terms the actual state of affairs arising from the class conflicts of bourgeois society.

The critique of all previous social formations and their ideological claims suddenly ground to a halt. It did not evolve into self-criticism. Marx suggests that all criticisms of the Communist party position were based on misunderstandings, because they emerged from the limited theoretical assumptions forged within the particular perspectives and directed by the particular interests of the bourgeois class. Conceptions of property, individuality, freedom, labor, or family that informed the various objections to communist theory had no validity for the proletariat, because the ideology of the proletariat produced the categories for its own analysis. The proletariat possessed its own internal criteria for discerning the achievement of freedom, community, productivity, individual enrichment, sexual equality, creative labor, and so on.

Communist theory, as a theory of history and social relations, was not, for Marx, the representation of an interest within a world of competing interests, a perspective among perspectives, a map among maps, but a construction of the world that defined the meanings of interests and the categories of analysis within it. Communism as the self-consciousness of a class was in fact the self-consciousness of a universal class that produced a world in which it recognized its own reality.

The communist revolution was in Marx's view a "total" qualitative transformation of the world. It changed in fundamental ways how individuals experienced themselves in relation to their finite existence, to the world of nature, to other individuals, and to the realm of general meaning that determined their sense of identity in the larger, cosmic order of things. In this sense, Marxian theory remained a "secularization" rather than an abolition of metaphysical and religious visions of human redemption.

In *The German Ideology,* Marx noted that "for the production on a mass scale of this communist consciousness and for the success of the cause itself, the alteration of men on a mass scale is necessary, an alteration which can only take place in a practical movement, a revolution." The masses of the proletariat would enter into a consciousness of the New World only in the violent activity of destroying the old. In this act, they would rid themselves of "the muck of ages and become fitted to found society anew."[30]

Some of the most problematic issues in Marxism emerge from its conceptualization of revolution—its view of the path and stages in the transition from the "old" world to the "new." Within the context of bourgeois society, the growth and organization of the proletariat as a self-conscious class involved a relation to politics and ideology that seems to fall into the model of what Marx called self-estrangement. The experience of the future community existed in the present in the form of a political community (the "movement" or "party") and of a theoretical system (Marxist ideology) that conformed to the rules of the existing order. Within bourgeois society, the proletariat existed as a limited class community with a particular class perspective. The class of universal humanity first needed to organize as a particular class to overthrow the political power of the bourgeoisie and assert its control over the sphere of social production. The "self-consciousness" of the proletariat needed to be inculcated as an ideological worldview that would only gradually emerge as an authentic self-understanding among the masses of workers.

The history of Marxism after Marx's death was haunted by a variety of specters. It was haunted by religious and philosophical commitments to realities transcending the material activity and conditions of finite human existence; by the persistence of the search for the experience of freedom and community in the realm of political power and law; by the resistance of ethnic, cultural, national, and gender differences to reduction to the universality of productive relations; and by the stubborn unwillingness of sexual desire and the will-to-power to integrate themselves into the all-encompassing drive to self-affirmation in productive labor. Those dimensions of human experience that had been excluded from Marx's historical vision in the process of its formation refused to disappear, to finally submit to a world defined by labor alone. But according to Marx, all the ghosts of freedoms past were to find their reality in the freedom of labor to produce a world in its own image, and all the ghosts of past communities were to find their fulfillment in the association of producers controlling both their own productive activity and the circulation and consumption of their products.

It was a powerful vision, relentlessly pursuing the logic of an analysis of human existence as productive labor, of "man" as *homo faber* (man the maker). It claimed to encompass the substance of freedom and community hidden in the totality of past political and cultural forms, and it invited the ghosts of the past to find their peace and return to their graves as ancestors of the communist revolution. It was not an eccentric vision. To grasp life as productive activity, and to define freedom and community in these terms, was to provide an illuminating map for a significant experienced reality in Marx and Engels's own time, and it can continue to do so today in more muted, qualified, and reconfigured forms. The development of new communications and information technology combined with the global penetration of constantly changing iterations of capitalism in the late twentieth and early twenty-first centuries has radically transformed many dimensions of production and exchange, but it has also been accompanied by a remarkable resurgence of public interest in the apparent relevance of Marx's description of the inner logic of the capitalist system as producing ultimately unsustainable inequalities of wealth with potentially revolutionary consequences.[31] However, the conflictual international relations between labor and capital in the era of market globalization and the relentless transformation of all forms and products of human activity into commodities for exchange even as this production becomes increasingly "immaterial" and encompasses all forms of creating the conditions of human biological and social existence, are only two of the many indications that it may be too early to abandon Marx completely as a guide to life. To dismiss the historical reality constructed in the *Manifesto* as an illusion of the past, a specter that has evaporated in the post-1989 world, would be to fall into the same misconceptions and self-deceptions as Marx did when he dismissed national identity as an obsolete historical form of community, gender difference as a subcategory of class, and the will-to-power as an offshoot of productive relations.

As a specter haunting the consciousness of inhabitants of the late twentieth century, the *Communist Manifesto* can be exorcised only through a dialogue that recognizes the legitimacy and power of its constitution of the world *as* a constitution of the world and also recognizes that this dialogue is one with a ghost from our own past, a part of ourselves. The encounter with the *Communist Manifesto* is an encounter with a story among the plurality of stories we have inherited from the past. It is a story about us, but, perhaps, only about one dimension of us. As one of the plurality of stories that constitute our inheritance from the past, it must be preserved in, rather than excised from, public memory, and it must form one of the foundations for any stories we will construct through our practices in the present.

FROM THE *MANIFESTO* TO *CAPITAL:* THE LESSONS OF HISTORY AND THE LAWS OF HISTORY

The *Communist Manifesto* was published at the historical moment, February 1848, when an insurrection in Paris inaugurated a new period of revolutionary turmoil on the European continent. The theory of historical development and the projections of revolutionary transformation contained in the *Manifesto* were thus immediately subjected to the test of historical reality. By 1851, it was clear that the revolutions in France and Central Europe had failed. The diverse array of revolutionary movements were stifled and repressed. Not only the communists and social democrats but also the moderate liberal constitutionalists and liberal and democratic nationalists fell victim to a conservative reaction supported by military force.

Marx and Engels, who participated actively as journalists and organizers in the Prussian and German revolutions, interpreted this failure as a validation of the principles of the *Manifesto,* thus salvaging triumph from apparent defeat. At the same time, the failures of the revolutionary movements and the emergence of a period of conservative stability throughout Western and Central Europe were not without their effects on both the Marxian theory of the historical evolution of capitalism and its projected scenario for revolutionary change.

The *Manifesto* presented the Marxian conception of communism as a conceptual understanding of "a historical movement going on under our very eyes." This historical movement, the unstoppable development of the capitalist mode of production on a global scale, provided both the material conditions for a qualitative, revolutionary social transformation and the historical agent, a self-conscious international proletariat, that would actively bring about this transformation. To validate their conception of revolution, Marx and Engels needed to interpret the political events of 1848–1850 as a revelation of class conflicts determined by the bourgeois or capitalist mode of production and an important stage in the educational formation of the revolutionary proletariat.

In his initial analysis of the events in France, Marx proclaimed that historical actuality had confirmed and revealed for all to see the validity of his historical theory. In a series of newspaper articles written in 1850 (see Document 20), Marx described the ways in which the violent confrontations between politically organized groups during the course of the revolution had stripped away the ideological veils hiding the realities of class conflict and had provided a practical education in Marxian theory for the working classes. Historical events seemed to confirm his assertion of 1847: "In the measure that history moves forward, and with it the struggle of the proletariat assumes clearer outlines, they no longer need to seek science in their minds; they have only to take note of what is happening before their eyes and to become its mouthpiece."[32]

By the time the revolution had run its course and collapsed with the installation of Napoleon's nephew as French emperor in 1852, however, Marx had to admit that the alleged education by reality had not taken hold. The veil of political and cultural ideology had returned to effectively hide the realities of class conflict from the eyes of observers and participants. In a pamphlet titled *The Eighteenth Brumaire of Louis Bonaparte* (see Document 21), published in 1852, Marx reflected on the power of illusions to hide historical reality from historical actors, on the ability of historical events to veil class struggle as well as reveal it.

Marx never stopped believing that the historical evolution of capitalist modes of production continued, with relentless necessity, to exacerbate the contradictions between social modes of productive labor and private ownership of the means of production, to simplify class conflict into conflicts between capital and labor, and generally to develop the conditions for a communist revolution. But he did recognize that this process was not empirically obvious and that it had not been recognized by the majority of the working classes after the failures of 1848. In a charter statement for the new Working Men's International Association in 1864, Marx both lamented this failure in education and reiterated his belief that the historical tendencies that would eventually bring about such an education were still in effect (see Document 22). The international communist revolution may not thus far have obviously and palpably revealed its emerging contours in historical events, thus dissipating the veil of ideological illusion in the light of day, but, to use one of Marx's own favorite metaphors, the revolutionary transformation of European society continued to develop underground, hidden from view, as a revolutionary "mole."

Marx and Engels displayed their own illusions about the revelatory character of revolutionary crisis in the scenarios they had developed for the course of revolution. The *Manifesto* had confidently predicted that once the revolutionary process had been set in motion by commercial crises in the global market and by the political will of Parisian street fighters, events would move rapidly toward the final collapse of bourgeois society and the onset of proletarian revolution. Tactical alliances with bourgeois liberals and petit bourgeois social democrats during the early stages of revolution would soon lead to a self-conscious assertion of proletarian hegemony under communist leadership. Germany was placed at the center of a general European revolution, not only because Marx and Engels were Germans (although this may very well have played a role) but also because they believed that the delayed bourgeois revolution in Germany would move rapidly through its liberal, democratic, and nationalist phases into a "permanent revolution" that would bring the communists into power and set off a tidal wave of working-class revolution moving from the periphery to the center of world capitalism.

Such optimistic scenarios were gradually abandoned after 1851. When Marx and Engels returned to their English exile after the repression of the continental revolutions, their attention was increasingly focused on a closer analysis of the long-term creation of the conditions of revolution through the full-scale development of the capitalist system of production. At the same time, Marx needed to explain the effectiveness of the ideological veil that hid these developments and their implications from common view. Although Marx and Engels were themselves convinced that all the complicated, disappointing turns of events between 1848 and 1851 in France and Germany could be explained through an analysis of the class conflicts created by the bourgeois system of production, they also were aware that recent historical events had not taught these lessons "for all to see." The perceptions of their contemporaries required guidance and education through a convincing demonstration of the "laws" of capitalist production underlying the confusing variety of empirical phenomena. Only then would they understand the workings of the revolutionary mole and be able to sustain their faith both in the historical inevitability of capitalism's collapse and in the historical need to mobilize and prepare the working classes for the day of reckoning.

The theoretical results of the lessons learned through the failures of the revolutions of 1848 were eventually articulated, after a series of preliminary studies, in the detailed analysis of the bourgeois system of production presented in Marx's unfinished masterpiece, *Capital,* the first and only completed volume of which was published in 1867. Two prominent shifts in theory made evident the historical lessons learned since the publication of the *Manifesto* in 1848.

First, the analysis of the bourgeois mode of production in *Capital* provided an explanation of how the development of fundamental class conflict and class exploitation (creating the conditions of inevitable collapse and revolutionary possibility) was veiled under capitalism by the appearance of equal exchange among commodities in a free market. Labor, Marx insisted, was a commodity unlike any other. When labor was bought on the market and consumed by the buyer, it created a greater value than its market cost. In buying labor, the capitalist was actually buying labor *power,* the potential to create value. The wages paid to labor by the capitalist paid for only part of the value gained from labor by the capitalist. The profits of capital were grounded in an appropriation or consumption of the "surplus value" produced in the labor process. This hidden law of the production of surplus value explained the vast private appropriation of social wealth and the creation of extreme class differences under capitalism, and it led to the contradictions and conflicts that would inevitably produce capitalism's collapse.

The unveiling of the secret workings of the revolutionary mole behind the appearances of free exchange, moreover, was based on a more general shift in Marx's conception of the relationship between theory and reality. In an 1873 afterword to a second edition of the first

Figure 5. Karl Marx in London in 1861, during the time he was working on *Capital*.

volume of *Capital* (see Document 23), Marx asserted that understanding the bourgeois system of production as a dynamic historical process moving inevitably toward crisis and revolutionary transformation required a knowledge of dialectical analysis. Grasping the diggings of the revolutionary mole entailed a rehabilitation of the Hegelian method for conceptualizing the negative, dynamic dimension in every historical phenomenon. The Hegel whom Marx revived in the 1860s was not, of course, the same Hegel he had rejected in the mid-1840s. It was a Hegel demystified and translated into the earthly terms of material existence. But the conscious revival of Hegel did reveal Marx's return to a belief, predating the confident empiricism of the *Manifesto,* that understanding the present historical situation required a method for understanding the long-term dynamics of historical change hidden by surface appearances that made the world seem as fixed in its forms and relations as a natural crystal. In *Capital,* the contrast with the historical analysis of the *Manifesto* is most obvious in the famous chapter "The Fetishism of Commodities and the Secret Thereof" (see Document 24), in which the historical dynamic of capitalist commodity exchange is revealed through a dialectical analysis of its "natural" appearances.

Engels recognized the importance of the shift in Marxian theory after 1848. On a number of occasions after Marx's death, he noted that the early use of the term *labor* in the context of labor exchange, as in the *Manifesto* (page 71), should be replaced with the term *labor-power* to conform to Marx's mature theory of surplus value. In his speech at Marx's graveside in 1883 (see Document 25), Engels highlighted the discovery of surplus value as the original contribution of Marx's explanation of the laws of capitalist production. Yet Engels attributed this discovery to Marx the scientist, worthy to be celebrated in the company of the great natural scientists of the nineteenth century, such as Darwin, rather than to Marx the philosopher and student of Hegel. In so doing, he provided fuel for the debate between scientific and philosophical interpretations of Marxism in general, and the *Communist Manifesto* in particular, which continues into our own day. For Engels and many later Marxists, it was not enough that Marx had created a powerful conceptual and historical narrative that gave meaning to the experience of history for many people in his own time. His texts, including the *Manifesto,* were presented not as interpretations of history, but as the truth about history. It is difficult to die or kill for a work of words that is recognized as a story about the meaning of existence from the perspective of a particular historical moment, rather than a truth that is valid for all times and places.

NOTES

[1] The title of the original German pamphlet, published in 1848, was *Manifest der Kommunistischen Partei.*

[2] Karl Marx and Frederick Engels, "Preface to the 1872 German Edition of the *Manifesto of the Communist Party,*" in Karl Marx and Frederick Engels, *Collected Works* (New York and London: International Publishers, 50 vols., 1975–2004), Vol. 23, 174–75.

[3] Georg Lukács, *History and Class Consciousness: Studies in Marxist Dialectics* (Cambridge, Mass.: MIT Press, 1971), 1.

[4] Marx and Engels, "Preface to the 1872 German Edition," 174.

[5] Dirk J. Struik, Introduction to *The Birth of the Communist Manifesto: With Full Text of the Manifesto, All Prefaces by Marx and Engels, Early Drafts by Engels and Other Supplementary Materials* (New York: International Publishers, 1971); David Fernbach, Introduction to *The Revolutions of 1848* by Karl Marx (New York: Random House, 1973).

[6] Attempts by various West European "Neo-Marxists" to reconfigure the basic dimensions of the *Communist Manifesto* for the new age of global finance capital had emerged in the last decades of the twentieth century, but it was the influential, widely disseminated and debated work by Michael Hardt and Antonio Negri published in the first decade of this century that systematically brought this position to public notice. In three substantial volumes they tried to recreate the Marxian analysis of the structures of the capitalist system, the emergence of a revolutionary class of the exploited producers, and the possibility for revolutionary transformation. Cf. Hardt and Negri, *Empire* (Cambridge, Mass.: Harvard University Press, 2000), *Multitude: War and Democracy in the Age of Empire* (New York: Penguin Press, 2004), and *Commonwealth* (Cambridge, Mass.: Harvard University Press, 2009). For a debate about Frederic Jameson's more recent version of a reconfigured postmodern Marxist *Manifesto* with a particular focus on the political conditions for transformative action, cf, *An American Utopia: Dual Power and the Universal Army,* edited by Slavoj Žižek (London: Verso, 2016).

[7] More correctly, "fairy tale."

[8] Karl Marx, "Preface to the First German Edition of *Capital,*" in Marx/Engels, *Collected Works,* Vol. 35 (1996), 8. Marx used the phrase to warn his German readers that his analysis of conditions that seemed selectively present in England also concerned them, that the recent story of England was the story of their own future.

[9] "Preface to the Fourth German Edition (1890) of the *Manifesto of the Communist Party,*" in Marx/Engels, *Collected Works,* Vol. 27 (1990), 58.

[10] Bert Andreas, *Gruendungsdokumente des Bundes der Kommunisten (Juni bis September 1847)* (Hamburg: Ernest Hauswedel & Co., 1969), 20–21.

[11] The two credos drafted by Engels and part of his letter to Marx are reprinted here as Documents 2 and 3.

[12] Frederick Engels, "Preface to the 1888 English Edition of the *Manifesto of the Communist Party,*" in Marx/Engels, *Collected Works,* Vol. 26 (1990), 517.

[13] Frederick Engels, "Outlines of a Critique of Political Economy," in Marx/Engels, *Collected Works,* Vol. 3 (1975), 418.

[14] "Reflections of a Young Man on the Choice of Profession," in Marx/Engels, *Collected Works,* Vol. 1 (1975), 3–9.

[15] Alexis de Tocqueville, *Recollections: The French Revolution of 1848,* ed. J. P. Mayer and A. P. Kerr, with a new introduction by Fernand Braudel (New Brunswick, N.J.: Transaction Books, 1987), 14–15.

[16] Karl Marx, "Difference between the Democritean and Epicurean Philosophy of Nature" (1841) in Marx/Engels, *Collected Works,* Vol. 1 (1975), 30–31.

[17] Karl Marx, "The Leading Article in No. 179 of the *Koelnische Zeitung*" (1842), in Marx/Engels, *Collected Works,* Vol. 1 (1975), 192.

[18] Karl Marx, "Economic and Philosophic Manuscripts of 1844," in Marx/Engels, *Collected Works,* Vol. 3 (1975), 296.

[19] Ibid., 302: ". . . The history of *industry* and the established *objective* existence of industry are the *open book* of man's *essential powers,* the exposure to the senses of human *psychology.*"

[20] Karl Marx, "Contribution to the Critique of Hegel's Philosophy of Law" (1842–1843), in Marx/Engels, *Collected Works,* Vol. 3 (1975), 29.

[21] Karl Marx, "Contribution to the Critique of Hegel's Philosophy of Law: Introduction" (1844), in Marx/Engels, *Collected Works,* Vol. 3 (1975), 186–87. In this case, I have used the translation of T. Bottomore included in Robert Tucker, ed., *The Marx-Engels Reader,* 2nd ed. (New York: Norton, 1978), 64–65.

[22] Marx, "Economic and Philosophic Manuscripts of 1844," 280.

[23] Karl Marx and Frederick Engels, "The Holy Family or Critique of Critical Criticism: Against Bruno Bauer and Company" (1845), in Marx/Engels, *Collected Works,* Vol. 4 (1975), 36.

[24] Marx, "Economic and Philosophic Manuscripts of 1844," 299.

[25] Preface to "A Contribution to the Critique of Political Economy" (1859), in Marx/Engels, *Collected Works,* Vol. 29 (1987), 264.

[26] Karl Marx and Frederick Engels, "The German Ideology," in Marx/Engels, *Collected Works,* Vol. 5 (1976), 54.

[27] Ibid., 50.

[28] Ibid., 51.

[29] Ibid., 51–52.

[30] Ibid., 52–53.

[31] For example in the intense public discussion surrounding the publication of Thomas Piketty's, *Capital in the Twenty-First Century,* translated from the French by Arthur Goldhammer (Cambridge, Mass., Harvard University Press, 2014).

[32] Karl Marx, "The Poverty of Philosophy: Answer to the *Philosophy of Poverty* by M. Proudhon" (1847), in Marx/Engels, *Collected Works,* Vol. 6 (1976), 177.

PART TWO

Manifesto of the Communist Party

A spectre is haunting Europe—the spectre of Communism. All the Powers of old Europe have entered into a holy alliance to exorcise this spectre: Pope and Czar, Metternich and Guizot, French Radicals and German police-spies.[1]

Where is the party in opposition that has not been decried as Communistic by its opponents in power? Where the Opposition that has not hurled back the branding reproach of Communism, against the more advanced opposition parties, as well as against its reactionary adversaries?

Two things result from this fact:

I. Communism is already acknowledged by all European Powers to be itself a Power.

II. It is high time that Communists should openly, in the face of the whole world, publish their views, their aims, their tendencies, and meet this nursery tale of the Spectre of Communism with a Manifesto of the party itself.

[1]The first part of this sentence would be more literally translated as "All the Powers of old Europe have joined together for a holy crusade against this spectre." In early 1848, Metternich was the conservative chancellor of the Austrian Empire, and Guizot was the liberal foreign minister of France. This list opposes secular and sacred rulers; Western, central, and Eastern European regions; conservative and liberal government leaders; and the democratic opposition and its prosecutors, as if to show that all the disparate elements in the current political scene were united in their common fear of the force that would destroy the system they inhabited.

Figure 6. Title page of the first German edition of the *Manifesto of the Communist Party,* published in London in February 1848.

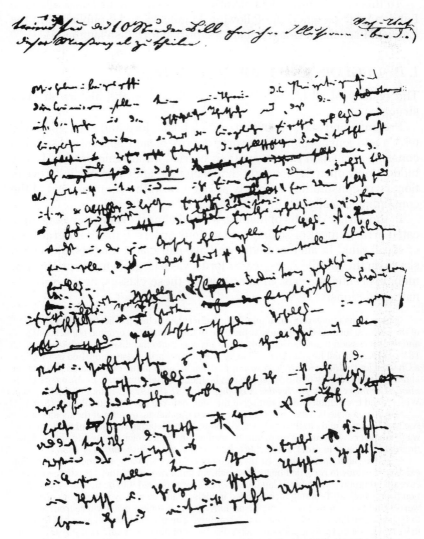

Figure 7. A page of the original draft of the *Communist Manifesto*. The top two lines are in the handwriting of Marx's wife, Jenny, indicating that Marx dictated parts of the manuscript.

To this end, Communists of various nationalities have assembled in London, and sketched the following Manifesto, to be published in the English, French, German, Italian, Flemish and Danish languages.[2]

I. BOURGEOIS AND PROLETARIANS*

The history of all hitherto existing society** is the history of class struggles.

Freeman and slave, patrician and plebeian, lord and serf, guildmaster*** and journeyman, in a word, oppressor and oppressed, stood in constant opposition to one another, carried on an uninterrupted, now hidden, now open fight, a fight that each time ended, either in a revolutionary re-constitution of society at large, or in the common ruin of the contending classes.

In the earlier epochs of history, we find almost everywhere a complicated arrangement of society into various orders, a manifold gradation of social rank. In ancient Rome we have patricians, knights, plebeians, slaves; in the Middle Ages, feudal lords, vassals, guild-masters, journeymen, apprentices, serfs; in almost all of these classes, again, subordinate gradations.[3]

[2] These translations represent intentions rather than actual publications. Because of the political turmoil that ensued at the time of the *Manifesto*'s original publication and the repression that followed, only one translation, into Swedish, was published in 1848–1849. A partial English translation by Helen MacFarlane was published in 1850 in a Chartist journal, *The Red Republican.* A detailed account of the complicated publication and translation history of the *Manifesto* can be found in Bert Andreas, *Le Manifeste Communiste de Marx et Engels: Histoire et Bibliographie, 1848–1919* (Milan: Feltrinelli, 1963). Widespread translation and reprinting of the *Manifesto* did not begin until after 1870.

*By bourgeoisie is meant the class of modern Capitalists, owners of the means of social production and employers of wage-labour. By proletariat, the class of modern wage-labourers who, having no means of production of their own, are reduced to selling their labour-power in order to live. [*Note by Engels to the English edition of 1888.*]

**That is, all *written* history. In 1847, the pre-history of society, the social organisation existing previous to recorded history, was all but unknown. Since then, Haxthausen discovered common ownership of land in Russia, Maurer proved it to be the social foundation from which all Teutonic races started in history, and by and by village communities were found to be, or to have been, the primitive form of society everywhere from India to Ireland. The inner organisation of this primitive Communistic society was laid bare, in its typical form, by Morgan's crowning discovery of the true nature of the *gens* and its relation to the *tribe.* With the dissolution of these primeval communities society begins to be differentiated into separate and finally antagonistic classes. I have attempted to retrace this process of dissolution in *Der Ursprung der Familie, des Privateigenthums und des Staats,* 2nd edition, Stuttgart, 1886. [*Note by Engels to the English edition of 1888.*]

* * * Guild-master, that is, a full member of a guild, a master within, not a head of a guild. [*Note by Engels to the English edition of 1888.*]

[3] Choosing precise terminology for defining social groupings was a significant problem not only for the translator but also for Marx and Engels in this section and

The modern bourgeois society that has sprouted from the ruins of feudal society has not done away with class antagonisms. It has but established new classes, new conditions of oppression, new forms of struggle in place of the old ones.

Our epoch, the epoch of the bourgeoisie, possesses, however, this distinctive feature: it has simplified the class antagonisms. Society as a whole is more and more splitting up into two great hostile camps, into two great classes directly facing each other: Bourgeoisie and Proletariat.

From the serfs of the Middle Ages sprang the chartered burghers of the earliest towns. From these burgesses the first elements of the bourgeoisie were developed.[4]

The discovery of America, the rounding of the Cape,[5] opened up fresh ground for the rising bourgeoisie. The East-Indian and Chinese markets, the colonisation of America, trade with the colonies, the increase in the means of exchange and in commodities generally, gave to commerce, to navigation, to industry, an impulse never before known, and thereby, to the revolutionary element in the tottering feudal society, a rapid development.

The feudal system of industry, under which industrial production was monopolised by closed guilds, now no longer sufficed for the growing wants of the new markets. The manufacturing system took its place. The guild-masters were pushed on one side by the manufacturing middle class; division of labour between the different corporate guilds vanished in the face of division of labour in each single workshop.

Meantime the markets kept ever growing, the demand ever rising. Even manufacture no longer sufficed. Thereupon, steam and machinery revolutionised industrial production. The place of manufacture was

throughout the *Manifesto*. Engels's reading of *Zunftbürger* (literally, a townsperson whose social status and citizenship rights were based on membership in a legally defined trade association, or guild) as "guild-master" is the first of a number of awkward attempts to describe the social world of the prerevolutionary, "old" society. This society was organized into a hierarchical structure of incorporated status groups, or "estates," but it also displayed the embryonic development of the modern bourgeois society, in which individuals were grouped into social classes defined by property ownership and position in the system of production. "Class" and "estate" terminology is often interchanged and overlapping in the text. This is revealing as well as confusing, since it indicates Marx and Engels's own interpretation of "class" as ultimately combining economic, social, political, and cultural dimensions, as in the older term "estate."

[4] The German term translated here first as "chartered burgher" and then as "burgess" is *Pfahlbürger,* which has the modern meaning of a narrow-minded, small-town philistine (a meaning used in translations later in the text) and derives from the conception of a town citizen whose rights and status are defined by the protection of a town wall or stockade (a fence of "stakes," or *Pfähle*).

[5] The Cape of Africa.

taken by the giant, Modern Industry, the place of the industrial middle class, by industrial millionaires, the leaders of whole industrial armies, the modern bourgeois.

Modern industry[6] has established the world market, for which the discovery of America paved the way. This market has given an immense development to commerce, to navigation, to communication by land. This development has, in its turn, reacted on the extension of industry; and in proportion as industry, commerce, navigation, railways extended, in the same proportion the bourgeoisie developed, increased its capital, and pushed into the background every class handed down from the Middle Ages.

We see, therefore, how the modern bourgeoisie is itself the product of a long course of development, of a series of revolutions in the modes of production and of exchange.

Each step in the development of the bourgeoisie was accompanied by a corresponding political advance of that class. An oppressed class under the sway of the feudal nobility, an armed and self-governing association in the medieval commune;* here independent urban republic (as in Italy and Germany), there taxable "third estate" of the monarchy (as in France), afterwards, in the period of manufacture proper, serving either the semi-feudal or the absolute monarchy as a counterpoise against the nobility, and, in fact, cornerstone of the great monarchies in general, the bourgeoisie has at last, since the establishment of Modern Industry and of the world market, conquered for itself, in the modern representative State,[7] exclusive political sway. The executive of the modern State is but a committee for managing the common affairs of the whole bourgeoisie.

The bourgeoisie, historically, has played a most revolutionary part.

The bourgeoisie, wherever it has got the upper hand, has put an end to all feudal, patriarchal, idyllic relations. It has pitilessly torn asunder the motley feudal ties that bound man to his "natural superiors," and has left remaining no other nexus between man and man than naked self-interest, than callous "cash payment." It has drowned the most heavenly ecstasies of religious fervour, of chivalrous enthusiasm, of philistine

---

[6]The German editions have "big" or "large-scale" industry.

*"Commune" was the name taken, in France, by the nascent towns even before they had conquered from their feudal lords and masters local self-government and political rights as the "Third Estate." Generally speaking, for the economical development of the bourgeoisie, England is here taken as the typical country; for its political development, France. [*Note by Engels to the English edition of 1888.*]

[7]A state whose political institutions are based on the legal recognition and political representation of individuals rather than social corporations or estates.

sentimentalism, in the icy water of egotistical calculation. It has resolved personal worth into exchange value, and in place of the numberless indefeasible chartered freedoms, has set up that single, unconscionable freedom — Free Trade. In one word, for exploitation, veiled by religious and political illusions, it has substituted naked, shameless, direct, brutal exploitation.

The bourgeoisie has stripped of its halo every occupation hitherto honoured and looked up to with reverent awe. It has converted the physician, the lawyer, the priest, the poet, the man of science, into its paid wage-labourers.

The bourgeoisie has torn away from the family its sentimental veil, and has reduced the family relation to a mere money relation.

The bourgeoisie has disclosed how it came to pass that the brutal display of vigour in the Middle Ages, which Reactionists so much admire, found its fitting complement in the most slothful indolence. It has been the first to show what man's activity can bring about. It has accomplished wonders far surpassing Egyptian pyramids, Roman aqueducts, and Gothic cathedrals; it has conducted expeditions that put in the shade all former Exoduses of nations and crusades.

The bourgeoisie cannot exist without constantly revolutionising the instruments of production, and thereby the relations of production, and with them the whole relations of society. Conservation of the old modes of production in unaltered form, was, on the contrary, the first condition of existence for all earlier industrial classes. Constant revolutionising of production, uninterrupted disturbance of all social conditions, everlasting uncertainty and agitation distinguish the bourgeois epoch from all earlier ones. All fixed, fast-frozen relations, with their train of ancient and venerable prejudices and opinions, are swept away, all new-formed ones become antiquated before they can ossify. All that is solid[8] melts into air, all that is holy is profaned, and man is at last compelled to face with sober senses, his real conditions of life, and his relations with his kind.

The need of a constantly expanding market for its products chases the bourgeoisie over the whole surface of the globe. It must nestle everywhere, settle everywhere, establish connexions everywhere.

The bourgeoisie has through its exploitation of the world market given a cosmopolitan character to production and consumption in every country. To the great chagrin of Reactionists, it has drawn from

[8] Moore condensed the phrase "customary and established" into "solid." The original phrase has a much more specific historical reference to the prerevolutionary European social order.

under the feet of industry the national ground on which it stood. All old-established national industries have been destroyed or are daily being destroyed. They are dislodged by new industries, whose introduction becomes a life and death question for all civilised nations, by industries that no longer work up indigenous raw material, but raw material drawn from the remotest zones; industries whose products are consumed, not only at home, but in every quarter of the globe. In place of the old wants, satisfied by the productions of the country, we find new wants, requiring for their satisfaction the products of distant lands and climes. In place of the old local and national seclusion and self-sufficiency, we have inter-course in every direction, universal inter-dependence of nations. And as in material, so also in intellectual production. The intellectual creations of individual nations become common property. National onesided-ness and narrow-mindedness become more and more impossible, and from the numerous national and local literatures, there arises a world literature.

The bourgeoisie, by the rapid improvement of all instruments of pro-duction, by the immensely facilitated means of communication, draws all, even the most barbarian, nations into civilisation. The cheap prices of its commodities[9] are the heavy artillery with which it batters down all Chinese walls, with which it forces the barbarians' intensely obsti-nate hatred of foreigners to capitulate. It compels all nations, on pain of extinction, to adopt the bourgeois mode of production; it compels them to introduce what it calls civilisation into their midst, i.e., to become bourgeois themselves. In one word, it creates a world after its own image.

The bourgeoisie has subjected the country to the rule of the towns. It has created enormous cities, has greatly increased the urban popu-lation as compared with the rural, and has thus rescued a considerable part of the population from the idiocy of rural life. Just as it has made the country dependent on the towns, so it has made barbarian and semi-barbarian countries dependent on the civilised ones, nations of peasants on nations of bourgeois, the East on the West.

The bourgeoisie keeps more and more doing away with the scattered state of the population, of the means of production, and of property. It has agglomerated population, centralised means of production, and has concentrated property in a few hands. The necessary conse-quence of this was political centralisation. Independent, or but loosely

[9] The contemporary reference here is to the British Opium War in China, which led to the opening of Chinese ports to foreign trade and the British occupation of Hong Kong.

connected provinces with separate interests, laws, governments and systems of taxation, became lumped together into one nation, with one government, one code of laws, one national class-interest, one frontier and one customs-tariff.

The bourgeoisie, during its rule of scarce one hundred years, has created more massive and more colossal productive forces than have all preceding generations together. Subjection of Nature's forces to man, machinery, application of chemistry to industry and agriculture, steam-navigation, railways, electric telegraphs, clearing of whole continents for cultivation, canalisation of rivers, whole populations conjured out of the ground—what earlier century had even a presentiment that such productive forces slumbered in the lap of social labour?

We see then: the means of production and of exchange, on whose foundation the bourgeoisie built itself up, were generated in feudal society. At a certain stage in the development of these means of production and of exchange, the conditions under which feudal society produced and exchanged, the feudal organisation of agriculture and manufacturing industry, in one word, the feudal relations of property became no longer compatible with the already developed productive forces;[10] they became so many fetters. They had to be burst asunder; they were burst asunder.

Into their place stepped free competition, accompanied by a social and political constitution adapted to it, and by the economical and political sway of the bourgeois class.

A similar movement is going on before our own eyes. Modern bourgeois society with its relations of production, of exchange and of property, a society that has conjured up such gigantic means of production and of exchange, is like the sorcerer, who is no longer able to control the powers of the nether world whom he has called up by his spells. For many a decade past the history of industry and commerce is but the history of the revolt of modern productive forces against modern conditions of production, against the property relations that are the conditions for the existence of the bourgeoisie and of its rule. It is enough to mention the commercial crises that by their periodical return put on its trial, each time more threateningly, the existence of the entire bourgeois society. In these crises a great part not only of the existing products, but also of the previously created productive forces, are periodically destroyed. In these crises there breaks out an epidemic that, in all earlier epochs, would have seemed an absurdity—the epidemic

[10] The original German edition has an added clarifying phrase: "They hindered production instead of furthering it."

of over-production. Society suddenly finds itself put back into a state of momentary barbarism; it appears as if a famine, a universal war of devastation had cut off the supply of every means of subsistence; industry and commerce seem to be destroyed; and why? Because there is too much civilisation, too much means of subsistence, too much industry, too much commerce. The productive forces at the disposal of society no longer tend to further the development of the conditions of bourgeois property; on the contrary, they have become too powerful for these conditions, by which they are fettered, and so soon as they overcome these fetters, they bring disorder into the whole of bourgeois society, endanger the existence of bourgeois property. The conditions of bourgeois society are too narrow to comprise the wealth created by them. And how does the bourgeoisie get over these crises? On the one hand by enforced destruction of a mass of productive forces; on the other, by the conquest of new markets, and by the more thorough exploitation of the old ones. That is to say, by paving the way for more extensive and more destructive crises, and by diminishing the means whereby crises are prevented.

The weapons with which the bourgeoisie felled feudalism to the ground are now turned against the bourgeoisie itself.

But not only has the bourgeoisie forged the weapons that bring death to itself; it has also called into existence the men who are to wield those weapons—the modern working class—the proletarians.

In proportion as the bourgeoisie, *i.e.*, capital, is developed, in the same proportion is the proletariat, the modern working class, developed—a class of labourers, who live only so long as they find work, and who find work only so long as their labour increases capital. These labourers, who must sell themselves piecemeal, are a commodity, like every other article of commerce, and are consequently exposed to all the vicissitudes of competition, to all the fluctuations of the market.

Owing to the extensive use of machinery and to division of labour, the work of the proletarians has lost all individual character, and, consequently, all charm for the workman. He becomes an appendage of the machine, and it is only the most simple, most monotonous, and most easily acquired knack, that is required of him. Hence, the cost of production of a workman is restricted, almost entirely, to the means of subsistence that he requires for his maintenance, and for the propagation of his race. But the price of a commodity, and therefore also of labour,[11] is equal to its cost of production. In proportion, therefore, as

[11] As Engels noted in 1891, the use of the phrase "price of labor" is inadequate to describe the meaning of the labor exchange as Marx developed it after 1850. In his

the repulsiveness of the work increases, the wage decreases. Nay more, in proportion as the use of machinery and division of labour increases, in the same proportion the burden of toil also increases, whether by prolongation of the working hours, by increase of the work exacted in a given time or by increased speed of the machinery, etc.

Modern industry has converted the little workshop of the patriarchal master into the great factory of the industrial capitalist. Masses of labourers, crowded into the factory, are organised like soldiers. As privates of the industrial army they are placed under the command of a perfect hierarchy of officers and sergeants. Not only are they slaves of the bourgeois class, and of the bourgeois State; they are daily and hourly enslaved by the machine, by the overlooker, and, above all, by the individual bourgeois manufacturer himself. The more openly this despotism proclaims gain to be its end and aim, the more petty, the more hateful and the more embittering it is.

The less the skill and exertion of strength implied in manual labour, in other words, the more modern industry becomes developed, the more is the labour of men superseded by that of women. Differences of age and sex have no longer any distinctive social validity for the working class. All are instruments of labour, more or less expensive to use, according to their age and sex.

No sooner is the exploitation of the labourer by the manufacturer, so far, at an end, and he receives his wages in cash, than he is set upon by the other portions of the bourgeoisie, the landlord, the shopkeeper, the pawnbroker, etc.

The lower strata of the middle class—the small tradespeople, shopkeepers, and retired tradesmen generally,[12] the handicraftsmen and peasants—all these sink gradually into the proletariat, partly because their diminutive capital does not suffice for the scale on which Modern Industry is carried on, and is swamped in the competition with the large capitalists, partly because their specialised skill is rendered worthless by new methods of production. Thus the proletariat is recruited from all classes of the population.

---

mature theory, "labor" would be defined as "labor-power," to indicate the peculiar quality of labor as a commodity that has the potential to increase in value as it is consumed. (See the last section of the introduction to this book, beginning on page 52.) Engels made his comments in the introduction to a publication of Marx's pre-1848 pamphlet, *Wage Labour and Capital.*

[12] Again, social categories cause problems in translation, The German reads "middle estate," not "middle class"; "small producers," not "small tradespeople"; and "people who live from investments, interest, or rent," not "retired tradespeople generally."

The proletariat goes through various stages of development. With its birth begins its struggle with the bourgeoisie. At first the contest is carried on by individual labourers, then by the workpeople of a factory, then by the operatives of one trade, in one locality, against the individual bourgeois who directly exploits them. They direct their attacks not against the bourgeois conditions of production, but against the instruments of production themselves; they destroy imported wares that compete with their labour, they smash to pieces machinery, they set factories ablaze, they seek to restore by force the vanished status of the workman of the Middle Ages.

At this stage the labourers still form an incoherent mass scattered over the whole country, and broken up by their mutual competition. If anywhere they unite to form more compact bodies, this is not yet the consequence of their own active union, but of the union of the bourgeoisie, which class, in order to attain its own political ends, is compelled to set the whole proletariat in motion, and is moreover yet, for a time, able to do so. At this stage, therefore, the proletarians do not fight their enemies, but the enemies of their enemies, the remnants of absolute monarchy, the landowners, the non-industrial bourgeois, the petty bourgeoisie. Thus the whole historical movement is concentrated in the hands of the bourgeoisie; every victory so obtained is a victory for the bourgeoisie.

But with the development of industry the proletariat not only increases in number; it becomes concentrated in greater masses, its strength grows, and it feels that strength more. The various interests and conditions of life within the ranks of the proletariat are more and more equalised, in proportion as machinery obliterates all distinctions of labour, and nearly everywhere reduces wages to the same low level. The growing competition among the bourgeois, and the resulting commercial crises, make the wages of the workers ever more fluctuating. The unceasing improvement of machinery, ever more rapidly developing, makes their livelihood more and more precarious; the collisions between individual workmen and individual bourgeois take more and more the character of collisions between two classes. Thereupon the workers begin to form combinations (Trades' Unions)[13] against the bourgeois; they club together in order to keep up the rate of wages; they found permanent associations in order to make provision beforehand

---

[13] The term used in the original version was "coalitions." The use of the phrase "combinations (Trades' Unions)" is an indication of how organizational structures in the labor movement had changed by 1888.

for these occasional revolts. Here and there the contest breaks out into riots.

Now and then the workers are victorious, but only for a time. The real fruit of their battles lies, not in the immediate result, but in the everexpanding union of the workers. This union is helped on by the improved means of communication that are created by modern industry and that place the workers of different localities in contact with one another. It was just this contact that was needed to centralise the numerous local struggles, all of the same character, into one national struggle between classes. But every class struggle is a political struggle. And that union, to attain which the burghers of the Middle Ages, with their miserable highways, required centuries, the modern proletarians, thanks to railways, achieve in a few years.

This organisation of the proletarians into a class, and consequently into a political party, is continually being upset again by the competition between the workers themselves. But it ever rises up again, stronger, firmer, mightier. It compels legislative recognition of particular interests of the workers, by taking advantage of the divisions among the bourgeoisie itself. Thus the ten-hours' bill in England was carried.[14]

Altogether collisions between the classes of the old society further, in many ways, the course of development of the proletariat. The bourgeoisie finds itself involved in a constant battle. At first with the aristocracy; later on, with those portions of the bourgeoisie itself, whose interests have become antagonistic to the progress of industry; at all times, with the bourgeoisie of foreign countries. In all these battles it sees itself compelled to appeal to the proletariat, to ask for its help, and thus, to drag it into the political arena. The bourgeoisie itself, therefore, supplies the proletariat with its own elements of political and general education, in other words, it furnishes the proletariat with weapons for fighting the bourgeoisie.

Further, as we have already seen, entire sections of the ruling classes are, by the advance of industry, precipitated into the proletariat, or are at least threatened in their conditions of existence. These also supply the proletariat with fresh elements of enlightenment and progress.

Finally, in times when the class struggle nears the decisive hour, the process of dissolution going on within the ruling class, in fact within the whole range of old society, assumes such a violent, glaring character, that a small section of the ruling class cuts itself adrift, and joins the

[14] This bill limiting the daily working hours for women and children was passed by Parliament because of the willingness of conservative British landowners to oppose the interests of the industrial bourgeoisie.

revolutionary class, the class that holds the future in its hands. Just as, therefore, at an earlier period, a section of the nobility went over to the bourgeoisie, so now a portion of the bourgeoisie goes over to the proletariat, and in particular, a portion of the bourgeois ideologists, who have raised themselves to the level of comprehending theoretically the historical movement as a whole.

Of all the classes that stand face to face with the bourgeoisie today, the proletariat alone is a really revolutionary class. The other classes decay and finally disappear in the face of Modern Industry; the proletariat is its special and essential product.

The lower middle class, the small manufacturer, the shopkeeper, the artisan, the peasant, all these fight against the bourgeoisie, to save from extinction their existence as fractions of the middle class.[15] They are therefore not revolutionary, but conservative. Nay more, they are reactionary, for they try to roll back the wheel of history. If by chance they are revolutionary, they are so only in view of their impending transfer into the proletariat, they thus defend not their present, but their future interests, they desert their own standpoint to place themselves at that of the proletariat.

The "dangerous class," the social scum,[16] that passively rotting mass thrown off by the lowest layers of old society may, here and there, be swept into the movement by a proletarian revolution; its conditions of life, however, prepare it far more for the part of a bribed tool of reactionary intrigue.

In the conditions of the proletariat, those of old society at large are already virtually swamped. The proletarian is without property; his relation to his wife and children has no longer anything in common with the bourgeois family relations; modern industrial labour, modern subjection to capital, the same in England as in France, in America as in Germany, has stripped him of every trace of national character. Law, morality, religion, are to him so many bourgeois prejudices, behind which lurk in ambush just as many bourgeois interests.

All the preceding classes that got the upper hand, sought to fortify their already acquired status by subjecting society at large to their conditions of appropriation. The proletarians cannot become masters of the

[15] More correctly, "middle estates," not "lower middle class"; "small producer," not "small manufacturer"; "small merchant," not "shopkeeper"; and "middle estates," not "fractions of the middle class."

[16] The German word translated by these two phrases is *Lumpenproletariat,* or "proletariat in rags," a word that has become part of the English vocabulary of social analysis in the century and a half since 1848.

productive forces of society, except by abolishing their own previous mode of appropriation, and thereby also every other previous mode of appropriation. They have nothing of their own to secure and to fortify; their mission is to destroy all previous securities for, and insurances of, individual property.

All previous historical movements were movements of minorities, or in the interest of minorities. The proletarian movement is the self-conscious, independent movement of the immense majority, in the interest of the immense majority. The proletariat, the lowest stratum of our present society, cannot stir, cannot raise itself up, without the whole superincumbent strata of official society being sprung into the air.

Though not in substance, yet in form, the struggle of the proletariat with the bourgeoisie is at first a national struggle. The proletariat of each country must, of course, first of all settle matters with its own bourgeoisie.

In depicting the most general phases of the development of the proletariat, we traced the more or less veiled civil war, raging within existing society, up to the point where that war breaks out into open revolution, and where the violent overthrow of the bourgeoisie lays the foundation for the sway[17] of the proletariat.

Hitherto, every form of society has been based, as we have already seen, on the antagonism of oppressing and oppressed classes. But in order to oppress a class, certain conditions must be assured to it under which it can, at least, continue its slavish existence. The serf, in the period of serfdom, raised himself to membership in the commune, just as the petty bourgeois, under the yoke of feudal absolutism, managed to develop into a bourgeois. The modern labourer, on the contrary, instead of rising with the progress of industry, sinks deeper and deeper below the conditions of existence of his own class. He becomes a pauper, and pauperism develops more rapidly than population and wealth. And here it becomes evident, that the bourgeoisie is unfit any longer to be the ruling class in society, and to impose its conditions of existence upon society as an over-riding law. It is unfit to rule because it is incompetent to assure an existence to its slave within his slavery, because it cannot help letting him sink into such a state, that it has to feed him, instead of being fed by him. Society can no longer live under this bourgeoisie, in other words, its existence is no longer compatible with society.

---

[17] More correctly, "domination" here and in the last paragraph of this section.

The essential condition for the existence, and for the sway of the bourgeois class, is[18] the formation and augmentation of capital; the condition for capital is wage-labour. Wage-labour rests exclusively on competition between the labourers. The advance of industry, whose involuntary promoter is the bourgeoisie, replaces the isolation of the labourers, due to competition, by their revolutionary combination, due to association. The development of Modern Industry, therefore, cuts from under its feet the very foundation on which the bourgeoisie produces and appropriates products. What the bourgeoisie, therefore, produces, above all, is its own grave-diggers. Its fall and the victory of the proletariat are equally inevitable.

II. PROLETARIANS AND COMMUNISTS

In what relation do the Communists stand to the proletarians as a whole?

The Communists do not form a separate party opposed to other working-class parties.

They have no interests separate and apart from those of the proletariat as a whole.

They do not set up any sectarian principles of their own, by which to shape and mould the proletarian movement.

The Communists are distinguished from the other working-class parties by this only: 1. In the national struggles of the proletarians of the different countries, they point out and bring to the front the common interests of the entire proletariat, independently of all nationality. 2. In the various stages of development which the struggle of the working class against the bourgeoisie has to pass through, they always and everywhere represent the interests of the movement as a whole.

The Communists, therefore, are on the one hand, practically, the most advanced and resolute section of the working-class parties of every country, that section which pushes forward all others; on the other hand, theoretically, they have over the great mass of the proletariat the advantage of clearly understanding the line of march, the conditions, and the ultimate general results of the proletarian movement.

The immediate aim of the Communists is the same as that of all the other proletarian parties: formation of the proletariat into a class, overthrow of the bourgeois supremacy, conquest of political power by the proletariat.

---

[18]The translation omits the phrase "the accumulation of wealth in the hands of private individuals."

The theoretical conclusions of the Communists are in no way based on ideas or principles that have been invented, or discovered by this or that would-be universal reformer.

They merely express, in general terms, actual relations springing from an existing class struggle, from a historical movement going on under our very eyes. The abolition of existing property relations is not at all a distinctive feature of Communism.

All property relations in the past have continually been subject to historical change consequent upon the change in historical conditions.

The French Revolution, for example, abolished feudal property in favour of bourgeois property.

The distinguishing feature of Communism is not the abolition of property generally, but the abolition of bourgeois property. But modern bourgeois private property is the final and most complete expression of the system of producing and appropriating products, that is based on class antagonisms, on the exploitation of the many by the few.

In this sense, the theory of the Communists may be summed up in the single sentence: Abolition of private property.

We Communists have been reproached with the desire of abolishing the right of personally acquiring property as the fruit of a man's own labour, which property is alleged to be the groundwork of all personal freedom, activity and independence.

Hard-won, self-acquired, self-earned property! Do you mean the property of the petty artisan and of the small peasant, a form of property that preceded the bourgeois form? There is no need to abolish that; the development of industry has to a great extent already destroyed it, and is still destroying it daily.

Or do you mean modern bourgeois private property?

But does wage-labour create any property for the labourer? Not a bit. It creates capital, *i.e.*, that kind of property which exploits wage-labour, and which cannot increase except upon condition of begetting a new supply of wage-labour for fresh exploitation. Property, in its present form, is based on the antagonism of capital and wage-labour. Let us examine both sides of this antagonism.

To be a capitalist is to have not only a purely personal, but a social *status*[19] in production. Capital is a collective product, and only by the united action of many members, nay, in the last resort, only by the united action of all members of society, can it be set in motion.

Capital is, therefore, not a personal, it is a social power.

[19] More correctly, "position."

When, therefore, capital is converted into common property, into the property of all members of society, personal property is not thereby transformed into social property. It is only the social character of the property that is changed. It loses its class character.

Let us now take wage-labour.

The average price of wage-labour is the minimum wage, *i.e.,* that quantum of the means of subsistence, which is absolutely requisite to keep the labourer in bare existence as a labourer. What, therefore, the wage-labourer appropriates by means of his labour, merely suffices to prolong and reproduce a bare existence. We by no means intend to abolish this personal appropriation of the products of labour, an appropriation that is made for the maintenance and reproduction of human life, and that leaves no surplus wherewith to command the labour of others. All that we want to do away with is the miserable character of this appropriation, under which the labourer lives merely to increase capital, and is allowed to live only in so far as the interest of the ruling class requires it.

In bourgeois society, living labour is but a means to increase accumulated labour. In Communist society, accumulated labour is but a means to widen, to enrich, to promote the existence[20] of the labourer.

In bourgeois society, therefore, the past dominates the present; in Communist society, the present dominates the past. In bourgeois society capital is independent and has individuality,[21] while the living person is dependent and has no individuality.

And the abolition of this state of things is called by the bourgeois abolition of individuality and freedom! And rightly so. The abolition of bourgeois individuality, bourgeois independence, and bourgeois freedom is undoubtedly aimed at.

By freedom is meant, under the present bourgeois conditions of production, free trade, free selling and buying.

But if selling and buying disappears, free selling and buying disappears also. This talk about free selling and buying, and all the other "brave words" of our bourgeoisie about freedom in general, have a meaning, if any, only in contrast with restricted selling and buying, with the fettered traders of the Middle Ages, but have no meaning when

---

[20] More literally, "life process." "Existence" is too easily confused with the Marxian notion of "merely" existing, or physically subsisting, which is clearly not what is meant here.

[21] More correctly, "personal" or "personality" here and below. In Marx's philosophical and linguistic context, "person" and "personality" define the characteristics of the individual as a subjective agent.

opposed to the Communistic abolition of buying and selling, of the bourgeois conditions of production, and of the bourgeoisie itself.

You are horrified at our intending to do away with private property. But in your existing society, private property is already done away with for nine-tenths of the population; its existence for the few is solely due to its non-existence in the hands of those nine-tenths. You reproach us, therefore, with intending to do away with a form of property, the necessary condition for whose existence is the non-existence of any property for the immense majority of society.

In one word, you reproach us with intending to do away with your property. Precisely so; that is just what we intend.

From the moment when labour can no longer be converted into capital, money, or rent, into a social power capable of being monopolised, *i.e.,* from the moment when individual property can no longer be transformed into bourgeois property, into capital, from that moment, you say, individuality vanishes.

You must, therefore, confess that by "individual" you mean no other person than the bourgeois, than the middle-class owner of property. This person must, indeed, be swept out of the way, and made impossible.

Communism deprives no man of the power to appropriate the products of society; all that it does is to deprive him of the power to subjugate the labour of others by means of such appropriation.

It has been objected that upon the abolition of private property all work will cease, and universal laziness will overtake us.

According to this, bourgeois society ought long ago to have gone to the dogs through sheer idleness; for those of its members who work, acquire nothing, and those who acquire anything, do not work. The whole of this objection is but another expression of the tautology: that there can no longer be any wage-labour when there is no longer any capital.

All objections urged against the Communistic mode of producing and appropriating material products, have, in the same way, been urged against the Communistic modes of producing and appropriating intellectual products. Just as, to the bourgeois, the disappearance of class property is the disappearance of production itself, so the disappearance of class culture is to him identical with the disappearance of all culture.

That culture, the loss of which he laments, is, for the enormous majority, a mere training to act as a machine.

But don't wrangle with us so long as you apply, to our intended abolition of bourgeois property, the standard of your bourgeois notions of freedom, culture, law, &c. Your very ideas are but the outgrowth of the conditions of your bourgeois production and bourgeois property, just as your jurisprudence is but the will of your class made into a law for all, a will, whose essential character and direction are determined by the economical conditions of existence of your class.

The selfish misconception that induces you to transform into eternal laws of nature and of reason, the social forms springing from your present mode of production and form of property—historical relations that rise and disappear in the progress of production—this misconception you share with every ruling class that has preceded you. What you see clearly in the case of ancient property, what you admit in the case of feudal property, you are of course forbidden to admit in the case of your own bourgeois form of property.

Abolition of the family! Even the most radical flare up at this infamous proposal of the Communists.

On what foundation is the present family, the bourgeois family, based? On capital, on private gain. In its completely developed form this family exists only among the bourgeoisie. But this state of things finds its complement in the practical absence of the family among the proletarians, and in public prostitution.

The bourgeois family will vanish as a matter of course when its complement vanishes, and both will vanish with the vanishing of capital.

Do you charge us with wanting to stop the exploitation of children by their parents? To this crime we plead guilty.

But, you will say, we destroy the most hallowed of relations, when we replace home education by social.

And your education! Is not that also social, and determined by the social conditions under which you educate, by the intervention, direct or indirect, of society, by means of schools, &c.? The Communists have not invented the intervention of society in education; they do but seek to alter the character of that intervention, and to rescue education from the influence of the ruling class.

The bourgeois clap-trap about the family and education, about the hallowed co-relation of parent and child, becomes all the more disgusting, the more, by the action of Modern Industry, all family ties among the proletarians are torn asunder, and their children transformed into simple articles of commerce and instruments of labour.

But you Communists would introduce community of women, screams the whole bourgeoisie in chorus.

The bourgeois sees in his wife a mere instrument of production. He hears that the instruments of production are to be exploited in common, and, naturally, can come to no other conclusion than that the lot of being common to all will likewise fall to the women.

He has not even a suspicion that the real point aimed at is to do away with the status of women as mere instruments of production.

For the rest, nothing is more ridiculous than the virtuous indignation of our bourgeois at the community of women which, they pretend, is to be openly and officially established by the Communists. The Communists have no need to introduce community of women; it has existed almost from time immemorial.

Our bourgeois, not content with having the wives and daughters of their proletarians at their disposal, not to speak of common prostitutes, take the greatest pleasure in seducing each other's wives.

Bourgeois marriage is in reality a system of wives in common and thus, at the most, what the Communists might possibly be reproached with, is that they desire to introduce, in substitution for a hypocritically concealed, an openly legalised[22] community of women. For the rest, it is self-evident that the abolition of the present system of production must bring with it the abolition of the community of women springing from that system, *i.e.*, of prostitution both public and private.

The Communists are further reproached with desiring to abolish countries and nationality.

The working men have no country. We cannot take from them what they have not got. Since the proletariat must first of all acquire political supremacy, must rise to be the leading class of the nation,[23] must constitute itself the nation, it is so far, itself national, though not in the bourgeois sense of the word.

National differences[24] and antagonisms between peoples are daily more and more vanishing, owing to the development of the bourgeoisie, to freedom of commerce, to the world market, to uniformity in the mode of production and in the conditions of life corresponding thereto.

The supremacy of the proletariat will cause them to vanish still faster. United action, of the leading civilised countries at least, is one of the first conditions for the emancipation of the proletariat.

In proportion as the exploitation of one individual by another is put an end to, the exploitation of one nation by another will also be put an end to. In proportion as the antagonism between classes within the nation vanishes, the hostility of one nation to another will come to an end.

[22] More literally, "official, candid" rather than "openly legalised." In the next sentence, "official and nonofficial" would be a more precise translation than "public and private."

[23] "Elevate itself to a national class" would be a more precise translation than "rise to be the leading class of the nation."

[24] More correctly, "divisions."

The charges against Communism made from a religious, a philosoph-ical, and, generally, from an ideological standpoint, are not deserving of serious examination.

Does it require deep intuition to comprehend that man's ideas, views and conceptions, in one word, man's consciousness, changes with every change in the conditions of his material existence, in his social relations and in his social life?

What else does the history of ideas prove, than that intellectual pro-duction changes its character in proportion as material production is changed? The ruling ideas of each age have ever been the ideas of its ruling class.

When people speak of ideas that revolutionise society, they do but express the fact, that within the old society, the elements of a new one have been created, and that the dissolution of the old ideas keeps even pace with the dissolution of the old conditions of existence.

When the ancient world was in its last throes, the ancient religions were overcome by Christianity. When Christian ideas succumbed in the 18th century to rationalist ideas,[25] feudal society fought its death battle with the then revolutionary bourgeoisie. The ideas of religious liberty and freedom of conscience merely gave expression to the sway of free competition within the domain of knowledge.

"Undoubtedly," it will be said, "religious, moral, philosophical and juridical ideas have been modified in the course of historical develop-ment. But religion, morality, philosophy, political science,[26] and law, con-stantly survived this change.

"There are, besides, eternal truths, such as Freedom, Justice, etc., that are common to all states of society. But Communism abolishes eter-nal truths, it abolishes all religion and all morality, instead of constitut-ing them on a new basis; it therefore acts in contradiction to all past historical experience."

What does this accusation reduce itself to? The history of all past society has consisted in the development of class antagonisms, antago-nisms that assumed different forms at different epochs.

But whatever form they may have taken, one fact is common to all past ages, *viz.*, the exploitation of one part of society by the other. No wonder, then, that the social consciousness of past ages, despite all the multiplicity and variety it displays, moves within certain common forms,

[25] Literally, "ideas of the Enlightenment," which is both historically more precise and intellectually less narrow than "rationalist ideas."
[26] "Politics," not "political science."

or general ideas,[27] which cannot completely vanish except with the total disappearance of class antagonisms.

The Communist revolution is the most radical rupture with traditional property relations; no wonder that its development involves the most radical rupture with traditional ideas.

But let us have done with the bourgeois objections to Communism.

We have seen above, that the first step in the revolution by the working class is to raise the proletariat to the position of ruling class, to win the battle of democracy.

The proletariat will use its political supremacy to wrest, by degrees, all capital from the bourgeoisie, to centralise all instruments of production in the hands of the State, *i.e.,* of the proletariat organised as the ruling class; and to increase the total of productive forces as rapidly as possible.

Of course, in the beginning, this cannot be effected except by means of despotic inroads on the rights of property, and on the conditions of bourgeois production; by means of measures, therefore, which appear economically insufficient and untenable, but which, in the course of the movement, outstrip themselves, necessitate further inroads upon the old social order, and are unavoidable as a means of entirely revolutionising the mode of production.

These measures will of course be different in different countries.

Nevertheless in the most advanced countries, the following will be pretty generally applicable:

1. Abolition of property in land and application of all rents of land to public purposes.
2. A heavy progressive or graduated income tax.
3. Abolition of all right of inheritance.
4. Confiscation of the property of all emigrants and rebels.
5. Centralisation of credit in the hands of the State, by means of a national bank with State capital and an exclusive monopoly.
6. Centralisation of the means of communication and transport[28] in the hands of the State.
7. Extension of factories and instruments of production owned by the State; the bringing into cultivation of waste-lands, and the

[27] "Forms of consciousness," not "general ideas."

[28] "All transport," not "the means of communication and transport." With the tremendous growth and significance of the communications media since 1888, Moore's naive attempt to add a simple clarifying phrase can easily produce confusion. Marx did not in this sentence advocate centralized control of the media.

improvement of the soil generally in accordance with a common plan.

8. Equal liability of all to labour. Establishment of industrial armies, especially for agriculture.

9. Combination of agriculture with manufacturing industries; gradual abolition of the distinction between town and country, by a more equable distribution of the population over the country.

10. Free education for all children in public schools. Abolition of children's factory labour in its present form. Combination of education with industrial production, &c., &c.

When, in the course of development, class distinctions have disappeared, and all production has been concentrated in the hands of a vast association of the whole nation,[29] the public power will lose its political character. Political power, properly so called, is merely the organised power of one class for oppressing another. If the proletariat during its contest with the bourgeoisie is compelled, by the force of circumstances, to organise itself as a class, if, by means of a revolution, it makes itself the ruling class, and, as such, sweeps away by force the old conditions of production, then it will, along with these conditions, have swept away the conditions for the existence of class antagonisms and of classes generally, and will thereby have abolished its own supremacy as a class.

In place of the old bourgeois society, with its classes and class antagonisms, we shall have an association, in which the free development of each is the condition for the free development of all.

III. SOCIALIST AND COMMUNIST LITERATURE

1. Reactionary Socialism

A. FEUDAL SOCIALISM

Owing to their historical position, it became the vocation of the aristocracies of France and England to write pamphlets against modern bourgeois society. In the French revolution of July 1830, and in the English reform agitation, these aristocracies again succumbed to the hateful upstart. Thenceforth, a serious political contest was altogether out of question. A literary battle alone remained possible. But even in the

---

[29] "Of the associated individuals," not "of a vast association of the whole nation."

domain of literature the old cries of the restoration period* had become impossible.

In order to arouse sympathy, the aristocracy were obliged to lose sight, apparently, of their own interests, and to formulate their indictment against the bourgeoisie in the interest of the exploited working class alone. Thus the aristocracy took their revenge by singing lampoons on their new master, and whispering in his ears sinister prophecies of coming catastrophe.

In this way arose feudal Socialism; half lamentation, half lampoon; half echo of the past, half menace of the future; at times, by its bitter, witty and incisive criticism, striking the bourgeoisie to the very heart's core; but always ludicrous in its effect, through total incapacity to comprehend the march of modern history.

The aristocracy, in order to rally the people to them, waved the proletarian alms-bag in front for a banner. But the people, so often as it joined them, saw on their hindquarters the old feudal coats of arms, and deserted with loud and irreverent laughter.

One section of the French Legitimists and "Young England"[30] exhibited this spectacle.

In pointing out that their mode of exploitation was different to that of the bourgeoisie, the feudalists forget that they exploited under circumstances and conditions that were quite different, and that are now antiquated. In showing that, under their rule, the modern proletariat never existed, they forget that the modern bourgeoisie is the necessary offspring of their own form of society.

For the rest, so little do they conceal the reactionary character of their criticism that their chief accusation against the bourgeoisie amounts to this, that under the bourgeois *régime* a class is being developed, which is destined to cut up root and branch the old order of society.

What they upbraid the bourgeoisie with is not so much that it creates a proletariat, as that it creates a *revolutionary* proletariat.

In political practice, therefore, they join in all coercive measures against the working class; and in ordinary life, despite their high-falutin phrases, they stoop to pick up the golden apples dropped from the tree

---

*Not the English Restoration 1660 to 1689, but the French Restoration 1814 to 1830. [*Note by Engels to the English edition of 1888.*]

[30] The French legitimists were advocates of a restoration of the French Bourbon dynasty after the revolution of 1830. In their defense of the rights of the old feudal landlords, they sometimes presented themselves as defenders of the working classes against the bourgeoisie. Young England was a wing of the Tory party in England during the 1840s. Its most prominent member was Benjamin Disraeli, and its adherents mixed their aristocratic attacks on bourgeois capitalism with philanthropy for the working classes.

of industry, and to barter truth, love, and honour for traffic in wool, beetroot-sugar, and potato spirits.*

As the parson has ever gone hand in hand with the landlord,[31] so has Clerical Socialism with Feudal Socialism.

Nothing is easier than to give Christian asceticism a Socialist tinge. Has not Christianity declaimed against private property, against marriage, against the State? Has it not preached in the place of these, charity and poverty, celibacy and mortification of the flesh, monastic life and Mother Church? Christian[32] Socialism is but the holy water with which the priest consecrates the heart-burnings of the aristocrat.

B. PETTY-BOURGEOIS SOCIALISM

The feudal aristocracy was not the only class that was ruined by the bourgeoisie, not the only class whose conditions of existence pined and perished in the atmosphere of modern bourgeois society. The medieval burgesses and the small peasant proprietors were the precursors of the modern bourgeoisie. In those countries which are but little developed, industrially and commercially, these two classes still vegetate side by side with the rising bourgeoisie.

In countries where modern civilisation has become fully developed, a new class of petty bourgeois has been formed, fluctuating between proletariat and bourgeoisie and ever renewing itself as a supplementary part of bourgeois society. The individual members of this class, however, are being constantly hurled down into the proletariat by the action of competition, and, as modern industry develops, they even see the moment approaching when they will completely disappear as an independent section of modern society, to be replaced, in manufactures, agriculture and commerce, by overlookers, bailiffs and shopmen.

In countries like France, where the peasants constitute far more than half of the population, it was natural that writers who sided with the proletariat against the bourgeoisie, should use, in their criticism of the bourgeois *régime*, the standard of the peasant and petty bourgeois, and

---

*This applies chiefly to Germany where the landed aristocracy and squirearchy have large portions of their estates cultivated for their own account by stewards, and are, moreover, extensive beetroot-sugar manufacturers and distillers of potato spirits. The wealthier British aristocracy are, as yet, rather above that; but they, too, know how to make up for declining rents by lending their names to floaters of more or less shady joint-stock companies. [*Note by Engels to the English edition of 1888.*]

[31] More correctly, "feudal lord," not "landlord."

[32] The original German edition has a typographical error here that was often misread as "contemporary." It was later corrected to *heilige* (meaning "holy" or "sacred"), not "Christian."

from the standpoint of these intermediate classes should take up the cudgels for the working class. Thus arose petty-bourgeois Socialism. Sismondi[33] was the head of this school, not only in France but also in England.

This school of Socialism dissected with great acuteness the contradictions in the conditions of modern production. It laid bare the hypocritical apologies of economists. It proved, incontrovertibly, the disastrous effects of machinery and division of labour; the concentration of capital and land in a few hands; over-production and crises; it pointed out the inevitable ruin of the petty bourgeois and peasant, the misery of the proletariat, the anarchy in production, the crying inequalities in the distribution of wealth, the industrial war of extermination between nations, the dissolution of old moral bonds, of the old family relations, of the old nationalities.

In its positive aims, however, this form of Socialism aspires either to restoring the old means of production and of exchange, and with them the old property relations, and the old society, or to cramping the modern means of production and of exchange, within the framework of the old property relations that have been, and were bound to be, exploded by those means. In either case, it is both reactionary and Utopian.

Its last words are: corporate guilds for manufacture; patriarchal relations in agriculture.

Ultimately, when stubborn historical facts had dispersed all intoxicating effects of self-deception, this form of Socialism ended in a miserable fit of the blues.

C. GERMAN, OR "TRUE," SOCIALISM

The Socialist and Communist literature of France, a literature that originated under the pressure of a bourgeoisie in power, and that was the expression of the struggle against this power, was introduced into Germany at a time when the bourgeoisie, in that country, had just begun its contest with feudal absolutism.

German philosophers, would-be philosophers, and *beaux esprits*, eagerly seized on this literature, only forgetting, that when these writings immigrated from France into Germany, French social conditions had not immigrated along with them. In contact with German social conditions, this French literature lost all its immediate practical significance, and

---

[33] Jean-Charles-Léonard Simonde de Sismondi (1773–1842) was a Swiss economic theorist and historian famous for his analysis of the commercial crises within the free-market system.

assumed a purely literary aspect.[34] Thus, to the German philosophers
of the Eighteenth Century, the demands of the first French Revolution
were nothing more than the demands of "Practical Reason"[35] in general,
and the utterance of the will of the revolutionary French bourgeoisie
signified in their eyes the laws of pure Will, of Will as it was bound to be,
of true human Will generally.

The work of the German *literati* consisted solely in bringing the new
French ideas into harmony with their ancient philosophical conscience,
or rather, in annexing the French ideas without deserting their own philosophic point of view.

This annexation took place in the same way in which a foreign language is appropriated, namely, by translation.

It is well known how the monks wrote silly lives of Catholic Saints
over the manuscripts on which the classical works of ancient heathen-
dom had been written. The German *literati* reversed this process with
the profane French literature. They wrote their philosophical nonsense
beneath the French original. For instance, beneath the French criticism
of the economic functions of money, they wrote "Alienation of Humanity," and beneath the French criticism of the bourgeois State they wrote,
"Dethronement of the Category of the General," and so forth.[36]

The introduction of these philosophical phrases at the back of the
French historical criticisms they dubbed "Philosophy of Action," "True
Socialism," "German Science of Socialism," "Philosophical Foundation
of Socialism," and so on.

The French Socialist and Communist literature was thus completely emasculated. And, since it ceased in the hands of the German
to express the struggle of one class with the other, he felt conscious of
having overcome "French one-sidedness" and of representing, not true
requirements, but the requirements of Truth; not the interests of the
proletariat, but the interests of Human Nature, of Man in general, who
belongs to no class, has no reality, who exists only in the misty realm of
philosophical fantasy.

---

[34] The translation omits the sentence "It must have appeared as idle speculation on
the true society, on the realization of humanity."

[35] The ethical treatise *Critique of Practical Reason* published by the German philosopher Immanuel Kant in 1788. In Kant's view, ethical life was grounded in the purity of
intention of the subjective will.

[36] "Overcoming the Domination of the Abstract Universal," not "Dethronement of the
Category of the General." Marx had formulated his critique of the bourgeois state in the
early 1840s as an attempt to overcome the conception of community as a purely formal
or "abstract" universality. (See pages 44–51.)

This German Socialism, which took its schoolboy task so seriously and solemnly, and extolled its poor stock-in-trade in such mountebank fashion, meanwhile gradually lost its pedantic innocence.

The fight of the German, and, especially, of the Prussian bourgeoisie, against feudal aristocracy and absolute monarchy, in other words, the liberal movement, became more earnest.

By this, the long wished-for opportunity was offered to "True" Socialism of confronting the political movement with the Socialist demands, of hurling the traditional anathemas against liberalism, against representative government, against bourgeois competition, bourgeois freedom of the press, bourgeois legislation, bourgeois liberty and equality, and of preaching to the masses that they had nothing to gain, and everything to lose, by this bourgeois movement. German Socialism forgot, in the nick of time, that the French criticism, whose silly echo it was, presupposed the existence of modern bourgeois society, with its corresponding economic conditions of existence, and the political constitution adapted thereto, the very things whose attainment was the object of the pending struggle in Germany.

To the absolute governments,[37] with their following of parsons, professors, country squires and officials, it served as a welcome scarecrow against the threatening bourgeoisie.

It was a sweet finish after the bitter pills of floggings and bullets with which these same governments, just at that time, dosed the German working-class risings.

While this "True" Socialism thus served the governments as a weapon for fighting the German bourgeoisie, it, at the same time, directly represented a reactionary interest, the interest of the German Philistines. In Germany the *petty-bourgeois* class, a relic of the sixteenth century, and since then constantly cropping up again under various forms, is the real social basis of the existing state of things.

To preserve this class is to preserve the existing state of things in Germany. The industrial and political supremacy of the bourgeoisie threatens it with certain destruction; on the one hand, from the concentration of capital; on the other, from the rise of a revolutionary proletariat. "True" Socialism appeared to kill these two birds with one stone. It spread like an epidemic.

The robe of speculative cobwebs, embroidered with flowers of rhetoric, steeped in the dew of sickly sentiment, this transcendental robe in which the German Socialists wrapped their sorry "eternal truths," all

---

[37] More specifically, "German absolute governments."

skin and bone, served to wonderfully increase the sale of their goods amongst such a public.

And on its part, German Socialism recognised, more and more, its own calling as the bombastic representative of the petty-bourgeois Philistine.

It proclaimed the German nation to be the model nation, and the German petty Philistine to be the typical man. To every villainous meanness of this model man it gave a hidden, higher, Socialistic interpretation, the exact contrary of its real character. It went to the extreme length of directly opposing the "brutally destructive" tendency of Communism, and of proclaiming its supreme and impartial contempt of all class struggles. With very few exceptions, all the so-called Socialist and Communist publications that now (1847) circulate in Germany belong to the domain of this foul and enervating literature.

2. Conservative, or Bourgeois, Socialism

A part of the bourgeoisie is desirous of redressing social grievances, in order to secure the continued existence of bourgeois society.

To this section belong economists, philanthropists, humanitarians, improvers of the condition of the working class, organisers of charity, members of societies for the prevention of cruelty to animals, temperance fanatics, hole-and-corner reformers of every imaginable kind. This form of Socialism has, moreover, been worked out into complete systems.

We may cite Proudhon's *Philosophie de la Misère* as an example of this form.[38]

The Socialistic bourgeois want all the advantages of modern social conditions without the struggles and dangers necessarily resulting therefrom. They desire the existing state of society minus its revolutionary and disintegrating elements. They wish for a bourgeoisie without a proletariat. The bourgeoisie naturally conceives the world in which it is supreme to be the best; and bourgeois Socialism develops this comfortable conception into various more or less complete systems. In requiring the proletariat to carry out such a system, and thereby to march straightway into the social New Jerusalem, it but requires in reality, that

---

[38] Marx had published *The Poverty of Philosophy: Answer to the Philosophy of Poverty by M. Proudhon,* a book-length critique of Proudhon's libertarian socialism, just a few months earlier, in the fall of 1847. Pierre-Joseph Proudhon (1809–1865), a French journalist and socialist philosopher, was one of the founders of nineteenth-century anarchism and a rival of Marx for the loyalties of the working classes.

the proletariat should remain within the bounds of existing society, but should cast away all its hateful ideas concerning the bourgeoisie.

A second and more practical, but less systematic, form of this Socialism sought to depreciate every revolutionary movement in the eyes of the working class, by showing that no mere political reform, but only a change in the material conditions of existence, in economical relations, could be of any advantage to them. By changes in the material conditions of existence, this form of Socialism, however, by no means understands abolition of the bourgeois relations of production, an abolition that can be effected only by a revolution, but administrative reforms, based on the continued existence of these relations; reforms, therefore, that in no respect affect the relations between capital and labour, but, at the best, lessen the cost, and simplify the administrative work, of bourgeois government.

Bourgeois Socialism attains adequate expression, when, and only when, it becomes a mere figure of speech.

Free trade: for the benefit of the working class. Protective duties: for the benefit of the working class. Prison Reform:[39] for the benefit of the working class. This is the last word and the only seriously meant word of bourgeois Socialism.

It is summed up in the phrase: the bourgeois is a bourgeois—for the benefit of the working class.

3. Critical-Utopian Socialism and Communism

We do not here refer to that literature which, in every great modern revolution, has always given voice to the demands of the proletariat, such as the writings of Babeuf[40] and others.

The first direct attempts of the proletariat to attain its own ends, made in times of universal excitement, when feudal society was being overthrown, these attempts necessarily failed, owing to the then undeveloped state of the proletariat, as well as to the absence of the economic conditions for its emancipation, conditions that had yet to be produced, and could be produced by the impending bourgeois epoch alone. The revolutionary literature that accompanied these first movements of the proletariat had necessarily a reactionary character. It inculcated universal asceticism and social levelling in its crudest form.

---

[39] Marx's reference was more specific and more negative: "Single-cell prisons" or "Solitary confinement," not "Prison Reform."

[40] François-Noël (Gracchus) Babeuf (1760–1797) was a revolutionary advocate of egalitarian communism during the French Revolution.

The Socialist and Communist systems properly so called, those of Saint-Simon, Fourier, Owen[41] and others, spring into existence in the early undeveloped period, described above, of the struggle between proletariat and bourgeoisie (see Section I. Bourgeois and Proletarians).

The founders of these systems see, indeed, the class antagonisms, as well as the action of the decomposing elements in the prevailing form of society. But the proletariat, as yet in its infancy, offers to them the spectacle of a class without any historical initiative or any independent political movement.

Since the development of class antagonism keeps even pace with the development of industry, the economic situation, as they find it, does not as yet offer to them the material conditions for the emancipation of the proletariat. They therefore search after a new social science, after new social laws, that are to create these conditions.

Historical[42] action is to yield to their personal inventive action, historically created conditions of emancipation to fantastic ones, and the gradual, spontaneous class organisation of the proletariat to an organisation of society specially contrived by these inventors. Future history resolves itself, in their eyes, into the propaganda and the practical carrying out of their social plans.

In the formation of their plans they are conscious of caring chiefly for the interests of the working class, as being the most suffering class. Only from the point of view of being the most suffering class does the proletariat exist for them.[43]

The undeveloped state of the class struggle, as well as their own surroundings, causes Socialists of this kind to consider themselves far superior to all class antagonisms. They want to improve the condition of every member of society, even that of the most favoured. Hence, they habitually appeal to society at large, without distinction of class; nay, by preference, to the ruling class. For how can people, when once they understand their system, fail to see in it the best possible plan of the best possible state of society?

Hence, they reject all political, and especially all revolutionary, action; they wish to attain their ends by peaceful means, and endeavour, by small experiments, necessarily doomed to failure, and by the force of example, to pave the way for the new social Gospel.

---

[41] Claude-Henri de Rouvroy, Comte de Saint-Simon (1760–1825), Charles Fourier (1772–1837), and Robert Owen (1771–1858) were utopian socialists whose followers played a prominent role in the debates within the socialist left in the 1840s.

[42] "Social action," not "historical action."

[43] As late as 1843, this had been Marx's own view. (See page 39.)

Such fantastic pictures of future society, painted at a time when the proletariat is still in a very undeveloped state and has but a fantastic conception of its own position, correspond with the first instinctive yearnings of that class for a general reconstruction of society.

But these Socialist and Communist publications contain also a critical element. They attack every principle of existing society. Hence they are full of the most valuable materials for the enlightenment of the working class. The practical measures proposed in them—such as the abolition of the distinction between town and country, of the family, of the carrying on of industries for the account of private individuals, and of the wage system, the proclamation of social harmony, the conversion of the functions of the State into a mere superintendence of production, all these proposals point solely to the disappearance of class antagonisms which were, at that time, only just cropping up, and which, in these publications, are recognised in their earliest indistinct and undefined forms only. These proposals, therefore, are of a purely Utopian character.

The significance of Critical-Utopian Socialism and Communism bears an inverse relation to historical development. In proportion as the modern class struggle develops and takes definite shape, this fantastic standing apart from the contest, these fantastic attacks on it, lose all practical value and all theoretical justification. Therefore, although the originators of these systems were, in many respects, revolutionary, their disciples have, in every case, formed mere reactionary sects. They hold fast by the original views of their masters, in opposition to the progressive historical development of the proletariat. They, therefore, endeavour, and that consistently, to deaden the class struggle and to reconcile the class antagonisms. They still dream of experimental realisation of their social Utopias, of founding isolated "phalanstères," of establishing "Home Colonies," of setting up a "Little Icaria"*—duodecimo editions of the New Jerusalem—and to realise all these castles in the air, they are compelled to appeal to the feelings and purses of the bourgeois.[44] By degrees they sink into the category of the reactionary [or] conservative Socialists depicted above, differing from these only by more systematic pedantry, and by their fanatical and superstitious belief in the miraculous effects of their social science.

Phalanstères were Socialist colonies on the plan of Charles Fourier; *Icaria* was the name given by Cabet to his Utopia and, later on, to his American Communist colony. [*Note by Engels to the English edition of 1888.*]

[44]"Home Colonies" was the name given to some of Robert Owen's model communities. Etienne Cabet (1788–1856) was a utopian communist whose *Voyage to Icaria: A Philosophical and Social Novel* (1839) was much discussed in the 1840s. "Duodecimo editions" are small or miniature versions.

They, therefore, violently oppose all political action on the part of the working class; such action, according to them, can only result from blind unbelief in the new Gospel.

The Owenites in England, and the Fourierists in France, respectively oppose the Chartists and the *Réformistes*.[45]

IV. POSITION OF THE COMMUNISTS IN RELATION TO THE VARIOUS EXISTING OPPOSITION PARTIES

Section II has made clear the relations of the Communists to the existing working-class parties, such as the Chartists in England and the Agrarian Reformers[46] in America.

The Communists fight for the attainment of the immediate aims, for the enforcement of the momentary interests of the working class; but in the movement of the present, they also represent and take care of the future of that movement. In France the Communists ally themselves with the Social-Democrats,* against the conservative and radical bourgeoisie, reserving, however, the right to take up a critical position in regard to phrases and illusions traditionally handed down from the great Revolution.

In Switzerland they support the Radicals, without losing sight of the fact that this party consists of antagonistic elements, partly of Democratic Socialists, in the French sense, partly of radical bourgeois.

In Poland they support the party that insists on an agrarian revolution as the prime condition for national emancipation, that party which fomented the insurrection of Cracow in 1846.[47]

[45] The *Réformistes,* who are also referred to as social democrats in Section IV of the *Manifesto,* were a political movement of left-wing republican democrats grouped around the Parisian journal *La Réforme.* Their leaders were Louis Blanc (1811–1882) and Alexandre Ledru-Rollin (1807–1874). Both became members of the provisional government installed in France after the February revolution in 1848.

[46] The National Reform Association was created in 1845 to agitate for a fair distribution of small holdings (160 acres) in the United States. The association had strong connections to the German emigrant radicals in the League of the Just.

*The party then represented in Parliament by Ledru-Rollin, in literature by Louis Blanc, in the daily press by the *Réforme.* The name of Social-Democracy signified, with these its inventors, a section of the Democratic or Republican party more or less tinged with Socialism. [*Note by Engels to the English edition of 1888.*]

[47] The reference is to a nationalist, republican uprising in that part of southern Poland jointly controlled after 1815 by Prussia, Austria, and Russia. The attempt to establish a Polish national government in Cracow in March 1846 was crushed by Austrian and Russian military force. Cracow was subsequently incorporated into the Austrian Empire.

In Germany they fight with the bourgeoisie whenever it acts in a revolutionary way, against the absolute monarchy, the feudal squirearchy, and the petty bourgeoisie.

But they never cease, for a single instant, to instil into the working class the clearest possible recognition of the hostile antagonism between bourgeoisie and proletariat, in order that the German workers may straightway use, as so many weapons against the bourgeoisie, the social and political conditions that the bourgeoisie must necessarily introduce along with its supremacy, and in order that, after the fall of the reactionary classes in Germany, the fight against the bourgeoisie itself may immediately begin.

The Communists turn their attention chiefly to Germany, because that country is on the eve of a bourgeois revolution that is bound to be carried out under more advanced conditions of European civilisation, and with a much more developed proletariat, than that of England was in the seventeenth, and of France in the eighteenth century, and because the bourgeois revolution in Germany will be but the prelude to an immediately following proletarian revolution.

In short, the Communists everywhere support every revolutionary movement against the existing social and political order of things.

In all these movements they bring to the front, as the leading question in each, the property question, no matter what its degree of development at the time.

Finally, they labour everywhere for the union and agreement of the democratic parties of all countries.

The Communists disdain to conceal their views and aims. They openly declare that their ends can be attained only by the forcible overthrow of all existing social conditions. Let the ruling classes tremble at a Communistic revolution. The proletarians have nothing to lose but their chains. They have a world to win.

WORKING MEN[48] OF ALL COUNTRIES, UNITE!

---

[48] "Proletarians," not "Working Men," thus corresponding to the recently approved motto of the Communist League.

PART THREE

Related Documents

1

ALEXIS DE TOCQUEVILLE

From *Recollections: The French Revolution of* 1848
1847–1848

---

*In October 1847, the French aristocratic liberal and Member of the
Chamber of Deputies, Alexis de Tocqueville, privately composed what he
himself described as a "manifesto" in defense of property rights in the hope
that he could organize his fellow deputies for a program of parliamentary
action that might begin to stem the tide of what he saw as an imminent
democratic and communist revolution that would dissolve those rights.
(part a) A few months later, on January 27, 1848, he publically articulated his vision of the "specter of Revolution" in a speech before the French
Chamber of deputies. (part b)*

---

a. "The time is coming when the country will again be divided between
two great parties. The French Revolution, which abolished all privileges
and destroyed all exclusive rights, did leave one, that of property. Property holders must not delude themselves about the strength of their
position, or suppose that, because it has so far been surmounted, the
right to property is an insurmountable barrier, for our age is not like
any other. When the right to property was merely the basis of many
other rights, it could easily be defended, or rather, it was not attacked:
it was like the encircling wall of a society whose other rights were the
advance defense posts; the shots did not reach it; there was not even
serious intention to reach it. But now that the right to property is the last
remnant of a destroyed aristocratic world, and it alone still stands, an
isolated privilege in a levelled society; when it no longer has the cover
of other more doubtful and more hated rights, it is in great danger; it
alone now has to face the direct and incessant impact of democratic
opinions...

Alexis de Tocqueville, *Recollections: The French Revolution of 1848*, ed. J. P. Mayer and A.
P. Kerr, with a new introduction by Fernand Braudel (New Brunswick, N.J.: Transaction
Books, 1987), 12–13.

Soon the political struggle will be between the Haves and the Have-nots, property will be the great battlefield and the main political questions will turn on the more or less profound modifications of the rights of property owners that are to be made. Then we shall again see great public agitations and great political parties.

Why is everybody not struck by the signs that are the harbingers of this future? Do you think it by chance, or by some passing caprice of the human spirit, that on every side we see strange doctrines appearing, which have different names, but which all deny the right of property, or at least, tend to limit, diminish or weaken the exercise of that right? Who can fail to recognize in this the last symptom of the old democratic disease of the times, whose crisis is perhaps approaching?"

b. It is said there is no danger because there is no riot, and that because there is no visible disorder on the surface of society, we are far from revolution.

Gentlemen, allow me to say that I think you are mistaken. True, there is no actual disorder, but disorder has penetrated far into men's minds. See what is happening among the working classes, who are, I realize, quiet now. It is true that they are not now tormented by what may properly be called political passions to the extent they once were; but do you not see that their passions have changed from political to social? Do you not see that opinions and ideas are gradually spreading among them that tend not simply to the overthrow of such-and-such laws, such-and-such a minister, of even such-and-such a government, but rather to the overthrow of society, breaking down the bases on which it rests? Do you not hear what is being said among them? Do you not hear them constantly repeating that all the people above them are incapable and unworthy to rule them? That the division of property in the world up to now is unjust? That property rests on bases of inequity? And do you not realize that when such opinions take root and spread, sinking deeply into the masses, they must sooner or later (I do not know when, I do not know how) bring in their train the most terrifying of revolutions?"

2

FREDERICK ENGELS

Draft of a Communist Confession of Faith

June 9, 1847

This draft of a programmatic "confession of faith" by Frederick Engels was discussed and approved at the Communist League's first congress in London on June 2–9, 1847. The program was distributed to League members for discussion after the congress and revised by Engels in late October for renewed discussion at the second congress in November-December. Its full text was discovered in Hamburg in 1968 among the papers of a former member of the Communist League and translated into English in 1971. The first six questions reflect the more traditional utopian socialist ideas of many members of the League, but the remainder of the document reveals how effective Engels was in shifting the program toward an affirmation of his own and Marx's more "historical" positions.

Question 1: *Are you a Communist?*
Answer: Yes.
Question 2: *What is the aim of the Communists?*
Answer: To organise society in such a way that every member of it can develop and use all his capabilities and powers in complete freedom and without thereby infringing the basic conditions of this society.
Question 3: *How do you wish to achieve this aim?*
Answer: By the elimination of private property and its replacement by community of property.
Question 4: *On what do you base your community of property?*
Answer: Firstly, on the mass of productive forces and means of subsistence resulting from the development of industry, agriculture, trade and colonisation, and on the possibility inherent in machinery, chemical and other resources of their infinite extension.

Secondly, on the fact that in the consciousness or feeling of every individual there exist certain irrefutable basic principles which, being the result of the whole of historical development, require no proof.

Karl Marx and Frederick Engels, *Collected Works* (New York: International Publishers, 1975–), Vol. 6, 96–103.

Question 5: *What are such principles?*

Answer: For example, every individual strives to be happy. The happiness of the individual is inseparable from the happiness of all, etc.

Question 6: *How do you wish to prepare the way for your community of property?*

Answer: By enlightening and uniting the proletariat.

Question 7: *What is the proletariat?*

Answer: The proletariat is that class of society which lives exclusively by its labour and not on the profit from any kind of capital; that class whose weal and woe, whose life and death, therefore, depend on the alternation of times of good and bad business; in a word, on the fluctuations of competition.

Question 8: *Then there have not always been proletarians?*

Answer: No. There have always been *poor* and *working classes;* and those who worked were almost always the poor. But there have not always been proletarians, just as competition has not always been free.

Question 9: *How did the proletariat arise?*

Answer: The proletariat came into being as a result of the introduction of the machines which have been invented since the middle of the last century and the most important of which are: the steam-engine, the spinning machine and the power loom. These machines, which were very expensive and could therefore only be purchased by rich people, supplanted the workers of the time, because by the use of machinery it was possible to produce commodities more quickly and cheaply than could the workers with their imperfect spinning wheels and hand-looms. The machines thus delivered industry entirely into the hands of the big capitalists and rendered the workers' scanty property which consisted mainly of their tools, looms, etc., quite worthless, so that the capitalist was left with everything, the worker with nothing. In this way the factory system was introduced. Once the capitalists saw how advantageous this was for them, they sought to extend it to more and more branches of labour. They divided work more and more between the workers so that workers who formerly had made a whole article now produced only a part of it. Labour simplified in this way produced goods more quickly and therefore more cheaply and only now was it found in almost every branch of labour that here also machines could be used. As soon as any branch of labour went over to factory production it ended up, just as in the case of spinning and weaving, in the hands of the big capitalists, and the workers were deprived of the last remnants of their independence.

We have gradually arrived at the position where almost *all* branches of labour are run on a factory basis. This has increasingly brought about the ruin of the previously existing middle class, especially of the small master craftsmen, completely transformed the previous position of the workers, and two new classes which are gradually swallowing up all other classes have come into being, namely:

I. The class of the big capitalists, who in all advanced countries are in almost exclusive possession of the means of subsistence and those means (machines, factories, workshops, etc.) by which these means of subsistence are produced. This is the *bourgeois* class, or the *bourgeoisie*.

II. The class of the completely propertyless, who are compelled to sell their labour to the first class, the bourgeois, simply to obtain from them in return their means of subsistence. Since the parties to this trading in labour are not *equal*, but the bourgeois have the advantage, the propertyless must submit to the bad conditions laid down by the bourgeois. This class, dependent on the bourgeois, is called the class of the *proletarians* or the *proletariat*.

Question 10: *In what way does the proletarian differ from the slave?*

Answer: The slave is sold once and for all, the proletarian has to sell himself by the day and by the hour. The slave is the property of one master and for that very reason has a guaranteed subsistence, however wretched it may be. The proletarian is, so to speak, the slave of the entire bourgeois *class,* not of one master, and therefore has no guaranteed subsistence, since nobody buys his labour if he does not need it. The slave is accounted a *thing* and not a member of civil society. The proletarian is recognised as a *person,* as a member of civil society. The slave *may,* therefore, have a better subsistence than the proletarian but the latter stands at a higher stage of development. The slave frees himself by *becoming a proletarian*, abolishing from the totality of property relationships *only* the relationship *of slavery.* The proletarian can free himself only by abolishing *property in general.*

Question 11: *In what way does the proletarian differ from the serf?*

Answer: The serf has the use of a piece of land, that is, of an instrument of production, in return for handing over a greater or lesser portion of the yield. The proletarian works with instruments of production which belong to someone else who, in return for his labour, hands over to him a portion, determined by competition, of the products. In the case of the serf, the share of the labourer is determined by his own labour, that is, by himself. In the case of the proletarian it is determined by competition, therefore in the first place by the bourgeois. The serf has guaranteed subsistence, the proletarian has not. The serf frees himself by driving out his feudal lord and becoming a property owner himself, thus entering into competition and joining for the time being the possessing class, the privileged class. The proletarian frees himself by doing away with property, competition, and all class differences.

Question 12: *In what way does the proletarian differ from the handicraftsman?*

Answer: As opposed to the proletarian, the so-called handicraftsman, who still existed nearly everywhere during the last century and still exists here and there, is at most a *temporary* proletarian. His aim is to acquire capital himself and so to exploit other workers. He can often achieve this aim where the craft guilds still exist or where freedom to follow a trade has not yet led to the organisation of handwork on a factory basis and to intense competition. But as soon as the factory system is introduced into handwork and competition is in full swing, this prospect is eliminated and the handicraftsman becomes more and more a proletarian. The handicraftsman therefore frees himself *either* by becoming a bourgeois or in general passing over into the middle class, *or*, by becoming a proletarian as a result of competition (as now happens in most cases) and joining the movement of the proletariat—i.e., the more or less conscious communist movement.

Question 13: *Then you do not believe that community of property has been possible at any time?*

Answer. No. Communism has only arisen since machinery and other inventions made it possible to hold out the prospect of an all-sided development, a happy existence, for all members of society. Communism is the theory of a liberation which was not possible for the slaves, the serfs, or the handicraftsmen, but only for the proletarians and hence it belongs of necessity to the 19th century and was not possible in any earlier period.

Question 14: *Let us go back to the sixth question. As you wish to prepare for community of property by the enlightening and uniting of the proletariat, then you reject revolution?*

Answer. We are convinced not only of the uselessness but even of the harmfulness of all conspiracies. We are also aware that revolutions are not made deliberately and arbitrarily but that everywhere and at all times they are the necessary consequence of circumstances which are not in any way whatever dependent either on the will or on the leadership of individual parties or of whole classes. But we also see that the development of the proletariat in almost all countries of the world is forcibly repressed by the possessing classes and that thus a revolution is being forcibly worked for by the opponents of communism. If, in the end, the oppressed proletariat is thus driven into a revolution, then we will defend the cause of the proletariat just as well by our deeds as now by our words.

Question 15: *Do you intend to replace the existing social order by community of property at one stroke?*

Answer: We have no such intention. The development of the masses cannot be ordered by decree. It is determined by the development of the conditions in which these masses live, and therefore proceeds gradually.

Question 16: *How do you think the transition from the present situation to community of property is to be effected?*

Answer: The first, fundamental condition for the introduction of community of property is the political liberation of the proletariat through a democratic constitution.

Question 17: *What will be your first measure once you have established democracy?*

Answer: Guaranteeing the subsistence of the proletariat.

Question 18: *How will you do this?*

Answer: I. By limiting private property in such a way that it gradually prepares the way for its transformation into social property, e.g., by progressive taxation, limitation of the right of inheritance in favour of the state, etc., etc.

II. By employing workers in national workshops and factories and on national estates.

III. By educating all children at the expense of the state.

Question 19: *How will you arrange this kind of education during the period of transition?*

Answer: All children will be educated in state establishments from the time when they can do without the first maternal care.

Question 20: *Will not the introduction of community of property be accompanied by the proclamation of the community of women?*

Answer: By no means. We will only interfere in the personal relationship between men and women or with the family in general to the extent that the maintenance of the existing institution would disturb the new social order. Besides, we are well aware that the family relationship has been modified in the course of history by the property relationships and by periods of development, and that consequently the ending of private property will also have a most important influence on it.

Question 21: *Will nationalities continue to exist under communism?*

Answer: The nationalities of the peoples who join together according to the principle of community will be just as much compelled by this union to merge with one another and thereby supersede themselves as the various differences between estates and classes disappear through the superseding of their basis—private property.

Question 22: *Do Communists reject the existing religions?*

Answer: All religions which have existed hitherto were expressions of historical stages of development of individual peoples or groups of peoples. But communism is that stage of historical development which makes all existing religions superfluous and supersedes them.

3

FREDERICK ENGELS

From *A Letter to Karl Marx*

November 23/24, 1847

After the Communist League's first congress in June 1847, Engels became more confident that he and Marx could convince the members of the League to accept their position without the compromises built into earlier program drafts. In late November 1847, Engels scribbled this note on the back of a letter to Marx, suggesting that a program conforming to their own principles would also require a different form from that of the question-and-answer format of conventional socialist "catechisms."

Tuesday evening

Give a little thought to the Confession of Faith. I think we would do best to abandon the catechetical form and call the thing Communist *Manifesto*. Since a certain amount of history has to be narrated in it, the form hitherto adopted is quite unsuitable. I shall be bringing with me the one from here, which I did; it is in simple narrative form, but wretchedly worded, in a tearing hurry. I start off by asking: What is communism? and then straight on to the proletariat—the history of its origins, how it differs from earlier workers, development of the antithesis between

Karl Marx and Frederick Engels, *Collected Works* (New York: International Publishers, 1982), Vol. 38:149.

the proletariat and the bourgeoisie, crises, conclusions. In between, all kinds of secondary matter and, finally, the communists' party policy, in so far as it should be made public. The one here has not yet been submitted in its entirety for endorsement but, save for a few quite minor points, I think I can get it through in such a form that at least there is nothing in it which conflicts with our views.

4

FREDERICK ENGELS

From *The Condition of the Working Class in England*

1845

Sent to Manchester, England, to continue his business training in the family firm of Ermen and Engels, Frederick Engels used his two-year stay (1842–1844) at the center of the British Industrial Revolution to pursue his own education in the reality, as well as the theory, of the economic revolution transforming British society. When he returned to Germany, he published his findings in a book titled The Condition of the Working Class in England. *The following excerpts from this book display both Engels's personal identification with the working classes and his general conception of the nature and implications of industrial production in a free-market society. The first excerpt is the book's dedication. The excerpts that follow are taken from the book's historical introduction.*

To the Working-Classes of Great-Britain

Working Men!
To you I dedicate a work, in which I have tried to lay before my German Countrymen a faithful picture of your condition, of your sufferings and struggles, of your hopes and prospects. I have lived long enough amidst

Karl Marx and Frederick Engels, *Collected Works* (New York: International Publishers, 1975), Vol. 4:296–301, 307, 312–13, 320–23.

you to know something about your circumstances; I have devoted to their knowledge my most serious attention, I have studied the various official and non-official documents as far as I was able to get hold of them—I have not been satisfied with this, I wanted more than a mere *abstract* knowledge of my subject, I wanted to see you in your own homes, to observe you in your every-day life, to chat with you on your condition and grievances, to witness your struggles against the social and political power of your oppressors. I have done so: I forsook the company and the dinner-parties, the port-wine and the champaign [sic] of the middle-classes, and devoted my leisure-hours almost exclusively to the intercourse with plain Working-Men; I am both glad and proud of having done so. Glad, because thus I was induced to spend many a happy hour in obtaining a knowledge of the realities of life—many an hour, which else would have been wasted in fashionable talk and tiresome etiquette; proud, because thus I got an opportunity of doing justice to an oppressed and calumniated class of men who with all their faults and under all the disadvantages of their situation, yet command the respect of every one but an English money-monger; proud, too, because thus I was placed in a position to save the English people from the growing contempt which on the Continent has been the necessary consequence of the brutally selfish policy and general behaviour of your ruling middle-class.

Having, at the same time, ample opportunity to watch the middle-classes, your opponents, I soon came to the conclusion that you are right, perfectly right in expecting no support whatever from them. Their interest is diametrically opposed to yours, though they always will try to maintain the contrary and to make you believe in their most hearty sympathy with your fates. Their doings give them the lie. I hope to have collected more than sufficient evidence of the fact, that—be their words what they please—the middle-classes intend in reality nothing else but to enrich themselves by your labour while they can sell its produce, and to abandon you to starvation as soon as they cannot make a profit by this indirect trade in human flesh. What have they done to prove their professed good-will towards you? Have they ever paid any serious attention to your grievances? Have they done more than paying the expenses of half-a-dozen commissions of inquiry, whose voluminous reports are damned to ever-lasting slumber among heaps of waste paper on the shelves of the Home Office? Have they even done as much as to compile from those rotting blue-books a single readable book from which everybody might easily get some information on the condition of the great majority of "free-born Britons"? Not they indeed, those are things they do not like to speak of—they have left it to a foreigner to inform the civilised world of the degrading situation you have to live in.

A foreigner to *them,* not to *you,* I hope. Though my English may not be pure, yet, I hope, you will find it *plain* English. No working-man in England—nor in France either, by-the-by—ever treated me as a foreigner. With the greatest pleasure I observed you to be free from that blasting curse, national prejudice and national pride, which after all means nothing but *wholesale selfishness*—I observed you to sympathise with every one who earnestly applies his powers to human progress—may he be an Englishman or not—to admire every thing great and good, whether nursed on your native soil or not—I found you to be more than mere *Englishmen,* members of a single, isolated nation, I found you to be *Men,* members of the great and universal family of Mankind, who know their interest and that of all the human race to be the same. And as such, as members of this Family of "One and Indivisible" Mankind, as Human Beings in the most emphatical meaning of the word, as such I, and many others on the Continent, hail your progress in every direction and wish you speedy success.

Go on then, as you have done hitherto. Much remains to be undergone; be firm, be undaunted—your success is certain, and no step you will have to take in your onward march, will be lost to our common cause, the cause of Humanity!

Introduction

The history of the proletariat in England begins with the second half of the last century, with the invention of the steam-engine and of machinery for working cotton. These inventions gave rise, as is well known, to an industrial revolution, a revolution which altered the whole civil society; one, the historical importance of which is only now beginning to be recognised. England is the classic soil of this transformation, which was all the mightier, the more silently it proceeded; and England is, therefore, the classic land of its chief product also, the proletariat. Only in England can the proletariat be studied in all its relations and from all sides. . . .

[After a somewhat idealized account of the living conditions of the worker under traditional preindustrial forms of production, Engels goes on to describe the various inventions, especially in textile production, that inaugurated a radical change in those conditions.]

With these inventions, since improved from year to year, the victory of machine-work over hand-work in the chief branches of English industry was won; and the history of the latter from that time forward simply relates how the hand-workers have been driven by machinery from one position after another. The consequences of this were, on the one hand, a rapid fall in price of all manufactured commodities, prosperity of commerce and manufacture, the conquest of nearly all the unprotected foreign markets, the sudden multiplication of capital and national wealth; on the other hand, a still more rapid multiplication of the proletariat, the destruction of all property-holding and of all security of employment for the working-class, demoralisation, political excitement, and all those facts highly repugnant to Englishmen in comfortable circumstances. . . . Having already seen what a transformation in the social condition of the lower classes a single such clumsy machine as the jenny had wrought, there is no cause for surprise as to that which a complete and interdependent system of finely adjusted machinery has brought about, machinery which receives raw material and turns out woven goods. . . .

[Engels goes on to describe the enormous increases in production, the expansion of trade, and the improvements in transportation that technological innovation and the transformation of the work process have made possible.]

The history of English industrial development in the past sixty years [is] a history which has no counterpart in the annals of humanity. Sixty, eighty years ago, England was a country like every other, with small towns, few and simple industries, and a thin but *proportionally* large agricultural population. Today it is a country like *no* other, with a capital of two and a half million inhabitants; with vast manufacturing cities; with an industry that supplies the world, and produces almost everything by means of the most complex machinery; with an industrious, intelligent, dense population, of which two-thirds are employed in trade and commerce, and composed of classes wholly different; forming, in fact, with other customs and other needs, a different nation from the England of those days. The industrial revolution is of the same importance for England as the political revolution for France, and the philosophical revolution for Germany; and the difference between England in 1760 and in 1844 is at least as great as that between France under the *ancien régime* and during the revolution of July. But the mightiest result of this industrial transformation is the English proletariat.

We have already seen how the proletariat was called into existence by the introduction of machinery. The rapid extension of manufacture demanded hands, wages rose, and troops of workmen migrated from the agricultural districts to the towns. Population multiplied enormously, and nearly all the increase took place in the proletariat. Further, Ireland had entered upon an orderly development only since the beginning of the eighteenth century. There, too, the population, more than decimated by English cruelty in earlier disturbances, now rapidly multiplied, especially after the advance in manufacture began to draw masses of Irishmen towards England. Thus arose the great manufacturing and commercial cities of the British Empire, in which at least three-fourths of the population belong to the working-class, while the lower middle-class consists only of small shop-keepers, and very very few handicraftsmen. For, though the rising manufacture first attained importance by transforming tools into machines, work-rooms into factories, and consequently, the toiling lower middle-class into the toiling proletariat, and the former large merchants into manufacturers, though the lower middleclass was thus early crushed out, and the population reduced to the two opposing elements, workers and capitalists, this happened outside of the domain of manufacture proper, in the province of handicraft and retail trade as well. In the place of the former masters and apprentices, came great capitalists and working-men who had no prospect of rising above their class. Hand-work was carried on after the fashion of factory work, the division of labour was strictly applied, and small employers who could not compete with great establishments were forced down into the proletariat. At the same time the destruction of the former organisation of hand-work, and the disappearance of the lower middle-class deprived the working-man of all possibility of rising into the middle-class himself. Hitherto he had always had the prospect of establishing himself somewhere as master artificer, perhaps employing journeymen and apprentices; but now, when master artificers were crowded out by manufacturers, when large capital had become necessary for carrying on work independently, the working-class became, for the first time, an integral, permanent class of the population, whereas it had formerly often been merely a transition leading to the bourgeoisie. Now, he who was born to toil had no other prospect than that of remaining a toiler all his life. Now, for the first time, therefore, the proletariat was in a position to undertake an independent movement.

In this way were brought together those vast masses of working-men who now fill the whole British Empire, whose social condition forces itself every day more and more upon the attention of the civilised world.

The condition of the working-class is the condition of the vast majority of the English people. The question: What is to become of those destitute millions, who consume today what they earned yesterday; who have created the greatness of England by their inventions and their toil; who become with every passing day more conscious of their might, and demand, with daily increasing urgency, their share of the advantages of society? . . .

[Engels goes on to describe the debates in Parliament that have elevated the condition of the working classes to the status of a national question.]

In spite of all this, the English middle-class, especially the manufacturing class, which is enriched directly by means of the poverty of the workers, persists in ignoring this poverty. . . . Hence also the deep wrath of the whole working-class, from Glasgow to London, against the rich, by whom they are systematically plundered and mercilessly left to their fate, a wrath which before too long a time goes by, a time almost within the power of man to predict, must break out into a revolution in comparison with which the French Revolution, and the year 1794, will prove to have been child's play.

5

ROBERT OWEN

From *Report to the County of Lanark*

1820

Robert Owen, the British manufacturer turned socialist prophet, submitted this report to the Committee of Magistrates in the county of Lanark as a plan for alleviating the severe distress of unemployed workers caused, in his view, by a commercial crisis of overproduction. It was published the following year and reprinted in 1832. The following passage expresses Owen's attempt both to oppose the principle of individual interest with that of social cooperation and to ground a new socialist order in a social "science" of human character formation through environmental management.

Robert Owen, *Report to the County of Lanark, of a Plan for Relieving Public Distress, and Removing Discontent, by Giving Permanent, Productive Employment, to the Poor and Working Classes* (Glasgow: Printed at the University Press, for Wardlaw & Cunninghame, 1821), 28–31.

It has been, and still is, a received opinion among theorists in political economy, that man can provide better for himself, and more advantageously for the public, when left to his own individual exertions, opposed to, and in competition with his fellows, than when aided by any social arrangement, which shall unite his interests individually and generally with society.

This principle of individual interest, opposed, as it is perpetually, to the public good, is considered by the most celebrated political economists, to be the corner stone to the social system, and without which society could not subsist. Yet when they shall know themselves, and discover the wonderful effects which combination and union can produce, they will acknowledge that the present arrangement of society is the most antisocial, impolitic, and irrational, that can be devised; that under its influence, all the superior and valuable qualities of human nature are repressed from infancy, and that the most unnatural means are used to bring out the most injurious propensities; in short, that the utmost pains are taken to make that which by nature is the most delightful compound for producing excellence and happiness, absurd, imbecile, and wretched.

Such is the conduct now pursued by those who are called the best and wisest of the present generation, although there is not one rational object to be gained by it.

From this principle of individual interest have arisen all the divisions of mankind, the endless errors and mischiefs of class, sect, party, and of national antipathies, creating the angry and malevolent passions, and all the crimes and misery with which the human race has been hitherto afflicted.

In short, if there be one closet doctrine more contrary to truth than another, it is the notion that individual interest, as that term is now understood, is a more advantageous principle on which to found the social system, for the benefit of all, or of any, than the principle of union and mutual co-operation. . . .

It is well known, that a combination of men and of interests can effect that which it would be futile to attempt, and impossible to accomplish, by individual exertions and separate interests. Then why, it may be inquired, have men so long acted individually, and in opposition to each other? This is an important question, and merits the most serious attention. Men have not yet been trained in principles that will permit them *to act in union,* except to defend themselves or to destroy others. For self-preservation, they were early compelled to unite for these purposes in war. A necessity, however, equally powerful, will now compel men to be trained to act together, to *create and conserve,* that in like manner they may preserve life in peace. Fortunately for mankind, the system of individual opposing interests has now reached the extreme point of error and inconsistency;—in the midst of the most ample means to create wealth, all are in poverty, or in imminent danger, from the effects of poverty upon others.

The reflecting part of mankind have admitted in theory, that the characters of men are formed chiefly by the circumstances in which they are placed; yet the science of the influence of circumstances, which is the most important of all the sciences, remains unknown for the great practical business of life. When it shall be fully developed, it will be discovered, that to unite the mental faculties of men for the attainment of pacific and civil objects, will be a far more easy task than it has been to combine their physical powers to carry on extensive war like operations.

The discovery of the distance and movements of the heavenly bodies; of the time-piece; of a vessel to navigate the most distant parts of the ocean; of the steam engine, which performs, under the easy control of one man, the labour of many thousands; and of the press, by which knowledge and improvements may be speedily given to the most ignorant in all parts of the earth; these have, indeed, been discoveries of high import to mankind; but important as these and others have been in their effects, on the condition of human society, their combined benefits in practice, will fall short of those which will be speedily attained by the new intellectual power, which men will acquire through the knowledge of "the science of the influence of circumstances over the whole conduct, character, and proceedings of the human race." By this latter discovery, more shall be accomplished in one year, for the well-being of human nature, including, without any exceptions, all ranks and descriptions of men, than has ever yet been effected in one or in many centuries. . . .

Are not the mental energies of the world at this moment in a state of high effervescence? Is not society at a stand, incompetent to proceed in its present course, and do not all men cry out that "something must be done"? That "something," to produce the effect desired, must be a complete renovation of the whole social compact; one not forced on prematurely, by confusion and violence. . . .

No! The change sought for must be preceded by the clear development of a great and universal principle, which shall unite in one, all the petty jarring interests, by which, till now, human nature has been made a most inveterate enemy to itself.

No! extensive, nay, rather, universal as the re-arrangement of society must be, to relieve it from the difficulties with which it is now overwhelmed, it will be effected in peace and quietness, with the goodwill

and hearty concurrence of all parties, and of every people. It will necessarily commence by common consent, on account of its advantages,
almost simultaneously among all civilized nations; and, once begun, will
daily advance with an accelerating ratio, unopposed, and bearing down
before it the existing systems of the world. The only astonishment then
will be that such systems could so long have existed.

6

CHARLES FOURIER

From *The Theory of the Four Movements and of the General Destinies*

1808

This short passage is from the introduction to The Theory of the Four
Movements and of the General Destinies, *in which Charles Fourier
lays out the general principles of his theory. It was first published in 1808
but appeared in expanded and revised form in a third edition published
by members of the Fourierist movement in 1846. After his death in
1837, Fourier became, along with Robert Owen, among the most influential utopian socialists, inspiring not only the creation of a movement
of intellectual disciples but also the experimental creation of Fourierist
communes in both Europe and America. In contrast to Owen's search for
a science of character formation, Fourier based his hopes for the future
on the belief that the release of the natural passions from social repression
would reveal their attractive, rather than their repulsive, qualities and
provide the foundations for a harmonious and cooperative "societary"
order. To German intellectuals such as Marx and Engels, Fourier's
emphasis on passionate attraction as the basis for communal association
made his theory appear related to Feuerbach's emphasis on sensuousness
and the concrete relations of the life of feeling (see Document 15).*

Jonathan Beecher and Richard Bienvenue, trans. and ed., *The Utopian Vision of Charles
Fourier: Selected Texts on Work, Love, and Passionate Attraction* (Boston: Beacon Press,
1971), 96–100.

More than once people have supposed that incalculable savings and ameliorations would result if one could bring together the inhabitants of a village in an industrial society, if one could associate two or three hundred families of unequal wealth according to their capital and their work. At first the idea seems completely impractical because of the obstacle that would be presented by the human passions. The obstacle seems particularly great because the passions cannot be overcome by gradual degrees. It is scarcely possible to create an agricultural association of twenty, thirty, forty or fifty individuals. But at least eight hundred are necessary to establish a NATURAL or ATTRACTIVE association. I mean by these words a society whose members would be inspired to work by rivalry, self-esteem and other stimuli compatible with self-interest. In the order to which I refer we will become passionately enthusiastic about agricultural work which is so irksome today that we only do it out of necessity and the fear of dying of hunger. . . .

Disputatious people are sure to raise objections. "How can you form an association out of families when one may have 1,000 livres and another may be penniless? How can you reconcile so many conflicting interests and desires? How can you absorb all their jealousies in such a way as to serve everyone's interest?" My reply to all this is: by the enticement of wealth and pleasure. The strongest passion of both peasants and city people is the love of profit. When they see that a societary community yields a profit THREE TIMES that of a community of incoherent families and provides all its members with the most varied pleasures, they will forget all their rivalries and hasten to form an association. The system will be adopted everywhere without the application of any form of constraint, for people everywhere are passionately devoted to wealth and pleasure.

To summarize, this theory of agricultural association, which is going to change the condition of the human race, appeals to the passions which are common to all men; it seduces them with the enticements of profit and sensual pleasure. That is why it is sure to succeed among the savages and barbarians as well as the civilized, for the passions are the same everywhere. . . .

People have regarded the passions as enemies of concord and have written thousands of volumes against them. These volumes are going to fall into nothingness. For the passions tend only to concord, to that social unity which we have thought was so alien to them. But the passions can only be harmonized if they are allowed to develop in an orderly fashion within the PROGRESSIVE SERIES or SERIES OF GROUPS.[1] Outside of this mechanism the passions are only unchained tigers, incomprehensible enigmas. . . .

The societary order which is going to replace the incoherence of civilization has no place for moderation or equality or any of the other philosophical notions. It requires ardent and refined passions. As soon as an association is formed, the passions will harmonize with greater ease if they are more intense and more numerous.

This is not to say that the new order will change the passions. Neither God nor man is capable of changing them; but it is possible to change their direction without changing their nature. . . .

The establishment of the societary order in a single community will be spontaneously imitated everywhere thanks to the immense profits and innumerable pleasures which that order will assure to all individuals, however poor or wealthy they may be.

[1] In Fourier's theory, a "group" is a collection of at least three individuals who share a common passion. A "series" is a carefully constructed collection of groups of individuals who are diverse in age, wealth, sex, and interests but who share a common passion, such as gardening. The organization of a harmonious or "societary" order was meant to bring individuals together into groups and series in such a fashion that all their passions could find opportunities for social realization. Any particular individual would be a member of many groups and series.

7

CHARLES FOURIER

From *The Theory of Universal Unity*

1841–1843

Charles Fourier's ideas about transforming the forced labor of a society organized according to free-market principles into the pleasurable labor of a society built around the principle of passionate attraction provide an interesting contemporary parallel to Marx's concerns about "alienated" labor within a capitalist system of production. The following excerpts were first published in a multivolume treatise on agricultural and domestic association in 1822 and were reprinted in the collected works of Fourier published after his death.

Jonathan Beecher and Richard Bienvenue, trans. and ed., *The Utopian Vision of Charles Fourier: Selected Texts on Work, Love, and Passionate Attraction* (Boston: Beacon Press, 1971), 274–75.

Until now politics and morality have failed in their attempts to make men love work. Wage-earners and the entire lower class are becoming more and more indolent. Sunday's idleness is being compounded with Monday's idleness. Men work without enthusiasm, slowly and with loathing.

Aside from slavery, the only means by which society can force men to work is to make them fear starvation and punishment. Yet if God has destined us to work, he should not have to use violent means. How can we believe that he is not able to employ a nobler device, an enticement capable of transforming work into pleasure?

Only God is invested with the power to distribute attraction. He wishes to guide his universe and its creatures by attraction alone. To attach us to agricultural and manufacturing work he has devised a system of *industrial attraction*. Once this system is put into practice, it will endow manufacturing and farming tasks with a host of charms. It may even make work more alluring than are the festivities, balls, and spectacles of today. In other words, the common people will derive so much pleasure and stimulation from work in the societary state that they will refuse to leave their jobs to attend balls and spectacles scheduled during work periods.

If it is to attract the people so forcefully, societary work must have none of the loathsome aspects that make work in the present state so odious. For societary work to become attractive it must fulfill the seven following conditions:

1. Each worker must be an associate who is compensated by dividend and not by wages.
2. Each person—man, woman, or child—must be paid in proportion to his contribution in *capital, work* and *talent.*
3. Work sessions must be varied about eight times a day because a man cannot remain enthusiastic about his job for more than an hour and a half or two when he is performing an agricultural or manufacturing task.
4. These tasks must be performed by groups of friends who have gathered together spontaneously and who are stimulated and intrigued by very active rivalries.
5. Workshops, fields and gardens must offer the worker the enticements of elegance and cleanliness.
6. The division of labor must be carried to the supreme degree in order to allot suitable tasks to people of each sex and of every age.

7. The distribution of tasks must assure each man, woman, or child the right to work or the right to take part at any time in any kind of work for which he or she is qualified.

X. Finally, in this new order the common people must enjoy a guarantee of well-being, a minimum income sufficient for present and future needs. This guarantee must free them from all anxiety either for their own welfare or that of their dependents.

8

ROBERT OWEN

From *Report to the County of Lanark*

1820

In this passage from his 1820 Report to the County of Lanark, *Robert Owen looks to a fair, scientific, and "natural" application of the labor theory of value to social exchange in order to abolish the inequalities produced by a market system of wages. If workers received fair value for the products they produced, they would have the wealth to consume their products, thus ending the cycle of crises of overproduction. A just exchange in the labor market would resolve the problem of unemployment and worker poverty that his report was intended to address. By the late 1840s, Marx and Engels had little confidence in the power of "natural" principles of justice to transform the relations of alienated labor within the capitalist system.*

To understand the subject on which your Reporter is now about to enter, requires much profound study of the whole circle of political economy. A knowledge of some of its parts, with ignorance of the remainder, will be found to be most injurious to the practical statesman; and it is

Robert Owen, *Report to the County of Lanark, of a Plan for Relieving Public Distress, and Removing Discontent, by Giving Permanent, Productive Employment, to the Poor and Working Classes* (Glasgow: Printed at the University Press, for Wardlaw & Cunninghame, 1821), 6–7, 9.

owing to this cause, perhaps, more than to any other, that the world has been so wretchedly governed; for the object of this science is to direct how the powers of men in community may be the most advantageously applied, whereas those powers have been combined, hitherto, chiefly to retard the improvements of society.

Your Reporter, then, after deeply studying these subjects, practically and theoretically, for a period exceeding thirty years, and during which, his practice, without a single exception, has confirmed the theory which practice first suggested, now ventures to state, as one of the results of this study and experience, *that the natural standard of value is, in principle, human labour, or the combined manual and mental powers of men called into action*; and that it would be highly beneficial, and has now become absolutely necessary, to reduce this principle into immediate practice.

It will be said by those who have taken a superficial or mere partial view of the question, that human labour or power is so unequal in individuals, that its average amount cannot be estimated.

Already, however, the average physical power of men as well as of horses (equally varied in the individuals) has been calculated for scientific purposes, and both now serve to measure inanimate powers.

On the same principle, the average of human labour or power may be ascertained; and as it forms the essence of all wealth, its value in every article of produce may be also ascertained, and its exchangeable value with all other values fixed accordingly; the whole to be permanent for a given period.

Human labour would thus acquire its natural or intrinsic value, which would increase as science advanced; and this is, in fact, the only really useful object of science.

The demand for human labour would be no longer subject to caprice, nor would the support of human life be made, as at present, a perpetually varying article of commerce, and the working classes made the slaves of an artificial system of wages, more cruel in its effects than any slavery ever practised by society, either barbarous or civilized.

This change in the standard of value would immediately open the most advantageous domestic markets, until the wants of all were amply supplied, nor while this standard continued, could any evil arise in future from the want of markets.

It would secure the means for the most unlimited and advantageous intercourse and exchange with other nations, without compromising national interests, and enable all Governments to withdraw every existing injurious commercial restriction.

It would render unnecessary and entirely useless the present demoralizing system of bargaining between individuals, and no practice perhaps tends more than this to deteriorate and degrade the human character.

It would speedily remove pauperism and ignorance from society, by furnishing time and means for the adequate instruction of the working classes, who might be rendered of far more commercial value to themselves and to society, than they have yet been, at any period of the world.

It would supply the means of gradually improving the condition of all ranks to an extent not yet to be estimated. And as it would materially improve human nature, and raise all in the scale of well-being and happiness, none could be injured or oppressed. . . .

It is the want of a profitable market that alone checks the successful and otherwise beneficial industry of the working classes.

The markets of the world are created solely by the remuneration allowed for the industry of the working classes, and those markets are more or less extended and profitable, in proportion as these classes are well or ill remunerated for their labour. But the existing arrangements of society will not permit the labourer to be remunerated for his industry, and in consequence all markets fail.

To re-create and extend demand in proportion as the late scientific improvements and others which are hourly advancing to perfection, extend the means of supply, the natural standard of value is required.

It will be found equal to the important task which it has to perform.

It will at once remove the obstruction which has paralyzed the industry of the country; and experience will prove, that this effect cannot be accomplished by any other expedient.

9

The Six Points of the People's Charter

1838

This list of the six major points of the People's Charter, formulated in 1838, constituted the basis for a powerful political movement mobilizing vast numbers of the politically excluded working classes throughout Great

F. C. Mather, ed., *Chartism and Society: An Anthology of Documents* (New York: Holmes and Meier, 1980), 47.

Britain for petition drives and public demonstrations. The Chartists looked to democratic politics as the way to institute reforms that would alleviate social inequalities and integrate the organization of labor into a public social policy. This version of the charter is from a broadsheet of 1838.

1. A VOTE for every man twenty-one years of age, of sound mind, and not undergoing punishment for crime.
2. THE BALLOT—To protect the elector in the exercise of his vote.
3. NO PROPERTY QUALIFICATION for Members of Parliament—thus enabling the constituencies to return the man of their choice, be he rich or poor.
4. PAYMENT OF MEMBERS, thus enabling an honest tradesman, working man, or other person, to serve a constituency, when taken from his business to attend to the interests of the Country.
5. EQUAL CONSTITUENCIES, securing the same amount of representation for the same number of electors, instead of allowing small constituencies to swamp the votes of large ones.
6. ANNUAL PARLIAMENTS, thus presenting the most effectual check to bribery and intimidation, since though a constituency might be bought once in seven years (even with the ballot), no purse could buy a constituency (under a system of universal suffrage) in each ensuing twelve-month; and since members, when elected for a year only, would not be able to defy and betray their constituents as now.

10

JAMES BRONTERRE O'BRIEN
Private Property
1841

This passage from an 1841 article by James Bronterre O'Brien, a prominent social theorist in the Chartist movement, provides a good example of the kind of theories of social justice based on the worker's right to enjoy the full value of his or her product that Marx and Engels were trying to transcend in the mid-1840s. Bronterre distinguishes between (1) the right to own the type of property that is a just return on one's own labor and (2) the private ownership of the means of production or the "produce" of social labor that allows an individual to control the labor of others. Marx and Engels distinguished the kind of private property that Bronterre rejects here as "bourgeois" property.

If all men are placed equal before the law—if the means of acquiring and retaining wealth are equally secured to all in proportion to the respective industry and services of each, I see no objection to private property. Every man has a right to the value of his own produce or services, be they more or less. If one man can and will do twice the work of another man, he ought certainly in justice to have twice the reward. But if his superior strength or skill gives him the means of acquiring more wealth than his neighbour, it by no means follows that he ought, therefore, to acquire a right or power over his neighbour's produce as well as his own. And here lies the grand evil of society—it is not in private property, but in the unjust and atrocious powers with which the existing laws of all countries invest it. If a man has fairly earned a hundred or a thousand pounds' worth of wealth beyond what he has consumed or spent, he has a sacred right to the exclusive use of it, if he thinks proper; but he has no right to use that wealth in such a way as to make it a sort of sucking-pump, or thumb-screw for sucking and screwing other people's produce into his possession. Sir John Cam Hobhouse, for example,

---

F. C. Mather, ed., *Chartism and Society: An Anthology of Documents* (New York: Holmes and Meier, 1980), 91–93.

has 60,000 £. in Whitbread's brewery. Now, supposing Sir John to have earned that money honestly, he has a right to use it, and live upon it, while it lasts; but he has no just right to make it the means of sucking 5,000 £. or 6,000 £. additional every year out of the public without a particle of labour or industry on his part. He has no just right to employ his money in usury or speculation. His money should not be allowed to grow money as cabbage grows cabbage, or weeds grows weeds. . . . Such are the effects of wealth as now administered. They result not from property, but from robbery—they are not rights of property, but wrongs on industry—they spring from bad laws—from depraved institutions. These laws and these institutions, instead of protecting industry from dishonest cupidity, have utterly sacrificed the former to the latter. The *employers* of labour and the *exchangers* of wealth are alone considered in the laws. The *producers* and active distributors are only thought of as slaves or criminals. Enormous fleets and armies are kept up to protect the merchants' gains. Enormous gaols and penitentiaries are kept up for the poor. Thus are the labourers forced to pay, not only for the protection of those who plunder them, but for the very instruments of their own torture and misery. Buonarroti[1] considers all these results inseparable from private property. So did Babeuf[2]—so did thousands of the French democrats of 1793—so do Robert Owen and his disciples of the present day. I think differently. I will never admit that private property is incompatible with public happiness, till I see it fairly tried. I never found an objection urged against it, which I cannot trace to the abuse, not to the use, of the institution. Assuredly, if men are allowed to acquire wealth by all manner of nefarious means, and to afterwards employ that wealth more nefariously still, there must be public ruin and misery; but I deny that these are the necessary effects of private property. Usury, for instance, has destroyed all the nations of antiquity, and is now undermining all modern states; but is usury essential to private property? I deny it. But, then it is necessary to, and inseparable from commerce. I deny that too. It is, certainly, inseparable from commerce as now conducted; but I deny that an enlightened Government, representing all classes, would allow commerce to be conducted as it is now. I assert, that such Government would place commerce and manufactures upon a

---

[1] Filippo Buonarroti (1761–1837) was an Italian revolutionary and utopian communist who was a comrade of Babeuf (see note 2) and carried his legacy into the nineteenth century.

[2] François-Noël (Gracchus) Babeuf (1760–1797) was a political agitator during the French Revolution who advocated equal distribution of land and income. He organized a "conspiracy of equals" to plan a revolutionary insurrection in 1796 and was arrested and executed in 1797.

totally different footing from the present, and make the land the common property of all the inhabitants, and that, without any real or material
injury to the existing proprietors. I hold, and I am sure I can prove, that
such a dispensation of things is within the power of an enlightened Leg-
islature, fairly representing all classes. I have no space to argue the question here, but assuming that I am right for the present, why should we
conclude that private property is the inevitable cause of the evils alluded
to, until the institution be fairly tried and tested?

11

G. W. F. HEGEL

From *Reason in History: A General Introduction to the Philosophy of History*

1837

*Although Georg Wilhelm Friedrich Hegel died in 1831, five years before
Marx arrived at the University of Berlin to engage in philosophical study,
Hegel's disciples dominated the teaching of philosophy, the social sciences,
and the humanities at the university during Marx's student years, and
Marx self-consciously "converted" to the Hegelian position in 1837. The
following passages, some of the clearest statements in Hegel's writings, are
taken from the introduction to* Hegel's Lectures on the Philosophy of
History. *These lectures were first published, on the basis of student notes,
in 1837 by Eduard Gans, a professor of law who was Marx's most important teacher during his first years at the university (1837–1839). Marx's
conception of labor developed as a materialistic translation of Hegel's
concept of spirit, just as his conception of social community emerged from
the conceptual framework of the Hegelian state.*

G. W. F. Hegel, *Reason in History,* trans. Robert S. Hartman (New York: Macmillan/
Library of Liberal Arts, 1953), 22–23, 25, 53.

I. The Idea of Freedom

The nature of Spirit may be understood by a glance at its direct opposite—Matter. The essence of matter is gravity, the essence of Spirit—its substance—is Freedom. It is immediately plausible to everyone that, among other properties, Spirit also possesses Freedom. But philosophy teaches us that *all* the properties of Spirit exist only through Freedom. All are but means of attaining Freedom; all seek and produce this and this alone. It is an insight of speculative philosophy that Freedom is the sole truth of Spirit. Matter possesses gravity by virtue of its tendency toward a central point; it is essentially composite, consisting of parts that exclude each other. It seeks its unity and thereby its own abolition; it seeks its opposite. If it would attain this it would be matter no longer, but would have perished. It strives toward ideality, for in unity it exists ideally. Spirit, on the contrary, is that which has its center in itself. It does not have unity outside of itself but has found it; it is in itself and with itself. Matter has its substance outside of itself; Spirit is Being-within-itself (self-contained existence). But this, precisely, is Freedom. For when I am dependent, I refer myself to something else which I am not; I cannot exist independently of something external. I am free when I am within myself. This self-contained existence of Spirit is self-consciousness, consciousness of self.

Two things must be distinguished in consciousness, first, *that* I know and, secondly, *what* I know. In self-consciousness the two coincide, for Spirit knows itself. It is the judgment of its own nature and, at the same time, the operation of coming to itself, to produce itself, to make itself (actually) into that which it is in itself (potentially). Following this abstract definition it may be said that world history is the exhibition of spirit striving to attain knowledge of its own nature. . . .

[Freedom] is the ultimate purpose toward which all world history has continually aimed. To this end all the sacrifices have been offered on the vast altar of the earth throughout the long lapse of ages. Freedom alone is the purpose which realizes and fulfills itself, the only enduring pole in the change of events and conditions, the only true efficient principle that pervades the whole. . . .

II. Freedom in the State

. . . Thus the State is the definite object of world history proper. In it freedom achieves its objectivity and lives in the enjoyment of this objectivity. For law is the objectivity of Spirit; it is will in its true form. Only the will that obeys the law is free, for it obeys itself and, being in itself, is free. In so far as the state, our country, constitutes a community of existence, and as the subjective will of man subjects itself to the laws, the antithesis of freedom and necessity disappears. The rational, like the substantial, is necessary. We are free when we recognize it as law and follow it as the substance of our own being.

[Hegel completes his discussion of the realization of the idea of freedom in history with the claim that the full realization of freedom occurs in the ethical community of the state.]

12

LUDWIG FEUERBACH

From *The Essence of Christianity*
1841

The "positive" demystification of traditional religion and philosophy as alienated forms of human self-affirmation in Feuerbach's The Essence of Christianity *(1841) was perceived as an epochal clarifying moment in Western thought by both Marx and Engels in the early 1840s.*

The necessary turning point of history is therefore the open confession that the consciousness of God is nothing else than the consciousness of the species; that man can and should raise himself only above the limits of his individuality and not above the laws, the positive essential conditions of his species; that there is no other essence which man can think, dream of, imagine, feel, believe in, wish for, love and adore as the absolute, than the essence of human nature itself. (Feuerbach's own footnote at this point: "Including external nature; for as man belongs to the essence of Nature—in opposition to common materialism; so nature belongs to the essence of man—in opposition to subjective idealism; which is also the secret of our '*absolute*' philosophy, at least in relation to Nature. Only by uniting man with Nature can we conquer the supranaturalistic egoism of Christianity.")

Ludwig Feuerbach, *The Essence of Christianity,* translated by George Eliot (New York: Harper and Brothers, 1957), 270–271.

Our relation to religion is therefore not a merely negative, but a critical one; we only separate the true from the false;—though we grant that the truth thus separated from falsehood is a new truth, essentially different from the old. Religion is the first form of self-consciousness. Religions are sacred because they are the traditions of the primitive self-consciousness. But that which in religion holds first place—namely God—is, as we have shown, in itself and according to truth, the second, for it is only the nature of man regarded objectively; and that which to religion is second—namely, man—must therefore be constituted and declared the first. Love to man must be no derivative love; it must be original. If human nature is the highest nature to man, then practically also the highest and first law must be the love of man to man. *Homo homini Deus est*;—this is the great practical principle:—this is the axis on which revolves the history of the world.

13

KARL MARX

From *Contribution to the Critique of Hegel's Philosophy of Law*

1844

Marx wrote this essay in late 1843 and published it in 1844 in the journal Deutsch-Französische Jahrbücher *(German-French Annals), which he co-edited with another exiled radical Hegelian intellectual, Arnold Ruge. The essay was originally intended as an introduction to a detailed analysis and critique of Hegel's philosophy of politics. It documents the way in which Marx's pursuit of the historical actualization of the idea of freedom moved from a criticism of religion to a criticism of politics as sites for human self-fulfillment.*

Introduction

For Germany the *criticism of religion* is in the main complete, and criticism of religion is the premise of all criticism.

Karl Marx and Frederick Engels, *Collected Works* (New York: International Publishers, 1975), Vol. 3:175–76.

The *profane* existence of error is discredited after its *heavenly oratio pro aris et focis** has been disproved. Man, who looked for a superhuman being in the fantastic reality of heaven and found nothing there but the *reflection* of himself, will no longer be disposed to find but the *semblance* of himself, only an inhuman being, where he seeks and must seek his true reality.

The basis of irreligious criticism is: *Man makes religion,* religion does not make man. Religion is the self-consciousness and self-esteem of man who has either not yet found himself or has already lost himself again. But *man* is no abstract being encamped outside the world. Man is *the world of man,* the state, society. This state, this society, produce religion, an *inverted world-consciousness,* because they are an *inverted world.* Religion is the general theory of that world, its encyclopaedic compendium, its logic in a popular form, its spiritualistic *point d'honneur,* its enthusiasm, its moral sanction, its solemn complement, its universal source of consolation and justification. It is the *fantastic realisation* of the human essence because the *human essence* has no true reality. The struggle against religion is therefore indirectly a fight against *the world* of which religion is the spiritual *aroma.*

Religious distress is at the same time the *expression* of real distress and also the *protest* against real distress. Religion is the sigh of the oppressed creature, the heart of a heartless world, just as it is the spirit of spiritless conditions. It is the *opium* of the people.

To abolish religion as the *illusory* happiness of the people is to demand their *real* happiness. The demand to give up illusions about the existing state of affairs is the *demand to give up a state of affairs which needs illusions.* The criticism of religion is therefore *in embryo the criticism of the vale of tears,* the *halo* of which is religion.

Criticism has torn up the imaginary flowers from the chain not so that man shall wear the unadorned, bleak chain but so that he will shake off the chain and pluck the living flower. The criticism of religion disillusions man to make him think and act and shape his reality like a man who has been disillusioned and has come to reason, so that he will revolve round himself and therefore round his true sun. Religion is only the illusory sun which revolves round man as long as he does not revolve round himself.

The *task of history,* therefore, once the *world beyond the truth* has disappeared, is to establish the *truth of this world.* The immediate *task of philosophy,* which is at the service of history, once the *holy form* of human

---

*Speech for the altars and hearths.

self-estrangement has been unmasked, is to unmask self-estrangement in its *unholy forms.* Thus the criticism of heaven turns into the criticism of the earth, the *criticism of religion* into the *criticism of law* and the *criticism of theology* into the *criticism of politics.*

14

KARL MARX

From *On the Jewish Question*
1843

In the context of a review of a book concerned with the question of the civic emancipation of the Jews, Marx developed his analysis of the illusory nature of political emancipation per se. This review was first published in the journal Deutsch-Französische Jahrbücher *in 1843. In this essay, Marx develops the conceptual distinctions between the state and civil society, and between the citizen and the bourgeois, to frame his own views of the need to move beyond political emancipation to a transformation of social relations.*

The limits of political emancipation are evident at once from the fact that the *state* can free itself from a restriction without man being *really* free from this restriction, that the state can be a *free state** without man being a *free man.* . . . .

It is possible, therefore, for the *state* to have emancipated itself from religion even if the *overwhelming majority* is still religious. And the overwhelming majority does not cease to be religious through being religious *in private.*

But the attitude of the state, and of the *republic** in particular, to religion is after all only the attitude to religion of the *men* who compose the state. It follows from this that man frees himself through the *medium of the state,* that he frees himself *politically* from a limitation when, in contradiction with himself, he raises himself above this limitation in an *abstract, limited,* and partial way. . . .

**A pun on the word *Freistaat,* i.e., a republic, for if it is taken literally, it means "free state."

Karl Marx and Frederick Engels, *Collected Works* (New York: International Publishers, 1975), Vol. 3:152–53, 167–68.

The *political* elevation of man above religion shares all the defects and all the advantages of political elevation in general. The state as a state annuls, for instance, *private property,* man declares by *political* means that private property is *abolished* as soon as the *property qualification* for the right to elect or be elected is abolished, as has occurred in many states of North America. . . .

Nevertheless the political annulment of private property not only fails to abolish private property but even presupposes it. The state abolishes, in its own way, distinctions of *birth, social rank, education, occupation,* when it declares that birth, social rank, education, occupation, are *non-political* distinctions, when it proclaims, without regard to these distinctions, that every member of the nation is an *equal* participant in national sovereignty, when it treats all elements of the real life of the nation from the standpoint of the state. . . .

The perfect political state is, by its nature, man's *species-life,* as *opposed* to his material life. All the preconditions of this egoistic life continue to exist in *civil society outside* the sphere of the state, but as qualities of civil society. Where the political state has attained its true development, man—not only in thought, in consciousness, but in *reality,* in *life*—leads a twofold life, a heavenly and an earthly life: life in the *political community,* in which he considers himself a *communal being,* and life in *civil society,* in which he acts as a *private individual,* regards other men as a means, degrades himself into a means, and becomes the plaything of alien powers. The relation of the political state to civil society is just as spiritual as the relation of heaven to earth. The political state stands in the same opposition to civil society, and it prevails over the latter in the same way as religion prevails over the narrowness of the secular world, i.e., by likewise having always to acknowledge it, to restore it, and allow itself to be dominated by it. In his *most immediate* reality, in civil society, man is a secular being. Here, where he regards himself as a real individual, and is so regarded by others, he is a *fictitious* phenomenon. In the state, on the other hand, where man is regarded as a species-being, he is the imaginary member of an illusory sovereignty, is deprived of his real individual life and endowed with an unreal universality. . . .

The *establishment of the political state* and the dissolution of civil society into independent *individuals*—whose relations with one another depend on *law,* just as the relations of men in the system of estates and guilds depended on *privilege*—is accomplished by *one and the same act.* Man as a member of civil society, *unpolitical* man, inevitably appears, however, as the *natural* man. The *droits de l'homme* appear as *droits naturels,* because *conscious activity* is concentrated on the *political act.*

Egoistic man is the *passive* result of the dissolved society, a result that is simply *found in existence,* an object of *immediate certainty,* therefore a *natural* object. The *political revolution* resolves civil life into its component parts, without *revolutionising* these components themselves or subjecting them to criticism. It regards civil society, the world of needs, labour, private interests, civil law, as the *basis of its existence,* as a *precondition* not requiring further substantiation and therefore as its *natural basis.* Finally, man as a member of civil society is held to be man *in the proper sense, homme* as distinct from the *citoyen,* because he is man in his sensuous, individual, *immediate* existence, whereas *political* man is only abstract, artificial man, man as an *allegorical, juridical* person. The real man is recognised only in the shape of the *egoistic* individual, the *true* man is recognised only in the shape *abstract citoyen.* . . .

All emancipation is a *reduction* of the human world and relationships to *man himself.*

Political emancipation is the reduction of man, on the one hand, to a member of civil society, to an *egoistic, independent* individual, and, on the other hand, to a *citizen,* a juridical person.

Only when the real, individual man re-absorbs in himself the abstract citizen, and as an individual human being has become a *species-being* in his everyday life, in his particular work, and in his particular situation, only when man has recognised and organised his *"forces propres"** as *social* forces, and consequently no longer separates social power from himself in the shape of *political* power, only then will human emancipation have been accomplished.

* "Own powers."

15

LUDWIG FEUERBACH

From *Principles of the Philosophy of the Future*

1843

These three paragraphs are taken from a short book of aphorisms published by the German post-Hegelian philosopher Ludwig Feuerbach (1804–1872) in 1843. Here Feuerbach states most clearly his attempt to

Zawar Hanfi, trans., *The Fiery Brook: Selected Writings of Ludwig Feuerbach* (Garden City, N.Y.: Doubleday, 1972), 227, 231–32.

ground philosophy in sensuous existence, a move that Engels and Marx viewed as a major revolution in philosophy. In his writings of 1843–1844, Marx tended to cite Feuerbach as the source of the general principle of sensuous naturalism or materialism informing his own critical views of political and social existence.

The old philosophy had its point of departure in the proposition: I am an abstract, a merely thinking being to which the body does not belong. The new philosophy proceeds from the principle: I am a real and sensuous *being; indeed, the whole of my body is my ego, my being itself.* The old philosopher, therefore, thought in a *constant contradiction to and conflict with the senses* in order to avoid sensuous conceptions, or in order not to pollute abstract concepts. In contrast, the new philosopher thinks *in peace and harmony with the senses.* The old philosophy conceded the truth of sensuousness *only in a concealed way,* only in terms of the *concept,* only *unconsciously* and *unwillingly,* only because it had to. This is borne out even by its concept of God as the being who encompasses all other beings within himself, for he was held to be distinct from a merely conceived being; that is, he was held to be existing outside the mind, outside thought—a really objective, sensuous being. In contrast, the new philosophy *joyfully* and *consciously* recognizes the truth of sensuousness: It is a *sensuous* philosophy with an *open heart.* . . .

It is not only "external" things that are objects of the senses. *Man,* too, is *given to himself only through the senses;* only as a sensuous object is he an object for himself. The *identity* of *subject and object*—in selfconsciousness only an abstract thought—has the character of *truth* and reality only in *man's sensuous perception of* man.

We feel not only stones and wood, not only flesh and bones, but also feelings when we press the hands or lips of a feeling being; we perceive through our ears not only the murmur of water and the rustle of leaves, but also the soulful voice of love and wisdom; we see not only mirror-like surfaces and specters of color, but we also gaze into the gaze of man. Hence, not only that which is external, but also that which is internal, not only flesh, but also spirit, not only things, but also the *ego* is an object of the senses. All is therefore capable of being perceived through the senses, even if only in a mediated and not immediate way, even if not with the help of crude and vulgar senses, but only through those that are cultivated; even if not with the eyes of the anatomist and the chemist, but only with those of the philosopher. Empiricism is therefore perfectly justified in regarding ideas as originating from the senses; but what it forgets is that the most essential sensuous object for man is *man himself;* that only in man's glimpse of man does the spark of consciousness and intellect spring. And this goes to show that idealism is right in so far as it sees the origin of ideas *in* man; but it is wrong in so far as it derives these ideas from man understood as an isolated being, as [a] mere soul existing for himself; in one word, it is wrong when it derives the ideas from an ego that is not given in the context of its togetherness with a perceptibly given You. Ideas spring only from conversation and communication. Not alone but only within a dual relationship does one have concepts and reason in general. It takes two human beings to give birth to a man, to physical as well as spiritual man; the togetherness of man with man is the first principle and the criterion of truth and universality. Even the certitude of those things that exist outside me is given to me through the certitude of the existence of other men besides myself. That which is seen by me alone is open to question, but that which is seen also by another person is certain.

16

MOSES HESS

From *A Communist Credo: Questions and Answers*
1844–1846

Moses Hess was a close intellectual and political associate of Marx and Engels through the mid- and late 1840s, and played an important role in their turn to Feuerbachian humanism, the interpretation of the human essence as productive labor and the examination of the conditions of a communist revolution. Hess suggested a broad, encompassing definition of labor as the production of life, an activity which included the inner drives toward sensual enjoyment and spiritual virtue. The Communist Credo, published in 1844 (anonymously) and then again in 1846, also marked an early attempt to translate philosophical concepts into a

Moses Hess, "A Communist Credo: Questions and Answers," *The Holy History of Mankind and Other Writings*, translated and edited with an introduction by Shlomo Avineri (Cambridge, U.K.: Cambridge University Press, 2004), 116–18.

*catechism of questions and answers in order to reach a broader audience.
This excerpt is from Part I: Of Labour and Enjoyment.*

1. What is the meaning of working?

Every transformation of matter for the life of mankind means working—
or acting, creating, generating, manufacturing, producing, taking action
and dealing, being active, in short: living. Because truly, all that lives,
works; and regarding human life, not only through the head and hands,
but also through all other limbs and organs of the human body which
transform for human life the materials which they receive from outside,
e.g. the mouth processes the received materials of the stomach, and
the latter does the same for the blood and so on. This means that each
organ of the human body, like each member of society, produces for
the whole or works and creates even while it appears to be consuming
and enjoying; at the same time it only enjoys its own life when it appears
to work or produce for the whole. This harmony of work and pleasure
takes place only in organic or organized life, not in the un-organized
one, as we shall presently show.

2. What kinds of work exist?

Organized and unorganized. In other words: free and coerced or forced
labour.

3. What is free activity and what is forced labour?

Free activity is all that grows out of an inner drive; forced labour, on the
other hand, is all that happens out of external drive or out of need. If
labour takes place out of an inner drive, it is a passion which promotes
the enjoyment of life, a virtue which carries its own reward in itself. If,
on the other hand, it is brought about through an external drive, then
it becomes a burden which degrades human nature and oppresses it, a
vice which can be carried out only for the vile wages of sin; it is wage or
slave labour. A man who looks for the wages of his work outside himself
is a slave who acts for alien goals, a mere machine driven (by others).

4. Which of these kinds of labour is understood today under work?

Forced Labour.

5. Which does one actually call free activity?

It is called either pleasure or virtue.

6. What does one understand today by pleasure?

Living according to certain sensuous inclinations, without regard for the whole of human nature.

7. What does one understand by virtue?

Living according to certain spiritual inclinations, without regard for the whole of human nature.

8. Can we nowadays act according to our true human nature or truly enjoy our human life?

Absolutely not. Almost every activity in our society comes not from an inner drive of our human nature. Not out of passion or love of labour, but out of external pressure, usually because of need or money. On the other hand, those life activities which are caused by inner drives, which we call pleasure or virtue, are perverted in such a way that they hurt the living enjoyment of human nature even more than this occurs through coercive labour. The excesses in the satisfaction of certain sensual and spiritual activities, which do not correspond to human nature and to which man now feels drawn only because his nature is not yet fully developed, but is being oppressed — such excesses cause all free-living activity of contemporary man to assume an inhuman or bestial character. Thus drinking turns into boozing, the act of procreation or sexual love into unbridled lasciviousness, taking a rest from work into laziness, scholarship into pedantry, the striving of the heart after a higher life into hypocritical piety, virtue into self-torture, and so on. All sensual as well as spiritual inclinations deteriorate into excesses and become diseased because not all of human nature is developed but is rather oppressed and therefore degenerates. This disease then replaces all other inclinations of human nature and degrades man into the level of the beast which possesses only one-sided urges.

9. Is it possible for all human beings to live and enjoy (life) according to their nature?

Not only is this possible, but the opposite would have been impossible had human nature developed in all men and not been violently oppressed through social conditions.

10. What kinds of work are possible in a society in which every man can apply all his faculties?

In such a society nothing but free activity is possible.

11. What kinds of work are possible in a society in which men are neither fully developed, nor can human activities be fully applied?

In such a society, nothing is possible except coercive labour, sloth, seeking of pleasure and false virtue.

12. Can, in our contemporary society, all human faculties be developed and the developed faculties applied?

No way. We are stunted both in our development as well as in the applications of our faculties and powers. General education and human development (*Bildung*), as well as the exchange and application of our faculties, are impossible in our society. Most human powers remain undeveloped and those which are developed are regularly crushed. The life of men in contemporary society is, in most cases, divided into coercive labour, deprivation and the seeking of pleasure. Here one splashes in luxury, there one lives in famine; sometimes it is scarcity, sometimes it is surplus which degrades man to the level of the beast.

13. Why is the development and application of our human powers not possible in contemporary society?

Because we turn each other into slaves by buying and selling ourselves, or—what is the same—all our human powers.

17

KARL MARX

From *The Economic and Philosophic Manuscripts of* 1844

1844

These draft fragments of an unfinished book were produced during the spring and summer of 1844, about six months after Marx had moved to Paris. The manuscripts were neglected and unknown until the late 1920s, when they were published first in a Russian translation in 1927 and then in a critical German edition in 1932. Their publication had a significant influence on the interpretation of Marx's later work, since they display so

---

Karl Marx and Frederick Engels, *Collected Works* (New York: International Publishers, 1975), Vol. 3:270–77.

clearly the formation of his principles, especially his theory of labor, within the context of his Hegelian philosophical heritage. In these excerpts, we can see how Marx used a form of Hegelian humanism (in which the universal essence of human existence was defined not as "reason" or "spirit" but as "species-being") to interpret the analysis of capitalism that he found in the writings of the British political economists. We also can see how he translates the Hegelian dynamics of freedom's self-realization into a description of the structure of human existence as creative labor.

We have proceeded from the premises of political economy. We have accepted its language and its laws. We presupposed private property, the separation of labour, capital and land, and of wages, profit of capital and rent of land—likewise division of labour, competition, the concept of exchange-value, etc. On the basis of political economy itself, in its own words, we have shown that the worker sinks to the level of a commodity and becomes indeed the most wretched of commodities; that the wretchedness of the worker is in inverse proportion to the power and magnitude of his production; that the necessary result of competition is the accumulation of capital in a few hands, and thus the restoration of monopoly in a more terrible form; and that finally the distinction between capitalist and land rentier, like that between the tiller of the soil and the factory worker, disappears and that the whole of society must fall apart into the two classes—the *property owners* and the propertyless *workers.*

Political economy starts with the fact of private property; it does not explain it to us. It expresses in general, abstract formulas the *material* process through which private property actually passes, and these formulas it then takes for *laws.* It does not *comprehend* these laws, i.e., it does not demonstrate how they arise from the very nature of private property. Political economy throws no light on the cause of the division between labour and capital, and between capital and land. When, for example, it defines the relationship of wages to profit, it takes the interest of the capitalists to be the ultimate cause, i.e., it takes for granted what it is supposed to explain. Similarly, competition comes in everywhere. It is explained from external circumstances. As to how far these external and apparently accidental circumstances are but the expression of a necessary course of development, political economy teaches us nothing. We have seen how exchange itself appears to it as an accidental fact. The only wheels which political economy sets in motion are *greed* and the *war amongst the greedy—competition.* . . .

Do not let us go back to a fictitious primordial condition as the political economist does, when he tries to explain. Such a primordial condition explains nothing; it merely pushes the question away into a grey nebulous distance. The economist assumes in the form of a fact, of an event, what he is supposed to deduce—namely, the necessary relationship between two things—between, for example, division of labour and exchange. Thus the theologian explains the origin of evil by the fall of man; that is, he assumes as a fact, in historical form, what has to be explained.

We proceed from an *actual* economic fact.

The worker becomes all the poorer the more wealth he produces, the more his production increases in power and size. The worker becomes an ever cheaper commodity the more commodities he creates. The *devaluation* of the world of men is in direct proportion to the *increasing value* of the world of things. Labour produces not only commodities: it produces itself and the worker as a *commodity*—and this at the same rate at which it produces commodities in general.

This fact expresses merely that the object which labour produces—labour's product—confronts it as *something alien,* as a *power independent* of the producer. The product of labour is labour which has been embodied in an object, which has become material: it is the *objectification* of labour. Labour's realisation is its objectification. Under these economic conditions this realisation of labour appears as *loss of realisation* for the workers; objectification as *loss of the object and bondage to it;* appropriation as *estrangement, as alienation.*

So much does labour's realisation appear as loss of realisation that the worker loses realisation to the point of starving to death. So much does objectification appear as loss of the object that the worker is robbed of the objects most necessary not only for his life but for his work. Indeed, labour itself becomes an object which he can obtain only with the greatest effort and with the most irregular interruptions. So much does the appropriation of the object appear as estrangement that the more objects the worker produces the less he can possess and the more he falls under the sway of his product, capital.

All these consequences are implied in the statement that the worker is related to the *product of his labour* as to an *alien* object. For on this premise it is clear that the more the worker spends himself, the more powerful becomes the alien world of objects which he creates over and against himself, the poorer he himself—his inner world—becomes, the less belongs to him as his own. It is the same in religion. The more man puts into God, the less he retains in himself. The worker puts his life into the object; but now his life no longer belongs to him but to the object.

Hence, the greater this activity, the more the worker lacks objects. Whatever the product of his labour is, he is not. Therefore the greater this product, the less is he himself. The *alienation* of the worker in his product means not only that his labour becomes an object, an *external* existence, but that it exists *outside him,* independently, as something alien to him, and that it becomes a power on its own confronting him. It means that the life which he has conferred on the object confronts him as something hostile and alien. . . .

What, then, constitutes the alienation of labour?

First, the fact that labour is *external* to the worker, i.e., it does not belong to his intrinsic nature; that in his work, therefore, he does not affirm himself but denies himself, does not feel content but unhappy, does not develop freely his physical and mental energy but mortifies his body and ruins his mind. The worker therefore only feels himself outside his work, and in his work feels outside himself. He feels at home when he is not working, and when he is working he does not feel at home. His labour is therefore not voluntary, but coerced; it is *forced labour.* It is therefore not the satisfaction of a need; it is merely a *means* to satisfy needs external to it. Its alien character emerges clearly in the fact that as soon as no physical or other compulsion exists, labour is shunned like the plague. External labour, labour in which man alienates himself, is a labour of self-sacrifice, of mortification. Lastly, the external character of labour for the worker appears in the fact that it is not his own, but someone else's, that it does not belong to him, that in it he belongs, not to himself, but to another. Just as in religion the spontaneous activity of the human imagination, of the human brain and the human heart, operates on the individual independently of him—that is, operates as an alien, divine or diabolical activity—so is the worker's activity not his spontaneous activity. It belongs to another; it is the loss of his self.

As a result, therefore, man (the worker) only feels himself freely active in his animal functions—eating, drinking, procreating, or at most in his dwelling and in dressing-up, etc.; and in his human functions he no longer feels himself to be anything but an animal. What is animal becomes human and what is human becomes animal. . . .

Man is a species-being, not only because in practice and in theory he adopts the species (his own as well as those of other things) as his object, but—and this is only another way of expressing it—also because he treats himself as the actual, living species; because he treats himself as a *universal* and therefore a free being.

The life of the species, both in man and in animals, consists physically in the fact that man (like the animal) lives on inorganic nature; and the more universal man (or the animal) is, the more universal is the sphere of inorganic nature on which he lives. Just as plants, animals, stones, air, light, etc., constitute theoretically a part of human consciousness, partly as objects of natural science, partly as objects of art—his spiritual inorganic nature, spiritual nourishment which he must first prepare to make palatable and digestible—so also in the realm of practice they constitute a part of human life and human activity. Physically man lives only on these products of nature, whether they appear in the form of food, heating, clothes, a dwelling, etc. The universality of man appears in practice precisely in the universality which makes all nature his *inorganic* body—both inasmuch as nature is (1) his direct means of life, and (2) the material, the object, and the instrument of his life activity. Nature is man's *inorganic body*—nature, that is, insofar as it is not itself human body. Man *lives* on nature—means that nature is his *body,* with which he must remain in continuous interchange if he is not to die. That man's physical and spiritual life is linked to nature means simply that nature is linked to itself, for man is a part of nature.

In estranging from man (1) nature, and (2) himself, his own active functions, his life activity, estranged labour estranges the *species* from man. It changes for him the *life of the species* into a means of individual life. . . .

For labour, *life activity, productive life* itself, appears to man in the first place merely as a *means* of satisfying a need—the need to maintain physical existence. Yet the productive life is the life of the species. It is life-engendering life. The whole character of a species—its species-character—is contained in the character of its life activity; and free, conscious activity is man's species-character. Life itself appears only as a *means to life.* . . .

In creating a *world of objects* by his practical activity, in his *work upon* inorganic nature, man proves himself a conscious species-being, i.e., as a being that treats the species as its own essential being, or that treats itself as a species-being. Admittedly animals also produce. They build themselves nests, dwellings, like the bees, beavers, ants, etc. But an animal only produces what it immediately needs for itself or its young. It produces one-sidedly, whilst man produces universally. It produces only under the dominion of immediate physical need, whilst man produces even when he is free from physical need and only truly produces in freedom therefrom. An animal produces only itself, whilst man reproduces the whole of nature. An animal's product belongs immediately to its physical body, whilst man freely confronts his product. An animal forms objects only in accordance with the standard and the need of the species to which it belongs, whilst man knows how to produce in accordance with the standard of every species, and knows how to apply everywhere the inherent standard to the object. Man therefore also forms objects in accordance with the laws of beauty.

It is just in his work upon the objective world, therefore, that man really proves himself to be a *species-being*. This production is his active species-life. Through this production, nature appears as *his* work and his reality. The object of labour is, therefore, the *objectification of man's species-life:* for he duplicates himself not only, as in consciousness, intellectually, but also actively, in reality, and therefore he sees himself in a world that he has created. In tearing away from man the object of his production, therefore, estranged labour tears from him his *species-life,* his real objectivity as a member of the species, and transforms his advantage over animals into the disadvantage that his inorganic body, nature, is taken away from him.

18

KARL MARX

Theses on Feuerbach

1845

These critical aphorisms show Marx setting out the principles of his own view of sensuous existence as social and historical (a position later described as "historical materialism") in opposition to what he saw as the ahistorical materialism of his former mentor Ludwig Feuerbach. They were written at approximately the same time as the more extensive elaboration of these principles in collaboration with Engels in The German Ideology *(see Document 19). They may have functioned as a preliminary outline of the first section of that larger study. Engels published the manuscript in an edited version in 1888 as an appendix to his work* Ludwig Feuerbach and the Decline of Classical German Philosophy. *The following excerpts are taken from a translation of the original unedited version that was first published in 1924. In these cryptic passages, we can see Marx trying to define his own form of "materialism" as both active (subjective) and social (as a form of social practice).*

Karl Marx and Frederick Engels, *Collected Works* (New York: International Publishers, 1976), Vol. 5:3–5.

1

The chief defect of all previous materialism (that of Feuerbach included) is that things *[Gegenstand]*, reality, sensuousness are conceived only in the form of the *object, or of contemplation,* but not as *sensuous human activity, practice,* not subjectively. Hence, in contradistinction to materialism, the *active* side was set forth abstractly by idealism—which, of course, does not know real, sensuous activity as such. Feuerbach wants sensuous objects, really distinct from conceptual objects, but he does not conceive human activity itself as *objective* activity. In *Das Wesen des Christenthums,*[1] he therefore regards the theoretical attitude as the only genuinely human attitude, while practice is conceived and defined only in its dirty-Jewish form of appearance. Hence he does not grasp the significance of "revolutionary," of "practical-critical," activity.

2

The question whether objective truth can be attributed to human thinking is not a question of theory but is a *practical* question. Man must prove the truth, i.e., the reality and power, the this-worldliness of his thinking in practice. The dispute over the reality or non-reality of thinking which is isolated from practice is a purely *scholastic* question.

3

The materialist doctrine concerning the changing of circumstances and upbringing forgets that circumstances are changed by men and that the educator must himself be educated. This doctrine must, therefore, divide society into two parts, one of which is superior to society. The coincidence of the changing of circumstances and of human activity or self-change can be conceived and rationally understood only as *revolutionary practice.*

4

Feuerbach starts out from the fact of religious self-estrangement, of the duplication of the world into a religious world and a secular one. His work consists in resolving the religious world into its secular basis.

[1] *The Essence of Christianity,* published in 1841. This work established Feuerbach's reputation as a radical humanist critic of Christian doctrine and ritual.

But that the secular basis lifts off from itself and establishes itself as an independent realm in the clouds can only be explained by the inner strife and intrinsic contradictoriness of this secular basis. The latter must, therefore, itself be both understood in its contradiction and revolutionised in practice. Thus, for instance, once the earthly family is discovered to be the secret of the holy family, the former must then itself be destroyed in theory and in practice.

5

Feuerbach, not satisfied with *abstract thinking,* wants *[sensuous] contemplation;* but he does not conceive sensuousness as *practical, human-sensuous* activity.

6

Feuerbach resolves the essence of religion into the essence of *man.* But the essence of man is no abstraction inherent in each single individual. In its reality it is the ensemble of the social relations.

Feuerbach, who does not enter upon a criticism of this real essence, is hence obliged:

1. To abstract from the historical process and to define the religious sentiment *[Gemüt]* by itself, and to presuppose an abstract — *isolated* — human individual.
2. Essence, therefore, can be regarded only as "species," as an inner, mute, general character which unites the many individuals *in a natural way.*

7

Feuerbach, consequently, does not see that the "religious sentiment" is itself a social product, and that the abstract individual which he analyses belongs to a particular form of society.

8

All social life is essentially *practical.* All mysteries which lead theory to mysticism find solution in human practice and in the comprehension of this practice.

9

The highest point reached by contemplative materialism, that is, materialism which does not comprehend sensuousness as practical activity, is the contemplation of single individuals and of civil society.

10

The standpoint of the old materialism is civil society; the standpoint of the new is human society, or social humanity.

11

The philosophers have only *interpreted* the world in various ways; the point is to *change* it.

19

KARL MARX AND FREDERICK ENGELS

From *The German Ideology*

1845–1846

Marx and Engels collaborated on The German Ideology *in 1845–1846. Most of the large manuscript was devoted to extremely detailed, polemical, satirical attacks on the radical German Hegelian theorists with whom Marx and Engels had been associated in the early 1840s. The first part of the work, organized as a critique of Feuerbach, is Marx's most systematic attempt to clarify the principles informing his conception of historical development. Here we can see him attempting to build a theory of progressive and ultimately unified historical development without the help of philosophical premises concerning universal reason, or human essence, but simply on what he saw as the empirical realities of human existence within the natural world. The manuscript was first published by the Marx-Engels Institute in Moscow in 1932. The following passages are from a slightly improved and expanded version. Although the larger text*

Karl Marx and Frederick Engels, *Collected Works* (New York: International Publishers, 1976), Vol. 5:31–32, 36–37.

is a collaborative work, these theoretical passages from its first section are commonly attributed to Marx.

The premises from which we begin are not arbitrary ones, not dogmas, but real premises from which abstraction can only be made in the imagination. They are the real individuals, their activity and the material conditions of their life, both those which they find already existing and those produced by their activity. These premises can thus be verified in a purely empirical way.

The first premise of all human history is, of course, the existence of living human individuals. Thus the first fact to be established is the physical organisation of these individuals and their consequent relation to the rest of nature. Of course, we cannot here go either into the actual physical nature of man, or into the natural conditions in which man finds himself—geological, oro-hydrographical, climatic and so on. All historical writing must set out from these natural bases and their modification in the course of history through the action of men.

Men can be distinguished from animals by consciousness, by religion or anything else you like. They themselves begin to distinguish themselves from animals as soon as they begin to *produce* their means of subsistence, a step which is conditioned by their physical organisation. By producing their means of subsistence men are indirectly producing their material life.

The way in which men produce their means of subsistence depends first of all on the nature of the means of subsistence they actually find in existence and have to reproduce.

This mode of production must not be considered simply as being the reproduction of the physical existence of the individuals. Rather it is a definite form of activity of these individuals, a definite form of expressing their life, a definite *mode of life* on their part. As individuals express their life, so they are. What they are, therefore, coincides with their production, both with *what* they produce and with *how* they produce. Hence what individuals are depends on the material conditions of their production.

This production only makes its appearance with the *increase of population*. In its turn this presupposes the *intercourse [Verkehr]* of individuals with one another. The form of this intercourse is again determined by production. . . .

The relations of different nations among themselves depend upon the extent to which each has developed its productive forces, the division of labour and internal intercourse. This proposition is generally

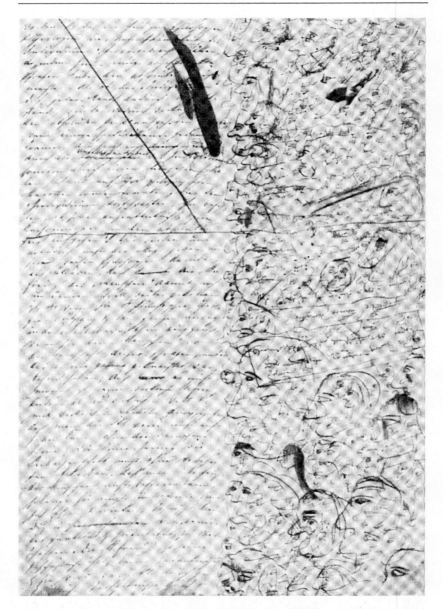

Figure 8. A page of the manuscript of *The German Ideology* discovered in the 1960s. The page is in Engels's script and displays his apparently irrepressible tendency both to doodle and to articulate his critical viewpoint in humorous caricature.

recognised. But not only the relation of one nation to others, but also the whole internal structure of the nation itself depends on the stage of development reached by its production and its internal and external intercourse. How far the productive forces of a nation are developed is shown most manifestly by the degree to which the division of labour has been carried. Each new productive force, insofar as it is not merely a quantitative extension of productive forces already known (for instance, the bringing into cultivation of fresh land), causes a further development of the division of labour.

The division of labour inside a nation leads at first to the separation of industrial and commercial from agricultural labour, and hence to the separation of *town* and *country* and to the conflict of their interests. Its further development leads to the separation of commercial from industrial labour. At the same time through the division of labour inside these various branches there develop various divisions among the individuals co-operating in definite kinds of labour. The relative position of these individual groups is determined by the way work is organised in agriculture, industry and commerce (patriarchalism, slavery, estates, classes). These same conditions are to be seen (given a more developed intercourse) in the relations of different nations to one another.

The various stages of development in the division of labour are just so many different forms of property, i.e., the existing stage in the division of labour determines also the relations of individuals to one another with reference to the material, instrument and product of labour. . . .

In direct contrast to German philosophy which descends from heaven to earth, here it is a matter of ascending from earth to heaven. That is to say, not of setting out from what men say, imagine, conceive, nor from men as narrated, thought of, imagined, conceived, in order to arrive at men in the flesh; but setting out from real, active men, and on the basis of their real life-process demonstrating the development of the ideological reflexes and echoes of this life-process. The phantoms formed in the brains of men are also, necessarily, sublimates of their material lifeprocess, which is empirically verifiable and bound to material premises. Morality, religion, metaphysics, and all the rest of ideology as well as the forms of consciousness corresponding to these, thus no longer retain the semblance of independence. They have no history, no development; but men, developing their material production and their material intercourse, alter, along with this their actual world, also their thinking and the products of their thinking. It is not consciousness that determines life, but life that determines consciousness. For the first manner of approach the starting-point is consciousness taken as the living individual; for the second manner of approach, which conforms to real life, it is the real living individuals themselves, and consciousness is considered solely as *their* consciousness.

This manner of approach is not devoid of premises. It starts out from the real premises and does not abandon them for a moment. Its premises are men, not in any fantastic isolation and fixity, but in their actual, empirically perceptible process of development under definite conditions. As soon as this active life-process is described, history ceases to be a collection of dead facts, as it is with the empiricists (themselves still abstract), or an imagined activity of imagined subjects, as with the idealists.

Where speculation ends, where real life starts, there consequently begins real, positive science, the expounding of the practical activity, of the practical process of development of men. Empty phrases about consciousness end, and real knowledge has to take their place. When the reality is described, a self-sufficient philosophy *[die selbständige Philosophie]* loses its medium of existence. At the best its place can only be taken by a summing-up of the most general results, abstractions which are derived from the observation of the historical development of men. These abstractions in themselves, divorced from real history, have no value whatsoever. They can only serve to facilitate the arrangement of historical material, to indicate the sequence of its separate strata. But they by no means afford a recipe or schema, as does philosophy, for neatly trimming the epochs of history.

20

KARL MARX

From *The Class Struggles in France,* 1848–1850

1850

In a series of articles that appeared in 1850 in Neue Rheinische Zeitung: Politsch-Oekonomische Revue (New Rhenish Gazette: Political-Economic Review), *an obscure and ephemeral monthly review published by the defeated radicals of the Communist League, Marx began*

Karl Marx and Frederick Engels, *Collected Works* (New York: International Publishers, 1978), Vol. 10:47, 54–57.

his postmortem of the failed revolutions of 1848. Here he attempts to interpret the series of defeats as a form of victory, as part of a historical process in which the obsolete forms of an antiquated society are swept away and the makers of a new world are educated for their future tasks. Marx was particularly concerned to show that the revolutionary defeats marked important stages in the progressive achievement of class consciousness among the working classes. The articles were collected under the title The Class Struggles in France, 1848–1850 *and republished as a pamphlet by Engels in 1895.*

With the exception of only a few chapters, every more important part of the annals of the revolution from 1848 to 1849 carries the heading: *Defeat of the Revolution!*

What succumbed in these defeats was not the revolution. It was the pre-revolutionary traditional appendages, results of social relationships which had not yet come to the point of sharp class antagonisms — persons, illusions, conceptions, projects from which the revolutionary party before the February Revolution was not free, from which it could be freed not by the *victory of February,* but only by a series of *defeats.*

In a word: the revolution made progress, forged ahead, not by its immediate tragi-comic achievements, but on the contrary by the creation of a powerful, united counter-revolution, by the creation of an opponent in combat with whom alone the party of insurrection ripened into a really revolutionary party. . . .

Even the memory of the limited aims and motives which drove the bourgeoisie into the February Revolution was extinguished by the proclamation of the republic on the basis of universal suffrage. Instead of only a few factions of the bourgeoisie, all classes of French society were suddenly hurled into the orbit of political power, forced to leave the boxes, the stalls and the gallery and to act in person upon the revolutionary stage! With the constitutional monarchy vanished also the semblance of a state power independently confronting bourgeois society as well as the whole series of subordinate struggles which this semblance of power called forth!

By dictating the republic to the Provisional Government and through the Provisional Government to the whole of France, the proletariat stepped into the foreground forthwith as an independent party, but at the same time challenged the whole of bourgeois France to enter the lists against it. What it won was the terrain for the fight for its revolutionary emancipation, but by no means this emancipation itself. . . .

In common with the bourgeoisie the workers had made the February Revolution, and *alongside* the bourgeoisie they sought to assert their interests, just as they had installed a worker in the Provisional Government itself alongside the bourgeois majority. . . . Just as the workers thought they would be able to emancipate themselves side by side with the bourgeoisie, so they thought they would be able to consummate a proletarian revolution within the national walls of France, side by side with the remaining bourgeois nations. But French relations of production are conditioned by the foreign trade of France, by her position on the world market and the laws thereof; how was France to break them without a European revolutionary war, which would strike back at the despot of the world market, England?

As soon as it has risen up, a class in which the revolutionary interests of society are concentrated finds the content and the material for its revolutionary activity directly in its own situation: foes to be laid low, measures dictated by the needs of the struggle to be taken; the consequences of its own deeds drive it on. It makes no theoretical inquiries into its own task. The French working class had not attained this level; it was still incapable of accomplishing its own revolution.

The development of the industrial proletariat is, in general, conditioned by the development of the industrial bourgeoisie. Only under its rule does the proletariat gain that extensive national existence which can raise its revolution to a national one, and does it itself create the modern means of production, which become just so many means of its revolutionary emancipation. Only its rule tears up the material roots of feudal society and levels the ground on which alone a proletarian revolution is possible. French industry is more developed and the French bourgeoisie more revolutionary than that of the rest of the Continent. But was not the February Revolution levelled directly against the finance aristocracy? This fact proved that the industrial bourgeoisie did not rule France. The industrial bourgeoisie can rule only where modern industry shapes all property relations to suit itself, and industry can win this power only where it has conquered the world market, for national bounds are inadequate for its development. But French industry, to a great extent, maintains its command even of the national market only through a more or less modified system of prohibitive tariffs. While, therefore, the French proletariat, at the moment of a revolution, possesses in Paris real power and influence which spur it on to an effort beyond its means, in the rest of France it is crowded into separate, scattered industrial centres, being almost lost in the superior numbers of peasants and petty bourgeois. The struggle against capital in its developed, modern form, in its decisive aspect, the struggle of the industrial wage-worker against the industrial bourgeois, is in France a partial phenomenon, which after the February days could so much the less supply the national content of the revolution, since the struggle against capital's secondary modes of exploitation, that of the peasant against usury and mortgages or of the petty bourgeois against the whole-sale dealer, banker and manufacturer, in a word, against bankruptcy, was still hidden in the general uprising against the finance aristocracy. Nothing is more understandable, then, than that the Paris proletariat sought to assert its own interests *side by side* with the interests of the bourgeoisie, instead of enforcing them as the revolutionary interests of society itself, that it let the *red* flag be dipped before the *tricolour.* The French workers could not take a step forward, could not touch a hair of the bourgeois order, until the course of the revolution had aroused the mass of the nation, the peasants and petty bourgeois, standing between the proletariat and the bourgeoisie, against this order, against the rule of capital, and had forced them to attach themselves to the proletarians as their protagonists. The workers could buy this victory only through the tremendous defeat in June.

21

KARL MARX

From *The Eighteenth Brumaire of Louis Bonaparte*

1852

In 1852, Marx was faced with the difficult task of demonstrating that the theory of history enunciated in the Communist Manifesto *could explain the sequence of events in France that led to the coup d'état of December 2, 1851, in which the elected French president, Napoleon's nephew Louis Bonaparte, seized dictatorial power. In a pamphlet titled* The Eighteenth Brumaire of Louis Bonaparte, *Marx tried to explain to himself as well as others how it was possible for bourgeois society to disavow its class structure after the revelations of the revolutionary*

Karl Marx and Frederick Engels, *Collected Works* (New York: International Publishers, 1979), Vol. 11:103–7.

year of 1848 and veil its realities under a caricature-like parody of the French Revolution of 1789–1799. His reconsideration of the relationships between appearance and reality and past and present in the making of historical events produced some of his most striking perceptions about the nature of historical development. The Eighteenth Brumaire was the date, according to the new calendar introduced in the French Revolution (November 9, 1799), on which Napoleon I had concentrated supreme power in his own hands.

Hegel remarks somewhere that all facts and personages of great importance in world history occur, as it were, twice. He forgot to add: the first time as tragedy, the second as farce. Caussidière for Danton, Louis Blanc for Robespierre, the Montagne of 1848 to 1851[1] for the Montagne of 1793 to 1795, the Nephew for the Uncle. And the same caricature occurs in the circumstances attending the second edition of the eighteenth Brumaire!

Men make their own history, but they do not make it just as they please; they do not make it under circumstances chosen by themselves, but under circumstances directly encountered, given and transmitted from the past. The tradition of all the dead generations weighs like a nightmare on the brain of the living. And just when they seem engaged in revolutionising themselves and things, in creating something that has never yet existed, precisely in such periods of revolutionary crisis they anxiously conjure up the spirits of the past to their service and borrow from them names, battle-cries and costumes in order to present the new scene of world history in this time-honoured disguise and this borrowed language. Thus Luther donned the mask of the Apostle Paul, the revolution of 1789 to 1814 draped itself alternately as the Roman Republic and the Roman Empire, and the revolution of 1848 knew nothing better to do than to parody, now 1789, now the revolutionary tradition of 1793 to 1795. In like manner a beginner who has learnt a new language always translates it back into his mother tongue, but he has assimilated the spirit of the new language and can freely express himself in it only when

---

[1]Marc Caussidiere (1808–1861) and Louis Blanc (1811–1882) were radical social democrats who played important roles in the regime instituted by the February 1848 revolution. Georges Danton (1759–1794) and Maximilien Robespierre (1758–1794) were political leaders during the radical phase (1793) of the French Revolution. The Montagne (the Mountain) was the name given to the bloc of Robespierre's social democratic supporters who sat in the National Assembly during the radical phase of the Revolution.

he finds his way in it without recalling the old and forgets his native tongue in the use of the new.

Consideration of this world-historical necromancy reveals at once a salient difference. Camille Desmoulins, Danton, Robespierre, Saint-Just,[2] Napoleon, the heroes as well as the parties and the masses of the old French Revolution, performed the task of their time in Roman costume and with Roman phrases, the task of unchaining and setting up modern *bourgeois* society. The first ones knocked the feudal basis to pieces and mowed off the feudal heads which had grown on it. The other created inside France the conditions under which free competition could first be developed, parcelled landed property exploited and the unchained industrial productive forces of the nation employed; and beyond the French borders he everywhere swept the feudal institutions away, so far as was necessary to furnish bourgeois society in France with a suitable up-to-date environment on the European Continent. The new social formation once established, the antediluvian Colossi disappeared and with them resurrected Romanity — the Brutuses, Gracchi, Publicolas, the tribunes, the senators, and Caesar himself. Bourgeois society in its sober reality had begotten its true interpreters and mouthpieces in the Says, Cousins, Royer-Collards, Benjamin Constants and Guizots;[3] its real commanders sat behind the counter, and the hogheaded Louis XVIII was its political chief. Wholly absorbed in the production of wealth and in peaceful competitive struggle, it no longer comprehended that ghosts from the days of Rome had watched over its cradle. But unheroic as bourgeois society is, it nevertheless took heroism, sacrifice, terror, civil war and battles of peoples to bring it into being. And in the classically austere traditions of the Roman Republic its gladiators found the ideals and the art forms, the self-deceptions that they needed in order to conceal from themselves the bourgeois limitations of the content of their struggles and to maintain their passion on the high plane of great historical tragedy. Similarly, at another stage of development, a century earlier, Cromwell and the English people had borrowed speech, passions and illusions from the Old Testament for their bourgeois revolution. When

[2]Camille Desmoulins (1760–1794), an associate of Danton, and Louis-Antoine Saint-Just (1767–1794), an associate of Robespierre, were radical leaders during the French Revolution.
[3]Jean-Baptiste Say (1767–1832), an economist; Victor Cousin (1792–1867), a philosopher; Pierre-Paul Royer-Collard (1763–1845), a politician and political theorist; Benjamin Constant (1767–1830), a writer and politician; and François Guizot (1787–1874), a historian and politician, were all important spokesmen for the French tradition of bourgeois liberalism that emerged during the 1820s and triumphed in the revolution of 1830.

the real aim had been achieved, when the bourgeois transformation of English society had been accomplished, Locke supplanted Habakkuk.[4]

Thus the resurrection of the dead in those revolutions served the purpose of glorifying the new struggles, not of parodying the old; of magnifying the given task in imagination, not of fleeing from its solution in reality; of finding once more the spirit of revolution, not of making its ghost walk about again. . . .

The social revolution of the nineteenth century cannot draw its poetry from the past, but only from the future. It cannot begin with itself before it has stripped off all superstition about the past. Earlier revolutions required recollections of past world history in order to dull themselves to their own content. In order to arrive at its own content, the revolution of the nineteenth century must let the dead bury their dead. There the words went beyond the content; here the content goes beyond the words. . . .

Bourgeois revolutions, like those of the eighteenth century, storm swiftly from success to success, their dramatic effects outdo each other, men and things seem set in sparkling brilliants, ecstasy is the everyday spirit, but they are short-lived, soon they have attained their zenith, and a long crapulent depression seizes society before it learns soberly to assimilate the results of its storm-and-stress period. On the other hand, proletarian revolutions, like those of the nineteenth century, criticise themselves constantly, interrupt themselves continually in their own course, come back to the apparently accomplished in order to begin it afresh, deride with unmerciful thoroughness the inadequacies, weaknesses and paltrinesses of their first attempts, seem to throw down their adversary only in order that he may draw new strength from the earth and rise again, more gigantic, before them, and recoil again and again from the indefinite prodigiousness of their own aims, until a situation has been created which makes all turning back impossible, and the conditions themselves cry out:

Hic Rhodus, hic salta!
Here is the rose, here dance![5]

---

[4] Habakkuk is an Old Testament prophet.
[5] The Latin saying *"Hic Rhodus, hic salta"* (Here is Rhodes, leap here) might be idiomatically translated as "Don't talk about feats you may have accomplished in the past. Show us what you can do here and now!" It is taken from one of Aesop's fables in which a braggart is called on his claims that he made astounding leaps over the colossi on the Greek island of Rhodes. The second saying is a paraphrase of the first (the Greek name "Rhodes" can also mean "rose") and was familiar to Marx from its usage in Hegel's introduction to his *Philosophy of Right* (1821).

22

KARL MARX

From *Inaugural Address of the Working Men's International Association*

October 1864

In the charter statement of the Working Men's International Association (later known as the First International) published in October 1864, Marx reviews the disillusioning collapse of the revolutionary working-class movement after 1848 and reiterates his claims that the appearance of expansive prosperity during the 1850s hid the stark realities of class conflict and impending crisis. The attempt to revive the movement for an international proletarian revolution collapsed very rapidly due to internecine squabbles. The headquarters of the association was transferred to New York in 1872, and the association was dissolved in 1874.

In all countries of Europe it has now become a truth demonstrable to every unprejudiced mind, and only denied by those, whose interest it is to hedge other people in a fool's paradise, that no improvement of machinery, no appliance of science to production, no contrivances of communication, no new colonies, no emigration, no opening of markets, no free trade, nor all these things put together, will do away with the miseries of the industrious masses; but that, on the present false base, every fresh development of the productive powers of labour must tend to deepen social contrasts and point social antagonisms. Death of starvation rose almost to the rank of an institution, during this intoxicating epoch of economical progress, in the metropolis of the British Empire. That epoch is marked in the annals of the world by the quickened return, the widening compass, and the deadlier effects of the social pest called a commercial and industrial crisis.

After the failure of the Revolutions of 1848, all party organisations and party journals of the working classes were, on the Continent, crushed by the iron hand of force, the most advanced sons of labour fled

Karl Marx and Frederick Engels, *Collected Works* (New York: International Publishers, 1985), Vol. 20:9–10.

in despair to the Transatlantic Republic,[1] and the short-lived dreams of emancipation vanished before an epoch of industrial fever, moral marasme,[2] and political reaction. The defeat of the Continental working classes, partly owed to the diplomacy of the English Government, acting then as now in fraternal solidarity with the Cabinet of St. Petersburg, soon spread its contagious effects to this side of the Channel. While the rout of their Continental brethren unmanned the English working classes, and broke their faith in their own cause, it restored to the landlord and the moneylord their somewhat shaken confidence. They insolently withdrew concessions already advertised. The discoveries of new goldlands[3] led to an immense exodus, leaving an irreparable void in the ranks of the British proletariat. Others of its formerly active members were caught by the temporary bribe of greater work and wages, and turned into "political blacks."[4] All the efforts made at keeping up, or remodeling, the Chartist Movement, failed signally; the press organs of the working class died one by one of the apathy of the masses, and, in point of fact, never before seemed the English working class so thoroughly reconciled to a state of political nullity. If, then, there had been no solidarity of action between the British and the Continental working classes, there was, at all events, a solidarity of defeat.

[1] United States of America.

[2] "Marasme" seems to be an idiosyncratic form of "marasmus," which means "wasting away."

[3] Marx appears to be referring to the lure of the California gold rush as one of the factors in encouraging labor emigration from Europe after 1848.

[4] Marx may have meant "black legs," an English term of opprobrium for workers who betray class solidarity in a strike by continuing to work. The term could be rephrased as "political scabs."

23

KARL MARX

Afterword to the Second German Edition of Capital

1873

As Marx turned, after the revolutionary failures of 1848–1850, to a more intensive study of the inner structures of the capitalist mode of production, he found himself increasingly in need of a philosophical method that

Karl Marx and Frederick Engels, *Collected Works* (New York: International Publishers, 1996), Vol. 35:19–20.

would reveal the hidden contradictions and revolutionary tendencies within the confusing appearances produced by a merely empirical description of a triumphant bourgeois society. In this afterword to a German edition of Capital *published in 1873, Marx consciously defends his use of a demystified Hegelian dialectic in revealing both the positive and negative dimensions, and thus the dynamic historical tendencies, of capitalist production and bourgeois society.*

Of course the method of presentation must differ in form from that of inquiry. The latter has to appropriate the material in detail, to analyse its different forms of development, to trace out their inner connection. Only after this work is done, can the actual movement be adequately described. If this is done successfully, if the life of the subject-matter is ideally reflected as in a mirror, then it may appear as if we had before us a mere a priori construction.

My dialectic method is not only different from the Hegelian, but is its direct opposite. To Hegel, the life process of the human brain, i.e., the process of thinking, which, under the name of "the Idea," he even transforms into an independent subject, is the demiurgos of the real world, and the real world is only the external, phenomenal form of "the Idea." With me, on the contrary, the ideal is nothing else than the material world reflected by the human mind, and translated into forms of thought.

The mystifying side of Hegelian dialectic I criticised nearly thirty years ago, at a time when it was still the fashion. But just as I was working at the first volume of *Das Kapital,* it was the good pleasure of the peevish, arrogant, mediocre Ἐπίγονοι[1] who now talk large in cultured Germany, to treat Hegel in same way as the brave Moses Mendelssohn in Lessing's time treated Spinoza, i.e., as a "dead dog."[2] I therefore openly avowed myself the pupil of that mighty thinker, and even here and there, in the chapter on the theory of value, coquetted with the modes of expression peculiar to him. The mystification which dialectic suffers in Hegel's hands, by no means prevents him from being the first to present its general form of working in a comprehensive and con-

---

[1] "Epigones," or the less distinguished successors of an illustrious generation.

[2] Marx appears to be referring to a statement reportedly made by the German philosopher and literary critic G. E. Lessing (1729–1781) to a friend in 1780 that many people no longer took the Dutch philosopher Baruch Spinoza (1632–1677) seriously but treated him like a dead dog. Why Marx tied Lessing's comments particularly to the Jewish philosopher Moses Mendelssohn (1729–1786) is not clear.

scious manner. With him it is standing on its head. It must be turned right side up again, if you would discover the rational kernel within the mystical shell.

In its mystified form, dialectic became the fashion in Germany, because it seemed to transfigure and to glorify the existing state of things. In its rational form it is a scandal and abomination to bourgeoisdom and its doctrinaire professors, because it includes in its comprehension and affirmative recognition of the existing state of things, at the same time also, the recognition of the negation of that state, of its inevitable breaking up; because it regards every historically developed social form as in fluid movement, and therefore takes into account its transient nature not less than its momentary existence; because it lets nothing impose upon it, and is in its essence critical and revolutionary.

The contradictions inherent in the movement of capitalist society impress themselves upon the practical bourgeois most strikingly in the changes of the periodic cycle, through which modern industry runs, and whose crowning point is the universal crisis. That crisis is once again approaching, although as yet but in its preliminary stage; and by the universality of its theatre and the intensity of its action it will drum dialectics even into the heads of the mushroom-upstarts of the new, holy Prusso-German empire.

24

KARL MARX

The Fetishism of Commodities and the
Secret Thereof

1867

In this famous chapter from the first volume of Capital, *published in 1867, Marx returns to many of the themes that informed his analysis of the relationship between producers and their products under capitalism in 1844–1845. The production of commodities for exchange in the capitalist system hides the social and historical character of labor from the producers. Instead of recognizing the social character of their labor in*

Karl Marx and Frederick Engels, *Collected Works* (New York: International Publishers, 1996), Vol. 35:81–94.

their products, the producers relate to their products as natural objects. Human products have become objective "things" that move according to their own laws and control the activity of their producers. Once again, Marx turns to religion as an analogy for the alienation of human beings from the products of their own activity and a mystification of the actual life processes of society, and he uses historical comparisons to unveil the "unnatural" or historically contingent character of the capitalist system of production and exchange.

A commodity appears, at first sight, a very trivial thing, and easily understood. Its analysis shows that it is, in reality, a very queer thing, abounding in metaphysical subtleties and theological niceties. So far as it is a value in use, there is nothing mysterious about it, whether we consider it from the point of view that by its properties it is capable of satisfying human wants, or from the point that those properties are the product of human labour. It is as clear as noon-day, that man, by his industry, changes the forms of the materials furnished by Nature, in such a way as to make them useful to him. The form of wood, for instance, is altered, by making a table out of it. Yet, for all that, the table continues to be that common, every-day thing, wood. But, so soon as it steps forth as a commodity, it is changed into something transcendent. It not only stands with its feet on the ground, but, in relation to all other commodities, it stands on its head, and evolves out of its wooden brain grotesque ideas, far more wonderful than "table-turning" ever was.

The mystical character of commodities does not originate, therefore, in their use value. Just as little does it proceed from the nature of the determining factors of value. For, in the first place, however varied the useful kinds of labour, or productive activities, may be, it is a physiological fact, that they are functions of the human organism, and that each such function, whatever may be its nature or form, is essentially the expenditure of human brain, nerves, muscles, &c. Secondly, with regard to that which forms the ground-work for the quantitative determination of value, namely, the duration of that expenditure, or the quantity of labour, it is quite clear that there is a palpable difference between its quantity and quality. In all states of society, the labour time that it costs to produce the means of subsistence, must necessarily be an object of interest to mankind, though not of equal interest in different stages of development. And lastly, from the moment that men in any way work for one another, their labour assumes a social form.

Whence, then, arises the enigmatical character of the product of labour, so soon as it assumes the form of commodities? Clearly from this form itself. The equality of all sorts of human labour is expressed objectively by their products all being equally values; the measure of the expenditure of labour power by the duration of that expenditure, takes the form of the quantity of value of the products of labour; and finally, the mutual relations of the producers, within which the social character of their labour affirms itself, take the form of a social relation between the products.

A commodity is therefore a mysterious thing, simply because in it the social character of men's labour appears to them as an objective character stamped upon the product of that labour; because the relation of the producers to the sum total of their own labour is presented to them as a social relation, existing not between themselves, but between the products of their labour. This is the reason why the products of labour become commodities, social things whose qualities are at the same time perceptible and imperceptible by the senses. In the same way the light from an object is perceived by us not as the subjective excitation of our optic nerve, but as the objective form of something outside the eye itself. But, in the act of seeing, there is at all events, an actual passage of light from one thing to another, from the external object to the eye. There is a physical relation between physical things. But it is different with commodities. There, the existence of the things *quâ* commodities, and the value relation between the products of labour which stamps them as commodities, have absolutely no connection with their physical properties and with the material relations arising therefrom. There it is a definite social relation between men, that assumes, in their eyes, the fantastic form of a relation between things. In order, therefore, to find an analogy, we must have recourse to the mist-enveloped regions of the religious world. In that world the productions of the human brain appear as independent beings endowed with life, and entering into relation both with one another and the human race. So it is in the world of commodities with the products of men's hands. This I call the Fetishism which attaches itself to the products of labour, so soon as they are produced as commodities, and which is therefore inseparable from the production of commodities.

This Fetishism of commodities has its origin, as the foregoing analysis has already shown, in the peculiar social character of the labour that produces them.

As a general rule, articles of utility become commodities, only because they are products of the labour of private individuals or groups of individuals who carry on their work independently of each other. The sum total of the labour of all these private individuals forms the aggregate labour of society. Since the producers do not come into social contact with each other until they exchange their products, the specific social character of each producer's labour does not show itself except in the act of exchange. In other words, the labour of the individual asserts itself as a part of the labour of society, only by means of the relations which the act of exchange establishes directly between the products, and indirectly, through them, between the producers. To the latter, therefore, the relations connecting the labour of one individual with that of the rest appear, not as direct social relations between individuals at work, but as what they really are, material relations between persons and social relations between things. It is only by being exchanged that the products of labour acquire, as values, one uniform social status, distinct from their varied forms of existence as objects of utility. This division of a product into a useful thing and a value becomes practically important, only when exchange has acquired such an extension that useful articles are produced for the purpose of being exchanged, and their character as values has therefore to be taken into account, before-hand, during production. From this moment the labour of the individual producer acquires socially a twofold character. On the one hand, it must, as a definite useful kind of labour, satisfy a definite social want, and thus hold its place as part and parcel of the collective labour of all, as a branch of a social division of labour that has sprung up spontaneously. On the other hand, it can satisfy the manifold wants of the individual producer himself, only in so far as the mutual exchangeability of all kinds of useful private labour is an established social fact, and therefore the private useful labour of each producer ranks on an equality with that of all others. The equalisation of the most different kinds of labour can be the result only of an abstraction from their inequalities, or of reducing them to their common denominator, viz., expenditure of human labour power or human labour in the abstract. The twofold social character of the labour of the individual appears to him, when reflected in his brain, only under those forms which are impressed upon that labour in every-day practice by the exchange of products. In this way, the character that his own labour possesses of being socially useful takes the form of the condition, that the product must be not only useful, but useful for others, and the social character that his particular labour has of being the equal of all other particular kinds of labour, takes the form that all the physically different articles that are the products of labour, have one common quality, viz., that of having value.

Hence, when we bring the products of our labour into relation with each other as values, it is not because we see in these articles the material receptacles of homogeneous human labour. Quite the contrary: whenever, by an exchange, we equate as values our different products, by that very act, we also equate, as human labour, the different kinds of labour expended upon them. We are not aware of this, nevertheless we do it. Value, therefore, does not stalk about with a label describing what it is. It is value, rather, that converts every product into a social hieroglyphic. Later on, we try to decipher the hieroglyphic, to get behind the secret of our own social products; for to stamp an object of utility as a value, is just as much a social product as language. The recent scientific discovery, that the products of labour, so far as they are values, are but material expressions of the human labour spent in their production, marks, indeed, an epoch in the history of the development of the human race, but, by no means, dissipates the mist through which the social character of labour appears to us to be an objective character of the products themselves. The fact, that in the particular form of production with which we are dealing, viz., the production of commodities, the specific social character of private labour carried on independently, consists in the equality of every kind of that labour, by virtue of its being human labour, which character, therefore, assumes in the product the form of value—this fact appears to the producers, notwithstanding the discovery above referred to, to be just as real and final, as the fact, that, after the discovery by science of the component gases of air, the atmosphere itself remained unaltered.

What, first of all, practically concerns producers when they make an exchange, is the question, how much of some other product they get for their own? in what proportions the products are exchangeable? When these proportions have, by custom, attained a certain stability, they appear to result from the nature of the products, so that, for instance, one ton of iron and two ounces of gold appear as naturally to be of equal value as a pound of gold and a pound of iron in spite of their different physical and chemical qualities appear to be of equal weight. The character of having value, when once impressed upon products, obtains fixity only by reason of their acting and reacting upon each other as quantities of value. These quantities vary continually, independently of the will, foresight and action of the producers. To them, their own social action takes the form of the action of objects, which rule the producers instead of being ruled by them. It requires a fully developed production of commodities before, from accumulated experience alone, the scientific conviction springs up, that all the different kinds of private labour, which are carried on independently of each other, and yet as spontaneously developed branches of the social division of labour, are continually being reduced to the quantitative proportions in which society requires them. And why?

Because, in the midst of all the accidental and ever fluctuating exchange relations between the products, the labour time socially necessary for their production forcibly asserts itself like an overriding law of Nature. The law of gravity thus asserts itself when a house falls about our ears. The determination of the magnitude of value by labour time is therefore a secret, hidden under the apparent fluctuations in the relative values of commodities. Its discovery, while removing all appearance of mere accidentality from the determination of the magnitude of the values of products, yet in no way alters the mode in which that determination takes place.

Man's reflections on the forms of social life, and consequently, also, his scientific analysis of those forms, take a course directly opposite to that of their actual historical development. He begins, *post festum,* * with the results of the process of development ready to hand before him. The characters that stamp products as commodities, and whose establishment is a necessary preliminary to the circulation of commodities, have already acquired the stability of natural, self-understood forms of social life, before man seeks to decipher, not their historical character, for in his eyes they are immutable, but their meaning. Consequently it was the analysis of the prices of commodities that alone led to the determination of the magnitude of value, and it was the common expression of all commodities in money that alone led to the establishment of their characters as values. It is, however, just this ultimate money form of the world of commodities that actually conceals, instead of disclosing, the social character of private labour, and the social relations between the individual producers. When I state that coats or boots stand in a relation to linen, because it is the universal incarnation of abstract human labour, the absurdity of the statement is self-evident. Nevertheless, when the producers of coats and boots compare those articles with linen, or, what is the same thing, with gold or silver, as the universal equivalent, they express the relation between their own private labour and the collective labour of society in the same absurd form.

The categories of bourgeois economy consist of such like forms. They are forms of thought expressing with social validity the conditions and relations of a definite, historically determined mode of production,

---

* After the feast, i.e., after the events reflected on have taken place.

viz., the production of commodities. The whole mystery of commodities, all the magic and necromancy that surrounds the products of labour as long as they take the form of commodities, vanishes therefore, so soon as we come to other forms of production.

Since Robinson Crusoe's experiences are a favourite theme with political economists, let us take a look at him on his island. Moderate though he be, yet some few wants he has to satisfy, and must therefore do a little useful work of various sorts, such as making tools and furniture, taming goats, fishing and hunting. Of his prayers and the like we take no account, since they are a source of pleasure to him, and he looks upon them as so much recreation. In spite of the variety of his work, he knows that his labour, whatever its form, is but the activity of one and the same Robinson, and consequently, that it consists of nothing but different modes of human labour. Necessity itself compels him to apportion his time accurately between his different kinds of work. Whether one kind occupies a greater space in his general activity than another, depends on the difficulties, greater or less as the case may be, to be overcome in attaining the useful effect aimed at. This our friend Robinson soon learns by experience, and having rescued a watch, ledger, and pen and ink from the wreck, commences, like a true-born Briton, to keep a set of books. His stock-book contains a list of the objects of utility that belong to him, of the operations necessary for their production; and lastly, of the labour time that definite quantities of those objects have, on an average, cost him. All the relations between Robinson and the objects that form this wealth of his own creation, are here so simple and clear as to be intelligible without exertion, even to Mr. Sedley Taylor.[1] And yet those relations contain all that is essential to the determination of value.

Let us now transport ourselves from Robinson's island bathed in light to the European Middle Ages shrouded in darkness. Here, instead of the independent man, we find everyone dependent, serfs and lords, vassals and suzerains, laymen and clergy. Personal dependence here characterises the social relations of production just as much as it does the other spheres of life organised on the basis of that production. But for the very reason that personal dependence forms the groundwork of society, there is no necessity for labour and its products to assume a fantastic form different from their reality. They take the shape, in the transactions of society, of services in kind and payments in kind. Here

---

[1] A British academic who became involved in a brief controversy in late 1883 with Marx's daughter Eleanor after Marx's death, and was punished in the English translation (1887) by being inserted at this point to replace Marx's own example of a thickheaded popular economist, the German "Mr. M. Wirth."

the particular and natural form of labour, and not, as in a society based on production of commodities, its general abstract form is the immediate social form of labour. Compulsory labour is just as properly measured by time, as commodity-producing labour; but every serf knows that what he expends in the service of his lord, is a definite quantity of his own personal labour power. The tithe to be rendered to the priest is more matter of fact than his blessing. No matter, then, what we may think of the parts played by the different classes of people themselves in this society, the social relations between individuals in the performance of their labour, appear at all events as their own mutual personal relations, and are not disguised under the shape of social relations between the products of labour.

For an example of labour in common or directly associated labour, we have no occasion to go back to that spontaneously developed form which we find on the threshold of the history of all civilised races. We have one close at hand in the patriarchal industries of a peasant family, that produces corn, cattle, yarn, linen, and clothing for home use. These different articles are, as regards the family, so many products of its labour, but as between themselves, they are not commodities. The different kinds of labour, such as tillage, cattle tending, spinning, weaving and making clothes, which result in the various products, are in themselves, and such as they are, direct social functions, because functions of the family, which, just as much as a society based on the production of commodities, possesses a spontaneously developed system of division of labour. The distribution of the work within the family, and the regulation of the labour time of the several members, depend as well upon differences of age and sex as upon natural conditions varying with the seasons. The labour power of each individual, by its very nature, operates in this case merely as a definite portion of the whole labour power of the family, and therefore, the measure of the expenditure of individual labour power by its duration, appears here by its very nature as a social character of their labour.

Let us now picture to ourselves, by way of change, a community of free individuals, carrying on their work with the means of production in common, in which the labour power of all the different individuals is consciously applied as the combined labour power of the community. All the characteristics of Robinson's labour are here repeated, but with this difference, that they are social, instead of individual. Everything produced by him was exclusively the result of his own personal labour, and therefore simply an object of use for himself. The total product of our community is a social product. One portion serves as fresh means of production and remains social. But another portion is consumed by the members as means of subsistence. A distribution of this portion amongst them is consequently necessary. The mode of this distribution will vary with the productive organisation of the community, and the degree of historical development attained by the producers. We will assume, but merely for the sake of a parallel with the production of commodities, that the share of each individual producer in the means of subsistence is determined by his labour time. Labour time would, in that case, play a double part. Its apportionment in accordance with a definite social plan maintains the proper proportion between the different kinds of work to be done and the various wants of the community. On the other hand, it also serves as a measure of the portion of the common labour borne by each individual, and of his share in the part of the total product destined for individual consumption. The social relations of the individual producers, with regard both to their labour and to its products, are in this case perfectly simple and intelligible, and that with regard not only to production but also to distribution.

The religious world is but the reflex of the real world. And for a society based upon the production of commodities, in which the producers in general enter into social relations with one another by treating their products as commodities and values, whereby they reduce their individual private labour to the standard of homogeneous human labour—for such a society, Christianity with its *cultus* of abstract man, more especially in its bourgeois developments, Protestantism, Deism, &c., is the most fitting form of religion. In the ancient Asiatic and other ancient modes of production, we find that the conversion of products into commodities, and therefore the conversion of men into producers of commodities, holds a subordinate place, which, however, increases in importance as the primitive communities approach nearer and nearer to their dissolution. Trading nations, properly so called, exist in the ancient world only in its interstices, like the gods of Epicurus in the Intermundia,[2] or like Jews in the pores of Polish society. Those ancient social organisms of production are, as compared with bourgeois society, extremely simple and transparent. But they are founded either on the immature development of man individually, who has not yet severed the umbilical cord that unites him with his fellowmen in a primitive tribal community, or upon direct relations of subjection. They can arise and exist only when the development of the productive power of labour has not risen beyond a low stage, and when, therefore, the social relations within the sphere

[2] The space between worlds.

of material life, between man and man, and between man and Nature, are correspondingly narrow. This narrowness is reflected in the ancient worship of Nature, and in the other elements of the popular religions. The religious reflex of the real world can, in any case, only then finally vanish, when the practical relations of every-day life offer to man none but perfectly intelligible and reasonable relations with regard to his fellowmen and to Nature.

The life-process of society, which is based on the process of material production, does not strip off its mystical veil until it is treated as production by freely associated men, and is consciously regulated by them in accordance with a settled plan. This, however, demands for society a certain material ground-work or set of conditions of existence which in their turn are the spontaneous product of a long and painful process of development.

Political economy has indeed analysed, however incompletely, value and its magnitude, and has discovered what lies beneath these forms. But it has never once asked the question why labour is represented by the value of its product and labour time by the magnitude of that value. These formulæ, which bear it stamped upon them in unmistakable letters that they belong to a state of society, in which the process of production has the mastery over man, instead of being controlled by him, such formulæ appear to the bourgeois intellect to be as much a self-evident necessity imposed by Nature as productive labour itself. Hence forms of social production that preceded the bourgeois form, are treated by the bourgeoisie in much the same way as the Fathers of the Church treated pre-Christian religions.

To what extent some economists are misled by the Fetishism inherent in commodities, or by the objective appearance of the social characteristics of labour, is shown, amongst other ways, by the dull and tedious quarrel over the part played by Nature in the formation of exchange value. Since exchange value is a definite social manner of expressing the amount of labour bestowed upon an object, Nature has no more to do with it, than it has in fixing the course of exchange.

The mode of production in which the product takes the form of a commodity, or is produced directly for exchange, is the most general and most embryonic form of bourgeois production. It therefore makes its appearance at an early date in history, though not in the same predominating and characteristic manner as now-a-days. Hence its Fetish character is comparatively easy to be seen through. But when we come to more concrete forms, even this appearance of simplicity vanishes. Whence arose the illusions of the monetary system? To it gold and silver, when serving as money, did not represent a social relation between producers, but were natural objects with strange social properties. And modern economy, which looks down with such disdain on the monetary system, does not its superstition come out as clear as noon-day, whenever it treats of capital? How long is it since economy discarded the physiocratic illusion, that rents grow out of the soil and not out of society?

But not to anticipate, we will content ourselves with yet another example relating to the commodity form. Could commodities themselves speak, they would say: Our use value may be a thing that interests men. It is no part of us as objects. What, however, does belong to us as objects, is our value. Our natural intercourse as commodities proves it. In the eyes of each other we are nothing but exchange values. Now listen how those commodities speak through the mouth of the economist.

"Value"— (i.e., exchange value) "is a property of things, riches"— (i.e., use value) "of man. Value, in this sense, necessarily implies exchanges, riches do not."

"Riches" (use value) "are the attribute of men, value is the attribute of commodities. A man or a community is rich, a pearl or a diamond is valuable. . . ." A pearl or a diamond is valuable as a pearl or a diamond.[3]

So far no chemist has ever discovered exchange value either in a pearl or a diamond. The economic discoverers of this chemical element, who by-the-bye lay special claim to critical acumen, find however that the use value of objects belongs to them independently of their material properties, while their value, on the other hand, forms a part of them as objects. What confirms them in this view, is the peculiar circumstance that the use value of objects is realised without exchange, by means of a direct relation between the objects and man, while, on the other hand, their value is realised only by exchange, that is, by means of a social process. Who fails here to call to mind our good friend, Dogberry, who informs neighbour Seacoal, that, "To be a well-favoured man is the gift of fortune; but reading and writing comes by Nature."[4]

---

[3] Marx's quotations are taken from an anonymous book on political economy published in 1821, and a work by Samuel Bailey (1791–1870) published in 1837.

[4] The quotations are from William Shakespeare's *Much Ado about Nothing,* Act III, Scene 3.

25

FREDERICK ENGELS

Speech at Karl Marx's Funeral

March 1883

Engels delivered this speech in English at Marx's graveside in Highgate Cemetery, London, three days after Marx's death on March 14, 1883. The eulogy revealed Engels's lifelong conviction that the Marxian theory of history and revolution was a scientific discovery, analogous to Darwin's theory of evolution. The speech was published in German translation in the German socialist newspaper Der Sozialdemokrat. *This version is thus a retranslation of the German into English.*

On the 14th of March, at a quarter to three in the afternoon, the greatest living thinker ceased to think. He had been left alone for scarcely two minutes, and when we came back we found him in his armchair, peacefully gone to sleep—but forever.

An immeasurable loss has been sustained both by the militant proletariat of Europe and America, and by historical science, in the death of this man. The gap that has been left by the departure of this mighty spirit will soon enough make itself felt.

Just as Darwin discovered the law of development of organic nature, so Marx discovered the law of development of human history: the simple fact, hitherto concealed by an overgrowth of ideology, that mankind must first of all eat, drink, have shelter and clothing, before it can pursue politics, science, art, religion, etc.; that therefore the production of the immediate material means of subsistence and consequently the degree of economic development attained by a given people or during a given epoch form the foundation upon which the state institutions, the legal conceptions, art, and even the ideas on religion, of the people concerned have been evolved, and in the light of which they must, therefore, be explained, instead of *vice versa,* as had hitherto been the case.

But that is not all. Marx also discovered the special law of motion governing the present-day capitalist mode of production and the bourgeois society that this mode of production has created. The discovery

Karl Marx and Frederick Engels, *Collected Works* (New York: International Publishers, 1989), Vol. 24:467–69.

of surplus value suddenly threw light on the problem, in trying to solve which all previous investigations, of both bourgeois economists and socialist critics, had been groping in the dark.

Two such discoveries would be enough for one lifetime. Happy the man to whom it is granted to make even one such discovery. But in every single field which Marx investigated—and he investigated very many fields, none of them superficially—in every field, even in that of mathematics, he made independent discoveries.

Such was the man of science. But this was not even half the man. Science was for Marx a historically dynamic, revolutionary force. However great the joy with which he welcomed a new discovery in some theoretical science whose practical application perhaps it was as yet quite impossible to envisage, he experienced quite another kind of joy when the discovery involved immediate revolutionary changes in industry and in historical development in general. For example, he followed closely the development of the discoveries made in the field of electricity and recently those of Marcel Deprez.

For Marx was before all else a revolutionist. His real mission in life was to contribute, in one way or another, to the overthrow of capitalist society and of the state institutions which it had brought into being, to contribute to the liberation of the modern proletariat, which *he* was the first to make conscious of its own position and its needs, conscious of the conditions of its emancipation. Fighting was his element. And he fought with a passion, a tenacity and a success such as few could rival. His work on the first *Rheinische Zeitung* (1842), the Paris *Vorwärts!* (1844), *Brüsseler Deutsche Zeitung* (1847), the *Neue Rheinische Zeitung* (1848–49), the *New-York Tribune* (1852–61), and in addition to these a host of militant pamphlets, work in organisations in Paris, Brussels and London, and finally, crowning all, the formation of the great International Working Men's Association—this was indeed an achievement of which its founder might well have been proud even if he had done nothing else.

And, consequently, Marx was the best-hated and most calumniated man of his time. Governments, both absolutist and republican, deported him from their territories. Bourgeois, whether conservative or ultrademocratic, vied with one another in heaping slanders upon him. All this he brushed aside as though it were cobweb, ignoring it, answering only when extreme necessity compelled him. And he died beloved, revered and mourned by millions of revolutionary fellow-workers—from the mines of Siberia to California, in all parts of Europe and America—and I make bold to say that though he may have had many opponents he had hardly one personal enemy.

His name will endure through the ages, and so also will his work!

Chronology for the Historical Contexts
of the *Manifesto*
(1765–1895)

1765   The invention of the spinning jenny by James Hargreaves inaugurated a period of technological innovation that would transform the production of textiles into a mechanized, large-scale modern industry by the time of Marx's birth. Textile manufacture in turn became the leading sector in the general transformation of first the British and then the European economy by what came to be called the Industrial Revolution.

1775–
1783   The American War of Independence.

1776   The Declaration of Independence is adopted by the Continental Congress in Philadelphia.

1789   The French Revolution begins. The calling of a meeting of the Estates General in May leads to the formation of the National Assembly in June. On August 4, feudal rights and privileges are abolished. On August 27, the Assembly approves the Declaration of the Rights of Man.

1792   The monarchy is abolished in France, and a republic is declared. Louis XVI is put on trial and eventually executed in January 1793.

French Revolutionary armies occupy the left bank of the Rhine, including Trier. Trier is eventually incorporated into the French state.

1793–
1794   Radical phase of the French Revolution: Reign of Terror and civil war within France; general war against the allied European powers that do not recognize the legitimacy of the new French regime.

1799   Napoleon Bonaparte begins his authoritarian rule in France, initially as first consul and then, in 1804, as emperor.

1805–
1806   Napoleon defeats Austria and Prussia and establishes dependent governments throughout Germany.

1807–
1812   Domestic reformers in Prussia exploit the crisis of French occupation to instigate major liberal reforms, including the emancipation of the serfs, the dissolution of traditional guild monopolies, and the civil emancipation of the Jews.

1813   The wars of liberation: Napoleon's armies are driven out of central Europe by a coalition of Prussians, Austrians, and Russians.

1815   The Congress of Vienna reconstructs Europe after the defeat of Napoleon. The liberal reform process ends and is reversed in some areas. The Rhineland is incorporated into Prussia.

1817   Karl Marx's father, Heinrich Marx (1782–1838), a prominent liberal Jewish lawyer, converts to Protestantism and is baptized in the Prussian Evangelical Church so as not to jeopardize his career.

1818   *May 5*   Karl Marx is born in Trier in the Prussian province of the Rhineland, the third of nine children. Both parents come from a distinguished lineage of rabbis and scholars.

1820   *November 28*   Frederick Engels is born in Barmen, near Düsseldorf in the Rhineland. He is baptized the following January in the Reformed (Calvinist) Evangelical Church.

1824   Seven of the Marx children, including Karl, are baptized into the Prussian-Evangelical Church. Their mother is baptized a year later. Karl will be confirmed in 1834.

1830   The first steam locomotive passenger railway line is opened between Manchester and Liverpool, England, inaugurating a new phase in the industrial transformation of Europe.

1830–
1833   Scattered liberal and democratic uprisings in southern and central Germany following the July revolution of 1830 in France produce the first small groups of German political exiles in Paris.

1834   The League of Outlaws is founded in Paris by refugee radicals.

1835   Marx completes his secondary school studies in Trier and enters the University of Bonn as a law student.

1836   Marx is secretly betrothed to Jenny von Westphalen, the daughter of a Prussian civil servant in Trier, whom he will marry in June 1843. He transfers to the University of Berlin in the fall, where he becomes involved with younger members of the Hegelian school and transfers his affiliation to the philosophical faculty.

The League of the Just is founded in Paris after a split in the League of Outlaws.

1837 Engels's secondary school studies in Elberfeld are cut short when his father withdraws him from school to learn the family business. Until 1841, he will work as a commercial apprentice in Bremen, where he also will begin to be published in literary journals.

1838 The Chartist movement, aiming at a democratic extension of parliamentary reform, is established in England.

1839 An unsuccessful uprising led by Auguste Blanqui in Paris leads to the expulsion of the leaders of the League of the Just, who set up headquarters in London.

1840 A dynastic change in Prussia raises hopes that the new king (Frederick William IV) will open the door to greater civil freedoms and constitutional government.

The German Worker's Education Society is founded in London.

1841 Marx receives his doctoral degree in absentia from the University of Jena for a dissertation titled "Difference between the Democritean and Epicurean Philosophy of Nature," but he abandons hope for an academic career after his friend Bruno Bauer is suspended from his job in Bonn because of his radical humanist views.

1841– 1842 Engels serves in the military in Berlin, associates with the Hegelian radicals, attends classes at the university, and becomes more active as a journalist.

1842 Marx begins to contribute articles to the *Rheinische Zeitung,* a liberal newspaper published in Cologne, and is appointed editor on October 15.

1842– 1844 Engels works in the textile firm Ermen and Engels, co-owned by his father in Manchester, England. He studies political economy and collects materials for his book *The Condition of the Working Class in England,* which is published in Germany in 1845. He begins associations with English utopian socialists, leaders of the Chartist movement, and the exiled leadership of the League of the Just.

1843 Marx resigns as editor of the *Rheinische Zeitung* in March because of Prussian censorship restrictions and moves to Paris at the end of October.

1844 Marx collaborates briefly with the Hegelian radical Arnold Ruge on the *Deutsch-Französische Jahrbücher* (German-French Annals). He studies the political economists and works on "The

Economic and Philosophic Manuscripts of 1844." The Silesian weavers revolt and its brutal military suppression focuses attention on the social immiserization of textile workers in Prussia. Marx begins his collaboration with Engels after Engels's ten-day visit to Paris at the end of August. They work together on the critique of their former Hegelian comrades, *The Holy Family,* which is published in February 1845.

1845   Marx is expelled from France and moves to Brussels in February. He travels to England with Engels in the summer and begins work on *The German Ideology* in the fall.

1846   The Communist Committees of Correspondence are established in March. Marx and Engels extend their polemic against utopian, moralistic, and messianic forms of socialism.

1847   Marx allies the Communist Committees of Correspondence with the Communist League. Engels takes part in the first league congress in June. Marx joins him at the November–December congress, where he is commissioned to write the *Communist Manifesto.*

The Prussian king summons the representatives of the provincial assemblies to a United Diet in Berlin, raising hopes for the establishment of constitutional government in Prussia.

In France, the parliamentary opposition exerts pressure on the constitutional monarchy for liberal reform through a campaign of "banquets," or demonstrations.

The British parliament passes a law fixing the ten-hour workday for women and children.

The European economy experiences a severe depression, as bad harvests coincide with a slump in business, exacerbating the poverty of the laboring classes and predisposing them to engage in desperate actions, including revolutionary violence.

1848   *February*   The *Manifesto of the Communist Party* is completed and published in London.

February 22–24   Revolution in Paris. King Louis Philippe abdicates, and a republic is proclaimed.

March 18–19   Revolution in Berlin. King Frederick William IV promises to grant a constitution.

Early March   Marx is expelled from Belgium. He moves to Paris and then to Cologne in April to take part in the revolutionary events in Germany. Beginning at the end of May, he edits the *Neue Rheinische Zeitung,* a radical republican journal that tries to pursue the strategies laid out at the end of the *Manifesto.*

1849   Marx is arrested and then acquitted of charges of inciting insurrection, but he is expelled from Prussia in May. After a brief stay in Paris, he begins what will become a permanent exile in London at the end of August. Engels participates in a futile military uprising in southern Germany, then emigrates to London.

1850   Engels resumes work at the firm of Ermen and Engels in Manchester, where he will be employed until 1869.

1852   The Communist League is dissolved after a number of its members are sentenced to jail terms in Cologne.

Louis Bonaparte, the president of the French republic, declares himself Emperor Napoleon III after a series of measures establishing his dictatorial power.

Marx writes *The Eighteenth Brumaire of Louis Bonaparte,* which first appears in a German periodical, *Die Revolution,* published in New York City.

1859   Marx publishes a preliminary installment of his systematic analysis of industrial capitalism in a short book titled *Contribution to a Critique of Political Economy.*

1864   The first Working Men's International Association is founded in London. Marx delivers the inaugural address. Although this organization will last only a few years, the 1860s mark the beginning of a new era in socialist politics based on the development of organized labor movements, trade unions, and social democratic parties in Western and Central Europe. The Second International Working Men's Association, founded in 1889, will be an expression of these new forms of labor organization and socialist politics.

1867   The first volume of Marx's *Capital* is published.

1870–
1871   The Prussian defeat of France in the Franco-Prussian War leads to the creation of a unified German Empire and the fall of Napoleon III. The postwar turmoil in France leads to a populist revolt in Paris and the temporary triumph of the Commune. Despite the violent suppression of this uprising, it once again confirms the belief of left-wing radicals that a communist revolution is inevitable.

1883   Marx dies peacefully in his study in London and is buried at Highgate Cemetery.

1895   Engels dies of throat cancer in London. His body is cremated, and his ashes are scattered in the sea off the English coast at Eastbourne.

Questions for Consideration

1. Considering the *Communist Manifesto* as a political action or political event, what were the historical preconditions for its appearance in February 1848? What were the causes and motives leading to its publication? What was it intended to accomplish?

2. The *Manifesto* was completed before the beginning of the 1848 Revolutions. How might one explain its consciousness of revolutionary expectancy, its confident belief that Europe was haunted by the "specter" of revolution?

3. What did Frederick Engels contribute to the making of the *Manifesto*? Would the *Manifesto* have been a different kind of work without his input?

4. How does Engels's 1847 "Draft of a Communist Confession of Faith" reveal the distinguishing characteristics of the Marxian position? What did Marx and Engels mean when they claimed the "historical" position for themselves against other socialist perspectives?

5. How did the revolutionary perspectives of contemporary radical thinkers like Charles Fourier, Robert Owen, Ludwig Feuerbach, Moses Hess, and James Bronterre O'Brien converge with, or diverge from, the perspective of Marx and Engels?

6. In what sense is the *Communist Manifesto* a proclamation of emancipation? What kind of liberation does it propose? Who is to be liberated?

7. Why did Marx reject the political realm as the appropriate site for the realization of the revolutionary ideals of liberty, equality, and fraternity? What were the implications of Marx's critique of political emancipation and political community?

8. What did Marx and Engels mean when they claimed that the bourgeois revolution dissolved all fixed relations and profaned everything previously held sacred? What fueled and motivated this corrosive power?

9. If all previous history had been characterized by class struggle, why would class conflict end with the victory of the proletariat in a communist revolution?

10. What was the role of labor in Marx's conceptions of individual and social existence? What dimensions of human experience were excluded by Marx's focus on the process of productive labor? What were the implications of these exclusions?

11. If workingmen had no country, where did they have a "home"? How did Marx imagine a fulfilled social existence — a fully realized life in community? Why could community not be found in the cultural and political framework of the nation?

12. According to Marx and Engels, why should the working classes choose the communist movement as the appropriate source for both enlightenment about their own condition and leadership in the battle against the bourgeoisie? What were the available alternatives? What principles informed Marx's and Engels's dismissal of the adequacy of these alternatives?

13. What were the lessons Marx learned through the historical testing of the *Manifesto* during the revolutions of 1848? Why did the impact of the failed revolutions lead Marx to reconsider his relationship to Hegel, his early philosophical mentor? Does the historical analysis of human alienation in *Capital* (1867) mark a shift in Marx's perspective from 1848, or from 1844?

14. On the basis of your own reading of the *Manifesto* and accompanying documents in this volume, how would you assess the claims of the eulogy Engels presented at Marx's graveside in 1883? Have the passing years turned Marx into a "dead dog"? (See Document 23, footnote 2, on p. 157.) Why might it be important for the present generation to read the *Communist Manifesto*?

Selected Bibliography

This list is intended as a guide to further reading for students. It is limited to works in English and focuses on studies directly relevant to the historical interpretation of the *Communist Manifesto*.

WORKS OF MARX AND ENGELS

Marx, Karl, and Frederick Engels. *Collected Works.* 50 vols. to date. New York: International Publishers, 1975–2004.

Marx, Karl. *Early Writings.* Introduced by Lucio Coletti and translated by Rodney Livingstone and Gregor Benton. New York: Random House, 1975.

Marx, Karl. *The Revolutions of 1848.* Edited and with an introduction by David Fernbach. New York: Random House, 1973.

Tucker, Robert C., ed. *The Marx-Engels Reader.* 2nd ed. New York: Norton, 1978.

STUDIES OF THE *COMMUNIST MANIFESTO*

A number of the previous editions of the *Manifesto* that include substantive introductions or critical secondary material have been included in this list.

Bender, Frederic L., ed. *Karl Marx: The Communist Manifesto.* 2nd ed. New York: Norton, 2013.

Cowling, Mark, ed. *The Communist Manifesto: New Interpretations.* New York: New York University Press, 1998.

Laski, Harold J. *The Communist Manifesto of Marx and Engels.* New York: Seabury Press, 1967.

Stedman Jones, Gareth, ed. Karl Marx and Friedrich Engels. *The Communist Manifesto,* Penguin Books, London, 2002.

Struik, Dirk. *The Birth of the Communist Manifesto.* New York: International Publishers, 1971.

Taylor, A. J. P. Introduction to *The Communist Manifesto,* by Karl Marx and Frederick Engels. Harmondsworth, England: Penguin Books, 1967.

BIOGRAPHICAL AND HISTORICAL STUDIES OF MARX AND ENGELS

Berlin, Sir Isaiah. *Karl Marx: His Life and Environment.* 4th ed. Oxford: Oxford University Press, 1978.

Hunt, Tristram. *Marx's General: The Revolutionary Life of Friedrich Engels.* Henry Holt and Company, New York, 2009.

McLellan, David. *Karl Marx: His Life and Thought.* New York: Harper and Row, 1977.

Seigel, Jerrold. *Marx's Fate: The Shape of a Life.* Princeton: Princeton University Press, 1978.

Sperber, Jonathan. *Karl Marx: A Nineteenth-Century Life.* New York: Liveright Publishing, 2013.

Stedman Jones, Gareth. *Karl Marx: Greatness and Illusion.* Cambridge, Mass.: Harvard University Press, 2016.

Wheen, Francis. *Karl Marx.* London: Fourth Estate, 1999.

HISTORICAL AND THEORETICAL CONTEXTS

Beecher, Jonathan. *Charles Fourier: The Visionary and His World.* Berkeley: University of California Press, 1986.

Breckman, Warren. *Marx, The Young Hegelians, and the Origins of Radical Social Theory: Dethroning the Self.* Cambridge, U.K.: Cambridge University Press, 1999.

Droz, Jacques. *Europe between Revolutions, 1815–1848.* Ithaca, N.Y.: Cornell University Press, 1980.

Harrison, J. F. C. *Quest for the New Moral World: Robert Owen and the Owenites in Britain and America.* New York: Scribners, 1969.

Hobsbawm, Eric J. *The Age of Revolution: Europe 1789–1848.* New York: Praeger, 1969.

Johnson, Christopher H. *Utopian Communism in France, 1839–1851.* Ithaca, N.Y.: Cornell University Press, 1974.

Lichtheim, George. *The Origins of Socialism.* New York: Praeger, 1969.

Manuel, Frank. *The Prophets of Paris.* Cambridge: Harvard University Press, 1962.

Sperber, Jonathan. *Rhineland Radicals: The Democratic Movement and the Revolution of 1848–1849.* Princeton, N.J.: Princeton University Press, 1991.

Sperber, Jonathan. *The European Revolutions, 1848–1851.* 2nd ed. Cambridge, U.K.: Cambridge University Press, 2005.

Thompson, E. P. *The Making of the English Working Class.* New York: Random House, 1966.

STUDIES OF THE THOUGHT OF MARX AND ENGELS

Avineri, Shlomo. *The Social and Political Thought of Karl Marx.* Cambridge: Cambridge University Press, 1970.

Carver, Terrell. *Marx and Engels: The Intellectual Relationship.* Bloomington: Indiana University Press, 1983.

Draper, Hal. *Karl Man's Theory of Revolution.* 4 vols. New York: Monthly Review Press, 1977–1990.

Leopold, David. *The Young Karl Marx: German Philosophy, Modern Politics, and Human Flourishing.* Cambridge University Press, Cambridge, 2007.

Megill, Allan. *Karl Marx: The Burden of Reason (Why Marx Rejected Politics and the Market).* Rowan and Littlefield, Lantham, Maryland, 2002.

Ollmann, Bertell. *Alienation: Marx's Conception of Man in Capitalist Society.* Cambridge: Cambridge University Press, 1976.

Ryan, Alan. *On Marx: Revolutionary and Utopian.* Liveright, New York, 2014.

Acknowledgments *(continued from p. ii)*

Alexis de Tocqueville. Excerpt from *Recollections: The French Revolution of 1848*, edited by J. P. Mayer and A. P. Kerr, with a new introduction by Fernand Braudel (New Brunswick, N.J.: Transaction Books, 1987), pp. 12–13. Copyright © 1987. Reproduced by permission of Taylor & Francis Group, LLC, a division of Informa plc.

Karl Marx and Frederick Engels. Excerpts from *Collected Works* by Karl Marx and Frederick Engels, Vols. 3–6, 10, 11, 20, 24, 35, and 38. Copyright © 1996 Progressive Publishing Group Corporation, Moscow; Lawrence & Wishart, London; and International Publishers, New York. By permission of International Publishers Company, Inc.

Charles Fourier. "The Theory of the Four Movements and of the General Destinies" and "The Theory of University Unity," excerpted from *The Utopian Vision of Charles Fourier: Selected Texts on Work, Love, and Passionate Attraction*, translated and edited by Jonathan Beecher and Richard Bienvenu. Copyright © 1971 by Jonathan Beecher and Richard Bienvenu. Reprinted by permission of Beacon Press, Boston.

"The Six Points of the People's Charter" (1838). From *Chartism and Society: An Anthology of Documents*, edited by F. C. Mather. Copyright © 1980 by Holmes and Meier Publishers, a division of Lynne Rienner Publishers Inc. Used with the permission of Lynne Rienner Publishers, Inc.

James Bronterre O'Brien. "Private Property" (1841). From *Chartism and Society: An Anthology of Documents*, edited by F. C. Mather. Copyright © 1980 by Holmes and Meier Publishers, a division of Lynne Rienner Publishers Inc. Used with the permission of Lynne Rienner Publishers, Inc.

G. W. F. Hegel. Excerpts taken from *Reason in History: A General Introduction to the Philosophy of History,* 1st ed., translated by Robert S. Hartman. Copyright © 1953. Reprinted by permission of Pearson Education, Inc., Upper Saddle River, NJ.

Ludwig Feuerbach. Excerpts from "Principles of the Philosophy of the Future" (1843), from *The Fiery Book: Selected Writings of Ludwig Feuerbach*, translated with an introduction by Zawar Hanfi. Copyright © 2012 Verso Books. First published in English by Anchor Books 1972. Translation and introduction © Zawar Hanfi 1972. All rights reserved.

Moses Hess. "I. Of Labour and Enjoyment," excerpted from "A Communist Credo: Questions and Answers." From *The Holy History of Mankind and Other Writings*, trans. and edited with an introduction by Shlomo Avineri. Copyright © 2004. Reprinted by permission of Cambridge University Press.

Index

abstract universality, 88n
accumulated labor, 78
active (subjective) materialism, 141, 142
Agrarian Reformers, 94
agricultural association, 115
alienation of labor, 136–41
    under capitalism, 34
    causes of, 43–44
    resolution of, 45
ancient property, 80
animals
    human beings *vs.*, 139–41, 145
aristocracy
    attempts to gain worker support, 84–85
    exploitation by, 85
artisans. *See also* handicraft workers
    industrial revolution and, 41
associated individuals
    human emancipation and, 28
attraction
    pleasurable labor and, 116
    societal order and, 114–16
authoritarianism, 12

Babeuf, François-Noël (Gracchus), 91, 123
ballots, 121
Blanc, Louis, 18, 94n, 152
Blanqui, Auguste, 169
Bonaparte, Louis, 151
bourgeoisie. *See also* capitalism
    abolition of private property of, 77–80
    basis of family in, 80
    class conflict and, 40

criticism of, 21
criticism of Marx by, 170
defined, 64n, 102
development of, 65–70
economic crises and, 69–70, 158
emancipation of, 22–23
in England, 105–6, 108
exploitation of world market by, 67–68
in France, 53, 149–50
historical roots of, 64–66
industrialization and, 65–70
Industrial Revolution and, 21
Marx's criticism of, 48
Marx's law of, 169–70
mode of production, 55
property, 122
revolution and, 9, 44, 154
struggle of proletariat with, 72–76
support of proletariat by, 73–74
unnatural character of society, 159–68
Bourgeois (conservative) socialism, 90–91
Brussels Committee of Correspondence, 9
Bund der Geaechteten (League of Outlaws), 7, 172
Bund der Gerechten (League of the Just), 7–8, 9, 94n, 173
Buonarroti, Filippo, 123

capital. *See also* private property
    accumulation of, 137
    as social power, 77
Capital (Marx), 6, 158, 176
    afterword to the Second German Edition, 157–58

Capital (Marx) *(cont.)*
  analysis of bourgeois mode of
    production in, 55
  "Fetishism of Commodities and the
    Secret Thereof, The," 57
capitalism. *See also* bourgeoisie; private
    property
  alienation of labor under, 34, 44, 45,
    137–141
  corruption of labor under, 17
  defined, 64n
  economic crises and, 69–70, 158
  expansion of, 45–46
  exploitation of proletariat by, 102–3
  as historical form, 5, 31, 76
  inevitability of overthrow of, 55
  Marx's law of, 169–70
  revolutionary movements and, 52–55
catechism
  communist confession of faith as, 10
Caussidière, Marc, 152
cells, 8
Central Committee, 8
Chartist movement, 18, 19, 94,
    156, 173
  People's Charter, 120–21
  social theory, 122–24
children
  division of labor and, 43
  exploitation of, 80
  industrial revolution and, 41
  working hours limitations, 73n
China, 68n
Christian Socialism, 86
citizenship rights, 26
civil servants, 38
civil society
  productive labor and, 32–37
class, 37–41
  community of, 40–41
  dominance by liberal democratic
    state, 29
  exploitation and, 55
  Marx's theory of, 38–41
class conflict
  individual interest and, 111–12
  interpretation of revolutionary
    movements as, 53–55
  theory of, 39–40

class struggle
  in history, 64–66
  industrialization and, 65, 92
  proletariat-bourgeoisie, 72–76
*Class Struggles in France, 1848–1850,
    The* (Marx), 148–51
coalitions, 72n
commodities
  concealment of value of, 163
  religion and, 166–67
  value associated with, 158–68
communal ownership, 8, 10, 17
commune, medieval, 66n
communication, centralization of, 83
communism
  aim of, 100
  bourgeoisie objections to, 79–82
  conditions for, 83–84
  emancipation of proletariat through,
    10
  Marx's use of term, 17
  opposition parties and, 94–95
  specter of, 3–5, 52
  structural organization and, 8
  use of term, 18
Communist Committees of the
    Correspondence, 9
*A Communist Credo: Questions and
    Answers* (Hess), 133–36
Communist League *(Bund der
    Kommunisten)*, 7–11, 95n, 148, 174
  Communist Manifesto accepted by, 11
  credo for, 100–5
  historical roots of, 7–10
Communist Manifesto
  accepted by Communist League,
    11–12
  adaptability of, 2–3
  chronology, 174
  contemporary relevance of, 1–6
  French coup d'état and, 151
  fundamental proposition of, 11
  as historical action, 1, 53
  historical contexts of, 6–21
  historical development and, 52–57
  as historical document, v–vi, 1–6
  historical premises of, 21–48
  pages from, 62, 63 illus.
  as political work, 48

politics and ideology of, 48–52
publication of, 52
purpose of, 1, 5
writing of, 6, 11
Communist party
aim of, 76–77
characteristics of, 76
Communist League and, 7–11
criticism of, 49–50
historical process and, 49
proletariats and, 48–49
communist revolution
emancipation and, 22–30
human emancipation through, 35–36
specter of, 2–5
world-historical cooperation and, 46
as world transformation, 50
community
division of labor and, 44
freedom in, 24, 26
goal of, 40
illusory forms of, 48
mutual identification, 28
personal freedom and, 16
community of property, 10, 101
conditions for, 103–4
transition to, 104
community of women, 81, 104
competition, 137
compulsory labor, 165
*Condition of the Working Class in England,
The* (Engels), 13, 106–11, 173–74
Congress of Vienna, 172
consciousness, 125
species-being as, 140
conservative (bourgeois) socialism, 90–91
Constant, Benjamin, 153
constituencies
People's Charter and, 120–21
contemplative materialism, 144
Contributions to the Critique of Hegel's Philosophy of Law (Marx), 127–31
cooperation
individual interest *vs.*, 111–14
countries. *See* nations
Cousin, Victor, 153n
creative power, transformation into products, 31

credit, centralization of, 83
Critical-utopian socialism, 91–94
Critique of Practical Reason (Kant), 88n

"dangerous class," 74
Danton, Georges, 152
Das Wesen des Christenthums (The Essence of Christianity) (Feuerbach), 142
democratic politics
People's Charter and, 120–21
democratic state
illusion of freedom in, 26–30
as means of class dominance, 29
democratization movements, 19
Desmoulins, Camille, 153
destitute populations, 19
Deutsch-Französische Jahrbücher (German-French Annals), 127, 129, 174
Disraeli, Benjamin, 85n
division of labor, 65
community and, 44
development of, 147
effects of, 147
influence of, 43
pleasurableness of work and, 116
rise of proletariat and, 102
value and, 165
domination, drive toward, 37
Draft of Communist Confession of Faith (Engels), 10, 100–5

"Economic and Philosophic Manuscripts of 1844, The" (Marx), 30, 137–41
economic crises
bourgeoisie role in, 69–70, 158
industrial revolution and, 18–21
economic theory, 13
education, under communism, 80, 84, 104
"Egoistic" exploitation, 22
Eighteenth Brumaire of Louis Bonaparte, The (Marx), 53, 151–54, 175
emancipation. *See also* human emancipation; political emancipation
criticism of past processes, 22
French Revolution and, 21

emancipation (*cont.*)
    of labor, 36–37
    Marx's concept of, 24
    principle of, 22–30
Engels, Frederick, vi, 14 illus., 141
    background of, 12–13
    birth of, 12
    chronology, 171–76
    clarification of Marx's views by, 15
    death of, 176
    interpretation of Marxism by, 57
    League of the Just and, 9
    manuscript page from *German
        Ideology, The,* 146 illus.
    Marx and, 7, 11–18
    predictions for communist
        revolution, 54–55
    publications
        *Condition of the Working Class in
            England, The,* 106–7
        *Draft of a Communist Confession of
            Faith,* 10, 100, 105
        German Ideology, The (with
            Marx), 144–48
        *Letter to Karl Marx, November
            23/24 ,* 1847, 105
        political cartoon, 20 illus.
        Speech at Karl Marx's funeral,
            169–70
    role of, 11–12
    studies Industrial Revolution in
        England, 106
    suggests Confession of Faith be
        redrafted as *Communist Manifesto,*
        105
    terms *Communist Manifesto* an
        historical document, 1, 3
England
    Industrial Revolution in, 106, 108–11
    middle classes in, 107–8, 111
    working classes in, 106–11
Enlightenment, 82n
The Essence of Christianity
    (Feuerbach), 126–27
eternal truths, abolition of, 82
exploitation
    by aristocracy, 85
    of children, 80
    of nations, 81

    of the proletariat, 71
    through free trade expansion, 67–68
    of women, 80–81
external labor, 139
external nature, 42

fair value, 118
family
    abolition of, 80
    community of property and, 104
*Fetishism of Commodities and the Secret
    Thereof, The (Capital)* (Marx),
    159–68
Feuerbachian humanism, 133
feudal socialism, 84–86
feudal society
    destruction of, 65, 69
    in history, 64–65
Feuerbach, Ludwig, 31, 32–33, 36, 41,
    131–32
    The Essence of Christianity, 126–27
    Marx's criticism of, 141–44
    *Principles of the Philosophy of the
        Future,* 132–33
First International, 155
forced labor, 134
Fourier, Charles, 17, 92n, 93n
    *Theory of the Four Movements and of
        General Destinies,* 114–16
    Theory of Universal Unity, The, 116–18
Fourierists, 94
France
    coup d'état (1851), 151–54
    failed French revolution (1848), 149–51
    French Revolution (1789–99), 15,
        20–22, 38, 152–53, 171
    French revolution (1830), 87–88
    opposition to communism in, 94, 95
    Paris uprising (1839), 8
    relevance of French Revolution
        (1789) in Germany, 87–88
    Restoration (1814–1830), 85
    revolutionary movements, 6, 52,
        171–76
Franco-Prussian War, 176
Frederick William IV, King of Prussia,
    20 illus.
free activity, 134
free association of moral beings, 24

freedom
    community and, 16
    Hegel on, 124–26
    importance of, 125
    Marx's concept of, 24, 28–29
    moral *vs.* individual, 24, 26
    philosophy and, 23–24
    religion and, 129
    self-determination, 28–29
    in the State, 125–26
    theory of, 22–30
free trade
    abolition of, 78
    exploitation through, 67
French Legitimists, 85
The French Revolution of 1848 (Toc-
    queville), 98–99

Gans, Eduard, 124
Gegenstand (things), 142
German Ideology, The (Marx and
    Engels), 42–44, 141, 144–48, 174
    manuscript page, 146 illus.
German Jews, 15
German ("true") socialism, 88–90
German Worker's Education Society, 173
Germany
    as central to communist revolution,
        54, 55
    expatriate intellectuals, 7
    parties in opposition to communism
        in, 94–95
    as site of communist revolution, 38
Gespenst (specter), 4–5
Great Britain. *See* England
greed, 137
groups, utopian socialist definition of,
    116n
guilds, 65
Guizot, Francois, 153

Habakkuk, 154
handicraft workers
    Communist League and, 7
    displacement of, in England, 110
    industrial revolution and, 71
    as proletariat, 71
    proletariat *vs.,* 103
Hargreaves, James, 171

Hegel, Georg Wilhelm Friedrich, 23,
    32, 33, 38, 57, 152
    *Reason in History: A General
        Introduction to the Philosophy of
        History,* 124–26
Hegelian philosophy, 31
    on distinctiveness of human beings, 32
    on freedom, 124–26
    Marx's criticism of, 127–29, 144
    Marx's return to, 156–58
    Marx's theory of human
        emancipation and, 23
Hess, Moses
    *A Communist Credo: Questions and
        Answers,* 133–36
historic materialism, 141–44
history
    capitalism as historical form, 31
    communist party as reflection of, 49
    goal of, 40
    as illusory form of community, 48
    man's making of, 152–53
    Marx's changing views on, 43–48
    Marx's law of development of,
        169–70
    productive labor and, 35, 44
    as reality of human existence, 41–48
Hobhouse, Sir John Cam, 122
Home Colonies, 93
homo faber (man the maker), 51
human artifacts, 33
human beings
    differentiation from animals, 139–40,
        145
    history as reality of existence,
        41–48
    species-being, 31–32, 40, 130–31,
        137, 139–41
human emancipation. *See also* emanci-
    pation; political emancipation
    agents of, 38
    Hegelian philosophy and, 23
    illusions of, 28–30, 38
    politics and, 29
    society and, 30
    state and, 38
    theory of, 22–30
    through communist revolution,
        35–36

human essence
    creation of, 47
    defined by labor, 31–37
    defined by productive labor, 32, 34
    defined by sex/love, 33, 36
    defined by thought, 32, 33
human rights, 26

Icaria, 93n
ideology
    abolition of, 81–82
    as illusory, 48
*Inaugural Address of the Working Men's
    International Association* (Marx),
    155–56
income tax, 83
individuals
    historical understanding of, 42–43
    rights, protection of, 26
    self-interest, societal problems and,
        112–13
industrial attraction, 117–18
Industrial Revolution
    bourgeoisie and, 66–70
    chronology, 171
    class struggle and, 92
    communism as managerial solution
        to, 15
    destructive effects of, 13
    economic crises resulting from,
        18–21
    in England, 106, 108–11
    rise of proletariat and, 101–2
    wages and, 70–71
    women as workers in, 44–45
inheritance, abolition of, 80, 83
inner nature, 42
intellectuals, German expatriates, 7
Intermundia, 166
Ireland, 110

Jews
    civic emancipation of, 129–31
    German, 15

Kant, Immanuel, 88n

labor. *See also* division of labor;
    wage-labor
    alienation of, 34, 136–41
    capitalism and, 17, 34, 101
    centralization of, 83
    as a commodity, 55
    as core of social exchange, 118–20
    cost of, 70–71
    demand for, 119
    distribution within family, 165
    emancipation of, 35–38
    external, 139
    forced, 139
    human essence defined by, 31–32
    Marx's theory of, 136–41
    objectification of, 138–41
    pleasurableness of, 116–18
    productivity by proletariat, 45–46
    product value, 158–68
    repossession of, 35
    transformation of objects by, 31–32
    universal unity theory and,
        116–18
    use of term, 57
    value and, 119, 158–68
    variation in, 117
labor-power
    defined, 55, 57, 70–71n
    sales of, 34, 55, 57, 64n
labor time, value and, 159–60, 163
land. *See also* private property
    as basis of wealth, 124
League of Outlaws *(Bund der
    Geaechteten),* 7, 172
League of the Just *(Bund der
    Gerechten),* 7, 94n, 173
    in France, 8, 9
    in London, 8
    motto of, 9
    organizational structure of, 8
    purpose of, 9
Ledru-Rollin, Alexandre, 18, 94n
Lessing, G. E., 157
liberation
    community and, 15
    individual self-interest and, 22
    from religion, 24
    true emancipation and, 23
liberty. *See* freedom
"Little Icaria," 93
love, human essence defined by, 33, 36

Ludwig Feuerbach and the Decline of the Classical German Ideology (Engels), 141
Lukács, Georg, 2
Lumpenproletariat (proletariat in rags), 74n

Manifesto of the Communist Party. See Communist Manifesto
Mankind as It Is and as It Should Be (Weitling), 8
marriage, 81. *See also* family
Marx, Eleanor, 164n
Marx-Engels Institute, 139
Marx, Heinrich, 172
Marxism
  authoritarianism of, 12
  clarification of, by Engels , 16
  as scientific discovery, 163–65
  as working-class movement, 10–11
Marx, Jenny, 63 illus.
Marx, Karl, 25 illus., 56 illus.
  birth of, 12
  chronology, 171–75
  conversion to Christianity, 16
  criticism of, 170
  death of, 169, 170, 176
  as discoverer of laws of human history, 169–70
  Engels and, 11–18
  failed French revolution (1848) and, 149–51
  French coup d'etat (1851) and, 151–54
  Hegelian philosophy and, 124, 156–58
  historic materialism, 141–44
  influences on, 15
  labor theory, 136–41
  League of the Just and, 9
  legacy of, 169–70
  as philosopher, 24
  political emancipation critique, 26–30
  predictions of communist revolution, 54–55
  publications
    Capital, afterword to the Second German Edition, 156–58
    Class Struggles in France, 1848–1850, The, 148–51
    Contribution to the Critique of Hege's Philosophy of Law, 127–29
    Economic and Philosophic Manuscripts of 1844, 136–41
    Eighteenth Brumaire of Louis Bonaparte, The, 151–54
    Fetishism of Commodities and the Secret Thereof, The (Capital), 158–68
    German Ideology, The (with Engels), 144–48
    Inaugural Address of the Working Men's International Association, 155–56
    On the Jewish Question, 129–31
    Theses on Feuerbach, 141–44
  self-criticism of former positions, 49
  terms *Communist Manifesto* an historical document, 3
  writes *Manifesto,* 6
materialism
  active (subjective), 141, 142
  contemplative, 144
  historic, 141–44
  social, 141
matter, 125
means of production
  centralization of, 68–69
  loss of control of, 69–70
men
  division of labor and, 43
  industrial revolution and, 41
Mendelssohn, Moses, 157
middle classes. *See* bourgeoisie
model communities, 17
mode of production, 17, 55, 145, 167–68
monetary system, 167–68
Montagne, 152
Moore, Samuel, vi, 11
moral beings, free association of, 24
moral freedom, 24, 26
mutual identification (community), 28
mutual interdependence, 44

Napoleon Bonaparte, 172
National Reform Association (U.S.), 94n

nations
    abolition of, 81
    under communism, 104
    division of labor and, 145
    productive development of, 145, 147
    relations among, 145
nature
    man's relationship to, 140, 167
*Neue Rheinische Zeitung: Politsch-
    Oekonomische Revue (New
    Rhenish Gazette: Political Eco-
    nomic Review),* 148, 175

objectification
    of labor, 138–41
    through labor, 32
O'Brien, James Bronterre
    Private Property, 122–24
On the Jewish Question (Marx),
    129–31
Opium War, 68n
oppression
    abolition of, 84
    conditions for, 75
    in history, 64, 66
    religion as sign of, 128
"Outlines of a Critique of Political
    Economy" (Engels), 13
Owenites, 94
Owen, Robert, 17, 92, 92n, 93n, 111–14,
    118–20
    labor theory, 118–20
    Report to the County of Lanark,
    111–14, 118–20

Paris
    insurrection (1848), 52
    uprising (1839), 8
parliaments, People's Charter points,
    120–21
patriarchal artisan culture, 41
People's Charter, 120–21
personal dependence, 164
petty-bourgeois socialism, 87, 89
Phalanstéres, 93
Philosophie de la Misère (Proudhon), 90
philosophy, role of, 23–26
pleasurable labor
    conditions for, 117–18

passionate attraction principle and,
    116
pleasure, 135
Poland, 94
political emancipation. *See also* emanci-
    pation; human emancipation
    limitations of, 129–31
    Marx's critique of, 26–29
political power
    abolition of, 84
    defined, 84
politics
    alienation of labor and, 136–41
    centralisation, 68
    human emancipation and, 28–29, 38
    as illusory, 48
population
    distribution of, 84
    growth of, 110, 145
populist movements, 19
pre-history, class in, 64n
Principles of the Philosophy of the Future
    (Feuerbach), 131–33
prison reform, 91
Private Property (O'Brien), 122–24
private property. *See also* capital; land;
    wealth
    abolition of, 10, 17, 34, 77–80, 83,
    104, 130
    acquisition of, 122–24
    bourgeois, 122
    confiscation of, 83
    creation through wage-labor, 78
    family and, 80
    fear of abolishing, 77–79
    inappropriate use of, 123
    political economy and, 137–38
    rights to, 122
    subjugation of others through, 79
production
    abolition of private property and, 79
    centralization of, 83
    means of, 54, 68–70
    mode of, 17, 55, 145, 167–68
    private ownership of, 54
productive labor
    bourgeoisie and, 44–45
    class conflict and, 40
    history of, 35, 43

human essence defined by, 31–37, 145

Marx's law of, 169–70

as organizing center of human existence, 30–37

primacy of, 37, 45

profession, arbitrary choice of, 45

proletariat
 characteristics of, 74–75
 class struggle, 40, 72–76
 Communist party and, 48–49
 defined, 64n, 101, 102
 defined by Marx, 38–39
 development of, 70–76, 150–51
 emancipation of, 10, 39–40, 81–84
 in England, 108–11
 exploitation of, 39, 71
 in France, 150–51
 handicraftsman *vs.*, 103
 industrialization and, 109–11
 Manifesto support for, 21
 organization of, 73
 political supremacy of, 83
 productivity and, 44–45
 revolution and, 50, 54, 103, 154
 rise of, 101–2
 serf *vs.*, 102
 slavery *vs.*, 102
 unity called for, 10, 95
 universal interest of, 38–39
 wage-labor of, 77–78
 world, 46–47

Prometheus, 23

Prometheus Bound, 27f

property. *See also* private property
 community of, 100, 103–5

propertyless class, 102. *See also* proletariat

prostitution, 81

Proudhon, M., 90

Prussia, 12, 172, 173, 174

public good
 individual interest *vs.*, 112–14

reactionary socialism, 84–90
 feudal socialism, 84–86
 German ("true") socialism, 87–90
 petty-bourgeois socialism, 86–87

Reagan, Ronald, 3

Reason in History: A General Introduction to the Philosophy of History (Hegel), 124–26

"Red" republican movement, 18

Réformistes, 94

religion
 abolition of, 82
 commodities and, 166–67
 criticism of, 128
 essence of, 143
 freedom of, 26
 free state and, 129
 liberation from, 24
 oppression and, 128
 replaced by communism, 104
 self-estrangement of, 142

Report to the County of Lanark (Owen), 111–14, 118–20

representative state, 66, 66n

revolutionary mole, 55, 57

revolutionary movements
 during 1845–48, 18–21
 chronology, 171–75
 class conflict and, 53–57
 communist position on, 105
 expectation of, 18–21
 failure of, 52, 55, 155–56
 in France, 9, 53–54, 149–54, 171–76
 inevitability of, 54–55
 Marx's commitment to, 170
 Marx's study of, 16
 type of, 154

Rheinische Zeitung, 27 illus., 170

Rhineland, 12

riches, 168. *See also* value; wealth

Robespierre, Maximilien, 152n

Royer-Collard, Pierre-Paul, 153, 153n

Ruge, Arnold, 127

Saint-Just, Louis-Antoine, 153n

Saint-Simon, Comte de, 92
 Rouvroy, Claude-Henri de, 92n

Say, Jean-Baptiste, 153n

secular democratic state, 26–27

self-assertion, 37

self-consciousness, 125

self-determination (freedom), 28

self-estrangement, 50

self-interest, 22
self-sufficiency, 148
sensuousness, 131–33, 142, 143
serfs, 103
series
    utopian socialist definition of, 116n
Sismondi, Jean-Charles-Léonard
        Simonde de, 87, 87n
Six Points of the People's Charter, The,
    120–21
slavery, 102
social democratic movement, 18
Social Democrats (France), 94, 94n
social exchange, labor and, 118–20
social intercourse, 42
socialism
    conservative (bourgeois), 90–91
    critical-utopian, 91–94
    Marx/Engels views of, 17
    reactionary, 84–90
    use of term, 18
    utopian, 17, 91–94, 111–20
society
    science of attraction and, 114–16
    as site for human emancipation, 30
species-being
    animals *vs.,* 140–41
    labor theory and, 137
    man as, 139–41
    objectification of, 141
    political emancipation and, 130–31
    productive labor and, 32, 40
specter of communism, 3–4, 52
Speech at Karl Marx's Funeral
        (Engels), 169–70
Spinoza, Baruch, 157
Spirit, 124–25
state
    bourgeoisie and, 66
    democratic, 29–30
    freedom in, 125–26
    Hegel's view of, 38
    religion and, 129
    representative, 66n
    secular democratic, 26–27
surplus value, 55, 57
Switzerland, 94

Taylor, Sedley, 164
ten-hours bill, 73
*Theory of the Four Movements and
    of General Destinies* (Fourier),
    114–16
Theory of Universal Unity, The
        (Fourier), 116–18
Theses on Feuerbach (Marx), 141–44
Third Estate, 66
thought, human essence defined by,
    32, 33
Tocqueville, Alexis de, 19
    The French Revolution of 1848, 98–99
town, 68, 147
tradespeople, 71
Trades' Unions, 72
transport, 83, 83n

United States, 94, 156, 170
urban development, 68
usury, 123
utopian communities, 93n
utopian socialism, 17, 91–94
    labor as core of social exchange,
        118–20
    labor process and, 117–18
    principle of cooperation and, 111–14
    science of attraction and, 114–16

value. *See also* wealth
    of commodities, 159–68
    compulsory labor and, 164–65
    defined, 168
virtue, 135
voting rights, 121

wage-labor. *See also* division of labor;
        labor
    as condition for capital, 76
    creation of private property through,
        77
    subsistence level of, 78
Wage Labor and Capital (Marx), 71n
wages
    fair value *vs.,* 118
    industrialization and, 70–71
    pleasurableness of work and, 117

value of human labor and, 119–20
wealth. *See also* capital; private
    property; value
    acquisition of, 123
    labor and, 137–38
    land as basis of, 124
    producers of, 123
Weitling, Wilhelm, 8
Westphalen, Jenny von, 173
Will, 88
will-to-power, 37
women
    community of, 80–81, 104
    division of labor and, 43
    exploitation of, 80–81
    industrial revolution and, 41
    as laborers, 44
    working hours limitations, 73n

Worker's Educational societies, 8, 9
workers. *See* proletariat
working, defined, 134
working classes
    conditions in England, 106–11
    Marxian theory and, 10–11
Working Men's International
    Association, 54, 155–56, 175
world market, 46
    bourgeoisie exploitation of, 67–68
    capitalism, 46
    competitive forces in, 46
    development of, 66

Young England, 85

Zunftbürger (guild members), 65n